Haida Gwaii
The Queen Charlotte Islands

Dennis Horwood and Tom Parkin

VICTORIA • VANCOUVER • CALGARY

Heritage House Publishing Company Ltd.
#108 – 17665 66A Avenue
Surrey, BC V3S 2A7
<www.heritagehouse.ca>

Library and Archives Canada Cataloguing in Publication

Horwood, Dennis, 1953–
    Haida Gwaii: the Queen Charlotte Islands/Dennis Horwood and Tom Parkin.—2nd ed.

Includes bibliographical references and index.

ISBN-13: 978-1-894974-11-0
ISBN-10: 1-894974-11-5

    1. Queen Charlotte Islands (B.C.)–Guidebooks. I. Parkin, Tom, 1951–
II. Title.

FC3845.Q3H67 2006   917.11'12044   C2006-901599-6
FC3845*

Edited by Karla Decker and Lesley Cameron
Book design by Catherine Mack
Layout and maps by Darlene Nickull
Cover design by Frances Hunter
Illustrations by Tom Parkin, unless otherwise noted
All photographs by the authors, unless otherwise noted

Printed in Canada

Heritage House acknowledges the financial support for its publishing program from the Government of Canada through the Book Publishing Industry Development Program (BPIDP), Canada Council for the Arts, and the British Columbia Arts Council.

The Canada Council | Le Conseil des Arts
for the Arts | du Canada

BRITISH
COLUMBIA
ARTS COUNCIL
We acknowledge the support of the Province of British Columbia
through the British Columbia Arts Council

This book is dedicated
to our enthusiastic field
companions, Brenda and Doug

ACKNOWLEDGEMENTS

This book involved the efforts of many people whose names do not appear on the cover. We have relied on the research of other authors, and the review of our text by numerous authorities. While accepting final responsibility for any errors that may have occurred, we'd like to thank the following people.

SECOND EDITION

The Gwaii Haanas National Park Reserve and Haida Heritage Site has been fully recognized for about 15 years. Our thanks go to Kate Alexander, Barb Wilson and Anna Gajda of Parks Canada for the time they spent advising us of the most recent changes to the reserve.

Andrew Merilees spent a considerable amount of time reviewing the Naikoon section as well as giving us insight into future park plans. Dan Bate was also of assistance in this regard.

Kimiko von Boetticher and Andrew Merilees spent many hours with us discussing changes and challenges on Haida Gwaii.

Brian Eccles from the BC Forest Service and Carl Johansen from the Ministry of Tourism helped us considerably with the latest information about the forest recreation sites.

Carolyn Hesseltine of the Village of Queen Charlotte Visitor Centre was most helpful in answering many questions and proofreading relevant sections of the text. We would also like to thank Drue Kendrick, who helped us sort out the fine details of orientations and reservations.

Moira Lemon of the Canadian Wildlife Service provided us with the latest results from Langara Island with regard to the revival of the seabird colonies.

Darcey Janes reviewed our Chartering and Tours section and offered some helpful suggestions. Walter Thorne gave freely of his time to explain the latest navigational aids and how they work.

Our sincere thanks to all of you!

FIRST EDITION

Archaeology: Kathryn Bernick and Bill Holme of the Burke Museum at the University of Washington made helpful comments. Dr. Jim Haggarty and Kevin Neary at the Royal BC Museum read chapters on the Haida.

Atmosphere and environment: Norman Dressler and Supervisor Earl Coatta of the Atmospheric Environment Service of Canada updated our climatic information.

BC Forest Service: Dr. Jim Pojar of the BC Ministry of Forests identified plant photos and checked botanical sections. Dr. Hans Roemer and John Pinder-Moss checked BC Ecological Reserves portions. Brian Eccles was very helpful with BC Forest Service campground updates and additions, and provided some great fishing tips.

Fisheries, oceans and marine: Captain David Littlejohn, Tom Rutherford and Richard Thomson kindly shared their knowledge of fishing and oceanography for the Hecate Strait and boating sections.

Geology: Dr. John Clague of the Geological Survey of Canada ensured the accuracy of Naikoon Park sedimentology.

Gwaii Haanas National Park Reserve and Haida Heritage Site: Doug Eastcott and Stephen Suddes of Parks Canada kept us abreast of developments in the National Park Reserve. We would also like to thank Michele Deakin and Barb Wilson for their comments from their review of this entire section.

Natural history: Don Blood, Dr. Jim Darling and David Nagorsen made recommendations on mammals. Dr. Wayne Nelson of the

University of Calgary provided details about Langara Island. Gary Kaiser brought us up to date with the rat extermination program on Langara Island. Ed Lochbaum and Graeme Ellis gave helpful suggestions for the marine mammal chapter.

Birds: Michael Brown, Mrs. Janet Gifford-Brown, Rick Howie, John Woods and Steven McConnell sent us bird records. Margo Hearne and Peter Hamel were especially helpful with numerous detailed bird observations. Wayne Campbell made constructive comments about the bird chapters and gave us additional unpublished bird records for the islands.

Photographs: Max Patzalt helped with his considerable photographic expertise, and Jeff King from the *Queen Charlotte Islands Observer* lent us photos.

Last but not least: Sheila Charneski and Rosemary and Ken Maitland proofread various sections. Ted Griff gave us his time and computer expertise. MaryAnn Zarichuk and Brenda Horwood took messages, made calls and kept us on track. Gerry Bindert provided logging information. Doug Steventon and Steve Aitkins contributed some interesting details. Lynda Jackson and Anne Day provided tasty tidbits for our beach recipes. Gord Nettleton proofread the biking section. Special thanks go to Joy LaFortune, who directed us to many residents and agencies that might otherwise have been overlooked.

When six new totem poles were raised in 2001 at Skidegate, they attracted national attention. One of the new poles is shown here.

CONTENTS

ACKNOWLEDGEMENTS   3
    Haida Gwaii: The Queen Charlotte Islands map   10

PART ONE: Welcome to Haida Gwaii   11
1.   Islands on the Edge   13
2.   European Discovery of Haida Gwaii   18
3.   The Haida People   20

PART TWO: Introduction to the Natural History of Haida Gwaii   23
4.   Birds of Haida Gwaii   25
5.   Marine Mammals and Reptiles of Haida Gwaii   35
6.   Land Mammals and Amphibians of Haida Gwaii   42

PART THREE: Where to Go   46
7.   Southern Graham Island (*Village of Queen Charlotte and area*)   47
    Crossing Hecate Strait   47
    Around Skidegate Inlet   52
       Skidegate Inlet map   53
    Rennell Sound   60
       Rennel Sound map   62
8.   Mid Graham Island (*Port Clements area*)   66
    Of Canoes and Culture   66
    Nadu—Trails to Tribulation   69
       Nadu map   71
9.   Northern Graham Island (*Langara Island and Masset area*)   74
    Langara Island Vicinity   74
       Langara Island map   75
    Delkatla Wildlife Sanctuary   79
       Delkata Wildlife Sanctuary map   80

Introduction to Naikoon Provincial Park 84

    Naikoon Provincial Park map 85

    Tow Hill Area 87

        Tow Hill map 88

    Tow Hill Bog 92

    North Beach 97

    Rose Spit 101

        North Beach and Rose Spit map 102

    East Beach 105

    Sand Dunes, Tlell River and Vicinity 110

10. North Moresby Island (*Gray Bay and Louise Island area*) 115

    Gray Bay 115

        Gray Bay to Cumshewa Head map 116

    Louise Island Circumnavigation 119

        Sandspit to Louise Island map 120

11. Gwaii Haanas National Park Reserve and Haida Heritage Site 130

    Gwaii Haanas National Park Reserve and Haida

    Heritage Site map 131

    Juan Perez and Darwin Sounds 135

        Darwin Sound to Juan Perez Sound map 136

    East Coast of Lyell Island—Hlk'yah G̲aawG̲a (*Windy Bay area*) 141

    Burnaby Narrows 146

    Skincuttle Inlet 150

        Skincuttle Inlet to Houston Stewart Channel map 151

    Houston Stewart Channel 155

    SG̲ang Gwaay World Heritage Site 158

PART FOUR: Their Place To Be 164

PART FIVE: Visiting Haida Gwaii 183

12. Overnighting on Haida Gwaii 184

    Bed & Breakfasts 185

    Fishing Lodges 190

    Camping 192

13. Planning Your Trip 194

    Transportation and Travel 194

    Chartering and Tours 197

    Navigation and Safety 200

    Museums 203

    Permits for Haida Reserves 203

    Orientation and Reservations for Gwaii Haanas 204
        National Park Reserve and Haida Heritage Site

    Communities and Facilities 207

    Emergency Services 209

    Climate and Clothing 210

    Cycling on Haida Gwaii 211

    Fishing 213

    On-the-Spot Preparation and Recipes for Crab and Clams 216

    Hunting 218

    The Five-Day Guide 220

    Useful Websites 221

APPENDICES 222

    Appendix 1: The Metric System 222

    Appendix 2: Birds of Haida Gwaii 223

    Appendix 3: Land Mammals and Amphibians of Haida Gwaii 231

    Appendix 4: Marine Mammals and Reptiles of Haida Gwaii 232

FURTHER READING 233

INDEX 235

HAIDA GWAII:
THE QUEEN CHARLOTTE ISLANDS

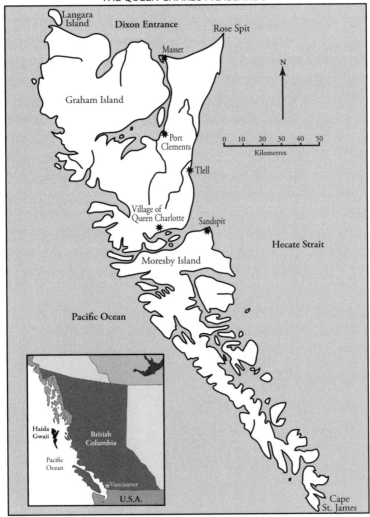

MAP LEGEND

✳ Community	🏛 Viewing tower	🏛 Watchmen site	– – – Park boundary
☆ Site of interest	🪣 Warden station	⚓ Anchorage	········· Trail
Ⓟ Parking	⋔ Picnic sites	🛥 Boat ramp	– – – – Indian reserve
🏠 Homestead	▪ Park hiking shelter	▲ Hill/mountain	······· Ecological reserve
◪ Divesite	⚠ Camping	🌿 Bog	▪▪▪▪▪▪ Ferry crossing
∧∧ Sand dunes	🚰 Fresh water from a pipe		– – – – Gravel road

PART ONE

WELCOME TO HAIDA GWAII

The area known as Haida Gwaii, the Queen Charlotte Islands or simply "the Charlottes," consists of a tight cluster of islands lying 50 to 150 kilometres off the northwestern coast of British Columbia. For millennia, it has been a remote, mysterious and inaccessible place, but developments during the last four decades have raised the profile of this unique and beautiful region.

Haida Gwaii has always been a distinctive place, and the first people to settle here developed an exceptional cultural identity. Long before European contact, the Haida were revered and feared, from what is now Alaska south to Washington State and beyond.

British and American sailors were drawn here to trade for the pelt of sea otters. When the fur trade eventually declined due to the otters' almost complete annihilation, the islands soon drew the attention of mining, fishing and forest companies.

The forest industry did well: the trees on Haida Gwaii are among the finest of any temperate rainforest. But as the rate of cut increased, so too did the clear-cuts. This motivated the Haida, along with many other residents and off-island groups, to lobby for a reduction in or an end to the logging. During the 1970s a series of articles, books and television programs began to publicize the exceptional nature of the islands' environment and the people who lived there. Suddenly, everyone seemed to be talking about "the Charlottes."

Native land claims and the struggle to protect the natural environment during the 1980s continued to promote national and international awareness of the islands, and in 1987 the Gwaii Haanas National Park Reserve and Haida Heritage Site was created. This remarkable park, with its ancient Haida village sites, is just one of the major attractions here. The superb beaches in Naikoon Provincial Park and excellent recreational fishing also draw visitors from around the world.

Tourists who visit Haida Gwaii tend to be adventure-oriented, recreation-focused and aware of the natural environment. They also tend to spend more time on these islands than tourists do in other, more typical, destinations. These visitors are eager to understand Haida Gwaii, and they often leave with a profound appreciation of their experience.

If that sounds appealing, this guidebook is for you.

ISLANDS ON THE EDGE

Haida Gwaii, the Queen Charlotte Islands, rise from the Pacific Ocean near the outer edge of the continental shelf. Although Canada's coast includes thousands of islands, the Charlottes are the most isolated. A broad inshore channel called Hecate Strait separates them from the mainland, and the heaving gap of Dixon Entrance lies between them and the islands to the north that form the Alaskan panhandle.

Viewed on a map, the roughly 150 islands in the archipelago form a scimitar-like shape, positioned 240 kilometres north of Vancouver Island. The largest island, Graham, is like the curving blade. A narrow but navigable channel separates it from the handle, Moresby Island, to the south. Smaller Langara, Louise, Lyell, Burnaby and Kunghit islands are like the encrusting jewels. The total land area of the archipelago is approximately 9,940 square kilometres. This is considerably smaller than Vancouver Island (the largest island along the west coast of the Americas), but almost twice the size of Prince Edward Island, Canada's smallest province.

In recent years, the name "Haida Gwaii" has come into common use when referring to these islands. This name, which means "Islands of the People," is not yet officially recognized by the provincial government. It is certainly more fitting than "Queen Charlotte," the name of a woman who never crossed the Atlantic, let alone visited the North Pacific islands named after her. It will, perhaps, take a few more years to get used to "Haida Gwaii," and even longer for officials to change the name and apply it to maps and charts. It is the name we use most often in this book when referring to the islands, although sometimes we just say "the Charlottes," as that is still the way many people in B.C. refer to the islands.

TOPOGRAPHY

The islands of Haida Gwaii encompass an enormously varied landscape. In a 1968 provincial research paper, geologist A. Sutherland Brown likened them to B.C. in miniature, since most of the terrain found elsewhere in the province is represented here. There are broad beaches of sand, rising columns of sandstone, sea-carved caves and cliffs of volcanic bedrock. There are glacial sediments and rock strata renowned for fossils.

Tow Hill is the most recognized landmark in Naikoon Provincial Park. A trail leads to the summit and offers excellent 360° views.

This is a wild place. The Queen Charlotte Mountains form a divide along the western edge of Graham and Moresby islands, a ridge of rugged and steep terrain incised by numerous straits and fjords. The surf-smashed west coast lies wide open to North Pacific winds, and its inaccessibility means that this beautiful area sees few visitors. Moresby Island is narrow, with steep slopes and few lakes, while Graham has rolling plateaus and muskeg lowlands on its eastern side. The heart of Graham Island is washed by the salt water of Masset Inlet, known to locals as "The Lake." Freshwater streams and rivers run everywhere.

Over all of this clambers verdant vegetation as dense as

Balance Rock, located just a few minutes away from Skidegate Village, is a glacial erratic—a leftover from the last Ice Age.

any tropical jungle. In grandeur, the giant conifers of Haida Gwaii are unsurpassed in Canada. These towering cedar, spruce and hemlock trees are among the best examples of temperate rainforest in North America and were essential to the development of Aboriginal culture. In 1987 some of these magnificent stands were protected when part of the Charlottes was designated the Gwaii Haanas National Park Reserve and Haida Heritage Site.

ECONOMY

Outside the parks and reserves, the huge conifers are still the chief measure of commerce on the islands. The forest industry is the biggest single employer here. Often, and quite understandably, the conservation of lands hasn't sat well with those whose livelihood depends on the harvesting of trees. While many residents are beginning to accept the long-term importance of conservation and careful land management, change comes at a price. The loss of forest jobs means full-time employment is harder to come by in a region that otherwise offers only commercial fishing or the rare mining job. No natural resources are processed here, and government employment and tourism previously represented only minor opportunities.

Many people feel that tourism now presents the greatest potential for economic growth. In the past, sport fishing was the main draw. More recently, however, eco-tourism has become firmly established and is expected to boost the islands' economy well into the new millennium.

COMMUNITY

Eight main communities dot the islands today, along with several logging camps and a number of former townsites that have retained a few occupants. From north to south, Graham Island has active communities at Old Massett, Masset, Port Clements, Tlell, Skidegate, Skidegate Landing and the Village of Queen Charlotte.

Masset is the largest centre. Commercial fishing is the economic mainstay here. Port Clements ("Port" for short) combines fishing with logging. Tlell is a hamlet, but is home to a collection of artisans and B&Bs, as well as the provincial park office and a small ranch. The Village of Queen Charlotte is simply dubbed "Charlotte." Its central location and government offices have made it the unofficial capital of the islands.

Sandspit, on Moresby Island, contests this supremacy because it has the largest airport, a small boat harbour and an information centre for Gwaii Haanas National Park Reserve and Haida Heritage Site.

PEOPLE

About 5,000 Canadians of varied ancestry live on Haida Gwaii today. Like islanders everywhere, they enjoy their isolation and lifestyle and are often resistant to change. They're particularly interested in maintaining local control over the developments that influence their lives. They prefer a certain amount of challenge to modern convenience.

Although islanders frequently demonstrate the *mañana* attitude, don't be fooled into thinking these are backwater folks. Many are multi-talented: being a jack-of-all-trades comes with the territory in a place where work and supplies are often expensive or in short supply. Here, financial achievement is not the only measure of success; personal accomplishment and individuality seem equally important. As a result, you'll find a high level of confidence and personality among the locals. "Characters" tend to find plenty of nourishment in this environment. Don't be surprised when you hear monikers such as Sid the Wrench, Huckleberry or Stickleback Tom.

A series of islander profiles in the section "Their Place To Be" offers a glimpse into the lifestyles and passions of some of the people we've had the pleasure of meeting over the course of numerous visits to Haida Gwaii. Since every islander seems to have several pearls in the closet, these profiles cannot possibly speak to the experiences of all. Instead, they present a snapshot of a few of the folks who make these islands their home, and, perhaps most importantly, give some insight into why they have stayed.

One thing is certain. Time spent meeting the people of Haida Gwaii will provide as many memorable moments as exploring the spectacular landscape.

ORIENTATION

To help you get around, we have included some brief directions ("Getting There") at the beginning of each destination chapter. For more general information about transportation, travel, permits, park orientation and reservations, community services, fishing and more, refer to the "Planning Your Trip" chapter at the end of the book.

In the event you're travelling on a tight schedule, we've also come up with recommendations for a five-day trip, and there's a metric conversion table back there, too, for those less familiar with the metric measurements used throughout this guide.

CAUTION

We would be remiss if we did not warn you at the outset about one particular feature of Haida Gwaii—the curious effect of the waters of St. Mary's Spring. The spring's location is marked by a chainsaw sculpture of a woman by the side of Yellowhead Highway (#16), just north of Lawn Hill. Legend has it that whoever partakes of the spring's cool, natural champagne will someday return to the islands. It has certainly had that effect on us.

We hope you, too, will find a reason to return to Haida Gwaii.

The small spring along Highway 16 has had a lasting effect on many travellers who have sipped the clear water.

2

EUROPEAN DISCOVERY
OF HAIDA GWAII

On July 17, 1774, a Spanish explorer, Captain Juan Perez of the ship *Santiago,* sighted a prominent headland on the archipelago's northwest tip. The next day a fleet of Haida dugout canoes paddled out to visit his ship. This historic event marked the first European contact with one of the most sophisticated Native societies in North America. It didn't take long for other navigators to follow Perez, venturing into the region from New Spain (now California) in 1775 and 1779.

The great British explorer Captain James Cook bypassed these islands altogether on his trip up this coast in 1778. Upon reaching Alaska, however, he traded for sea otter pelts that eventually sold in China for an astronomical sum. So began the maritime fur trade, an enterprise so profitable it ultimately annihilated all the sea otters in the area, and very nearly extinguished the entire species.

By 1786, British ships direct from England, India and the Far East were competing for trade with Natives all along the Pacific Northwest coast. Captain George Dixon sailed close to Hippa Island along the west coast of Haida Gwaii that year. The following year he returned and, after further exploration, named the entire group of islands after his ship and his king's consort: Queen Charlotte.

The islands eventually became a trading territory for Americans as well. Sadly, the aggressive attitude of these efficient competitors had serious consequences for both the Haida and other traders. The intimidation and force used by one Captain Robert Gray initiated a series of violent reprisals by the Natives. As the sea otter population declined, trade methods became more ruthless. There was murder on both sides.

Less hostile relations were re-established in 1831 when British traders of the Hudson's Bay Company (HBC) began constructing permanent trading posts on the north coast. The company restricted the sale of firearms, ammunition, and liquor. Although this reduced HBC profits, it resulted in a good deal more stability. With the British establishing colonies on the south coast and the Russians firmly in control of the north, the Americans eventually left the territory.

For the Haida, the introduction of western civilization was devastating. Disease, illegal alcohol, firearms and money combined to destroy what had been one of the strongest Native cultures on the coast. Missionaries also arrived to Christianize the Natives. In their fervour, some of these missionaries did more damage than good; others were trusted and respected.

The first was an Irish clergyman named William Henry Collison. His memoir, *In the Wake of the War Canoe*, offers a fascinating insight into many aspects of traditional Haida life before further European influence resulted in major cultural changes.

The early post-contact history of the islands follows a fairly typical pattern characterized by the usual retinue of missionaries, resource developers and homesteaders. Nothing came easily in this rugged and isolated environment. Certainly, the churches were successful in their search for souls, and the lumber industry still survives. Only a few homesteaders, however, found the climate hospitable.

The early exploration and pioneering history of the Charlottes has been well documented by island resident Kathleen (Betty) Dalzell in three volumes (see "Further Reading" and "Their Place to Be").

THE HAIDA PEOPLE

Geography made it easy for Haida society to develop. The islands enjoy a relatively warm maritime climate with plenty of rain, which enables rich stands of spruce, hemlock and cedar to flourish. Meanwhile, island shores are washed by nutrient-rich waters teeming with intertidal life, where fish, birds and mammals feed in abundance. Surrounded by such generous natural resources, the Haida developed a self-sustaining hunting and gathering society, rich in oral language and tradition.

The western red cedar was pivotal to Haida society. The species' immense size, straight grain, soft wood and resistance to rot made it ideal for house construction. The Haida cut the trees, selected a house site and undertook the actual construction with great care and precision. Houses had a dual purpose. They were practical, in that they provided their occupants with shelter, and they were also ceremonial centres. Entering their oval doorways marked passage into the spiritual world, bringing occupants into close association with their cultural traditions.

The final act in house building, along with a potlatch celebration, was the raising of a frontal pole bearing the crests of the resident family. Poles carved from cedar were erected both inside and outside houses. The figures on poles depict more than just animals: some represent natural phenomena; others are supernatural beings. The crests belonged to specific families and were jealously guarded. New crests could be added during a potlatch.

Sadly, few original poles remain in their original locations. The villages of K̲'uuna llnagaay (formerly Skedans) and SG̲ang Gwaay llnagaay (formerly Ninstints) have the most poles still on site. The museum at Skidegate Village displays a few more. (In 2001, six new poles were raised next to the museum.) Others can be viewed at the Royal British Columbia

Old Haida villages are one of the main attractions on the islands. This eagle mortuary stands at K̲'uuna Llnagaay (formerly called Skedans).

Museum in Victoria. In 1981 UNESCO granted SG̲ang Gwaay (formerly Anthony Island) World Heritage Site status. This ranks the Village of SG̲ang Gwaay llnagaay with the Egyptian pyramids (see "SG̲ang Gwaay World Heritage Site").

As impressive as their houses and poles were, the Haida were unequalled in canoe building. From massive cedars they carved graceful craft varying in length from 22 metres to the more manoeuvrable 4- and 7-metre models. The largest could easily transport 40 people and two tonnes of supplies.

With these boats, Haida men and women paddled through temperamental Dixon Entrance and crossed the treacherous shallows of Hecate Strait. On trading or raiding forays they travelled as far south as present-day Victoria and Puget Sound, Washington. They were superlative seafarers, staying out of sight of land for days without navigational aids. See "Of Canoes and Culture" for more about these historic vessels.

No discussion of West Coast Native culture would be complete without mention of potlatches. These were ceremonial celebrations held to mark significant cultural events. In preparation for such an event, guests from other villages were invited and huge feasts were prepared.

These celebrations were an extremely important part of Haida culture. They allowed marriages to be witnessed, families to intermix, a chief's successor to be named and an individual's or family's status to be confirmed. Eating, gift giving, dancing and storytelling were an integral part of each gathering. Since the Haida relied heavily on their oral history, much was irretrievably lost during the colonial period when their villages were ravaged by European diseases. Later, when the Canadian government outlawed potlatches, Haida culture was further diminished. During the last 50 years, however, the Haida have revived and reshaped many age-old traditions.

The resurgence of their art is one of the most appreciated aspects of this renaissance. Many Native artisans, among them weavers and carvers of silver, gold, argillite (a soft black shale quarried on Slatechuck Mountain) and wood, have gained international reputations. An item from one of these master crafters makes an great conversation piece when you talk about your visit to Haida Gwaii. Equally memorable is viewing the cedar canoe next to the museum in Skidegate, or visiting K̲'uuna or SG̲ang Gwaay. An invitation to a potlatch will deepen your understanding of Haida heritage and may serve as a reminder that the world came close to losing this magnificent culture.

Cumshewa Village once had about 280 inhabitants. This was one of the last village sites to be deserted in the southern islands.

Courtesy of BC Archives, circa 1890 C-09294

PART TWO

INTRODUCTION TO THE
NATURAL HISTORY OF HAIDA GWAII

The unusual natural history of Haida Gwaii, not to mention its promise of superlative outdoor recreation, has made these islands one of Canada's most desirable adventure-travel destinations. Provincial, national and international designation of reserves to protect landscapes and heritage sites as well as various species and their habitats has ensured the preservation of this region's many special attributes.

The islands' distance from the mainland has restricted the natural influx of animals and plants. As a result, the islands have significantly fewer species than the mainland. There are, however, many endemic subspecies of birds, mammals, fish and invertebrates. At one time these islands even supported a subspecies of caribou that, tragically, is now extinct. Several species of insects are found only here, and more unique species may be discovered as research continues.

When it comes to plants, there are a dozen species unique to Haida Gwaii. Not surprisingly in this moist climate, many are mosses. Another two dozen plants provide examples of disjunctive populations—that is, species separated from their relatives by great distances. For example, some local specimens are associated with species normally found in Japan, other parts of Asia and Scotland. Possibly they found refuge on an unglaciated part of the islands during the Ice Age.

Such ecological oddities have led to promotion of the islands as the "Galapagos of Canada." This is a reference to the Galapagos Islands, off the coast of Ecuador, which are famous for the evolutionary distinctions of their wildlife, originally studied by Charles Darwin. Biological parallels between the Charlottes and the Galapagos are evident, as they are on any isolated islands. For the most part, however, we feel the phrase works better in promotion than in application, because it creates a distorted expectation of the wildlife to be encountered. That said, knowledgeable birders, botanists, nature photographers and other enthusiasts will be delighted with what they can find here. You can enhance your pleasure by doing some reading before your arrival. *Islands at the Edge: Preserving the Queen Charlotte Islands Wilderness*, by the Island Protection Society, is an excellent introduction to the outstanding natural history of these islands.

The scent of Indian paintbrush on Rose Spit can be smelled downwind long before one sees the flowers.

BIRDS OF HAIDA GWAII

The Charlottes are among the richest islands for bird study in Canada. Millions of birds visit or nest around the archipelago every year, although the number of species to be found here is actually less than on the adjacent mainland. (Remote islands predictably have fewer species.) By the year 2006, 283 species had been recorded on Haida Gwaii, compared to more than 477 throughout B.C. Similarly, of about 300 species that breed in B.C., only 77 breed here. However, the unusual and rare birds of these islands are guaranteed to delight casual birdwatchers, and compulsive bird listers will have an opportunity to record Asian strays.

Birdwatching on Haida Gwaii doesn't always require binoculars. As you walk along the beaches you'll pass beneath bald eagles perched on overhanging branches, while song sparrows, dark-eyed juncos and even hermit thrushes will boldly continue feeding among the driftwood as you approach. On the water, common loons and white-winged scoters are easily identified before they dive.

If, on the other hand, you want to see sandhill cranes dancing, witness the flight of a peregrine falcon or search for Siberian shorebirds, you'll probably need a field guide, a good pair of binoculars or a spotting scope.

Bird enthusiasts come here specifically to see rare, colonial or unusual birds. Of the 283 recorded species, more than 70 percent are non-perching birds. Many of these are associated with aquatic habitats: loons, albatross, shearwaters, shorebirds and alcids fall into this category. During migration, hundreds of thousands of birds from these families visit Haida Gwaii.

Black oystercatchers are unmistakable with their robust red bill and pink feet. The name oystercatcher is a misnomer. They relish limpets, chitons, snails and other small shellfish.

Of the four species of loon, both the common and the red-throated breed on lakes in the Charlottes. The smaller, lighter, red-throated loon can take off from short stretches of water, which enables it to inhabit small lakes and ponds. Although they raise their young here, they fly to the ocean for food. An estimated 400 pairs of red-throated loons nest throughout the islands—one of the highest breeding densities in the world for this species .

Birders seem to have an even keener desire to see a third species, the yellow-billed loon. Although they breed exclusively in the high Arctic, individuals remain scattered along B.C.'s coast throughout the year, especially on the Charlottes. Numerous sightings occur during spring and summer, with fewer during autumn and winter. Look for them year-round in Skidegate Inlet, off Rose Spit, in sheltered bays or even on the open water of Old Massett.

Some birds travel to Haida Gwaii from more distant places. After breeding throughout the southern and eastern Pacific, shearwaters and albatross head to northern latitudes, where they may be sighted from spring through fall. Of the six species of shearwater, the sooty shearwaters are the most numerous. At least a million of these birds spend the summer in Hecate Strait. Due to upwelling currents, Rose Spit is also a favourite feeding place for sooty and several other species of shearwater.

While searching for shearwaters, you might spot a much larger, dark-bodied bird with a 2-metre wing span. Sightings of black-footed albatross (and the even rarer Laysan albatross) are well documented on

Pigeon guillemots in summer plumage. Of the eight species of breeding alcids, these birds are usually the easiest to find.

the Charlottes. A few have been spotted in Hecate Strait, but most occur off the west coast, particularly in spring and summer.

Of the 44 species of shore-birds recorded, only 8 are known as breeders. Two of these have made significant extensions to their normal breeding range. Semipalmated plovers nest each spring along North and East beaches. This is a long way south of their main Arctic breeding grounds, and one of only a few known B.C. breeding sites. Least sandpipers also normally nest on the tundra, but researchers have counted as many as 90 pairs nesting at Delkatla Wildlife Sanctuary at Masset—probably a

Glaucous-winged gulls nest on several small islets throughout Skidegate Inlet. Watch for them from the ferry MV *Kwuna*.

very high breeding density for this shorebird. Sanderlings do not breed here, but many stay on through the winter. Annual Christmas bird counts have recorded the highest winter number of this species anywhere in Canada. Look for them sprinting along the water's edge on sandy beaches, or on mud flats.

More than half of B.C.'s total seabird population, an estimated two million pairs, breeds on small wooded or sparsely vegetated islands here. Seabirds flourish on these islands partly because their colonies remain isolated from the mainland. The islands are protected from most predators, have direct access to the ocean and, equally important, offer a variety of nesting sites.

Isolation has also been an important factor in the evolution of three unique subspecies. The northern saw-whet owl, hairy woodpecker and Steller's jay all live in forested areas. They can be distinguished from their mainland relatives by their darker colours or by markings their relatives don't possess. Steller's jay here is darker and lacks the noticeable white eyebrow typical of mainland birds; saw-whet owls and hairy woodpeckers have darker pigmentation than off-island individuals.

As most birdwatchers know, the thrill of finding a "life bird"—a bird never previously sighted by that birdwatcher—is perhaps surpassed only by discovering a "new" species—a bird never before recorded in that area. Since Haida Gwaii lies along the migratory path of many birds, vagrant birds (unusual wanderers) occasionally appear. A great-tailed grackle identified at Cape St. James must have flown here from the Gulf Coast. The red-faced cormorant, Aleutian tern and black-tailed gull possibly arrived from Alaska or Siberia. A magnificent frigatebird, sighted off Langara Island in 1981, may have come from the Galapagos Islands on the equator.

Finding migrant and resident birds on the islands is a pleasant task. If you come by ferry, be sure to watch for oceanic birds as soon as you reach open water. The ferry docks in Skidegate Inlet, which is one of the better island birding spots. Kagan Bay, Sandspit and numerous islets host some nesting birds, as well as many migrating ducks and shorebirds. A Baikal teal, red-legged kittiwake, black-and-white warbler and red-throated pipits were recent rarities sighted at Sandspit.

Almost all seabird colonies are located in the Gwaii Haanas region or along the west coast north to Langara Island. You'll require a boat or aircraft to reach them. Many have landing restrictions and should be viewed only from the water.

North of Skidegate Inlet, scan the Yakoun River estuary near Port Clements. Sandhill cranes are regulars here throughout the summer, while wintering birds include trumpeter swans, ducks, geese and eagles. Delkatla Wildlife Sanctuary at Masset shouldn't be missed as its combination of water, shore and forest habitats has attracted more than 113 species. This list includes unusual vagrants such as cattle egrets, marbled godwits, ruffs and wood sandpipers. Nearby, Masset Sound, McIntyre Bay and waters to the west have an equal number of interesting birds. Black-tailed gulls, Aleutian terns and king eider have been found in these areas.

For us, Rose Spit remains the undisputed birding hot spot. Its sandy nose hooking into Hecate Strait attracts sea and land birds alike. Shearwaters, fulmars, auklets and diving ducks can number into the thousands. One summer afternoon more than a hundred sooty shearwaters crossed our spotting-scope view in less than a minute. On a brisk autumn day, after waiting three hours for a pea-soup fog to lift, we checked off 37 species in short order. Among them: red knot, wandering tattler, black-legged kittiwake, sandhill crane and two peregrine falcons. Only a Caspian tern, seen the day before, could have made us happier.

SEABIRD ISLANDS

The Charlottes are particularly well known for 12 species of nesting seabirds: two species of storm-petrel, a cormorant, a gull and eight species of alcids, or diving seabirds. They nest on smaller islands using a variety of wooded and open habitats ranging from barren rocks a few metres above high tide to cliffs, grassy knolls and heavily wooded islands. Although most are difficult to spot due to their nocturnal habits and underground nests, estimated numbers range from one million to two million pairs.

These birds use more than a hundred islands. Major breeding stations with more than 25,000 breeding pairs exist on Langara, Hippa, Lyell, Rankine, SGang Gwaay and Kerouard islands. Seabirds have selected these sites for good reason: in most cases the colonies are isolated from predators and free of human disturbance. Birds select sites as close as possible to their feeding areas—the pelagic waters of the eastern North Pacific. A variety of habitats exist on most islands, making it possible for several species to nest without seriously affecting one another.

Leach's and fork-tailed storm-petrels are the smallest of all the seabirds on the Charlottes. Sometimes called "sea swallows," they are barely larger than those more familiar insect eaters, and they have a similar light, fluttery flight. They nest in burrows and lay a single white egg. Both sexes share incubation, which lasts about 50 days. Every few nights, in complete darkness, the colonies come alive with activity. After foraging at sea, one parent returns to relieve its mate deep within the burrow. They apparently locate each other by call. The returning adult takes over while the other flies off.

Compared to the secretive storm-petrels, pelagic cormorants and glaucous-winged gulls are large and conspicuous breeding birds. Both species prefer rocky islets with little or no vegetation. The gulls occupy the flatter ground, while cormorants prefer ledges and cliff faces. Flocks of gulls circling over an islet or cliffs plastered with white excrement mark the colonies from a long way off and give the impression that the birds are abundant. A surprisingly low number actually breed on Haida Gwaii, however: less than 500 pairs of cormorants and 2,000 pairs of gulls.

Cormorants have the distinction of being the seabird with the greatest reproductive potential. They can lay as many as six eggs, and will lay a second clutch to replace any that are damaged or stolen. Crows and gulls frequently grab cormorant eggs if the adults are inattentive or have been scared off the nest. It's interesting to note that cormorants and gulls, despite being egg enemies, sometimes share the same nesting islet.

Many seabirds have solved the problem of exposed nests, laying their eggs in rock crevices or at the end of long burrows. The largest and most colourful burrow-nesting seabirds are tufted puffins and rhinoceros auklets. Both are dark bodied, but can be distinguished by their bills. The puffin has a bright yellow-and-orange triangle similar to a parrot, hence its nickname "sea parrot." The rhinoceros auklet's thinner bill bears a small horn near the base during breeding season. Both species feed near shore, returning to their burrows on grassy slopes or the forest floor once the sun has set. Their colonies on the Charlottes exist only in southern areas at this time. (Although only one nest of the less common horned puffin has ever been found here, probably there are more.)

Ancient murrelets and Cassin's auklets give no indication as to their actual abundance on Haida Gwaii. They number into the hundreds of thousands (nearly 75 percent of the entire world population of the species), yet are among the most secretive birds along our coast. They feed well offshore during the day, returning in total darkness to their burrows beneath the mossy forest floor. Bill snapping and twittering calls are heard as the adults crash-land beneath the trees. These vocalizations may help them orient themselves and locate their young.

Cassin's auklets feed a single black chick on regurgitated crustaceans. Forty days after hatching, the chicks fly away from the colony. Ancient murrelet young are precocial (they can feed themselves soon after birth). Within two days of hatching, the two murrelet chicks leave their burrow by night. Guided by their parents' calls, they scramble through the forest to the shoreline. Once on the water, they swim with their parents directly out to sea.

Marbled murrelets have so far eluded every attempt to locate their nests on the Charlottes. (Nests have been found on mossy branches of conifers in old-growth forests in other B.C. coastal locations.) Small groups of these chocolate-coloured murrelets gather offshore, where they dive for fish. At dusk they fly inland to highly secretive destinations. Evidence strongly suggests they nest in the branches of tall trees on the Charlottes. In 1953, amid the debris of a large hemlock felled near Masset, an adult marbled murrelet was discovered dazed but alive. Eggshell fragments were found nearby, but there was no sign of a nest. This tiny bird continues to keep its nesting sites a secret on Haida Gwaii.

Any discussion of seabird colonies on Haida Gwaii would be incomplete without mention of peregrine falcons and bald eagles, the seabirds' main predators. Somewhere between 60 and 80 pairs of peregrine falcons nest here. If non-breeding birds are added in, the falcon population probably exceeds 200 individuals—the greatest density in Canada. Their high numbers are supported by an abundance of food, especially seabirds. They hunt ancient murrelets, Cassin's auklets and both species of storm-petrels. Shorebirds and smaller waterbirds are preyed upon at other times of the year.

Peregrines are highly specialized predators. They pursue prey directly, catching or knocking it out of the air. During the nesting period, this activity begins at dusk, directly from the eyrie. As darkness closes in, nocturnal seabirds appear from either the sea or their burrows. Peregrine falcons wait aloft, and as the seabirds' shadowy silhouettes appear, the hunter makes a swift, headlong stoop. Speed, surprise and height give deadly advantage to the predator. Falcons often make successive kills whether hungry or not, judging from the littered remains of seabirds found below their favourite plucking perches.

Naturally, most eyries are located close to a seabird colony. Peregrines prefer to nest on a ledge near the top of a steep cliff, using overhanging roots or plants for shelter. Sometimes they'll take over an old eagle or hawk nest. Adults share parental duties, feeding three or four young even after they've become skilled fliers. Such added care may be crucial to maintaining their population, since young falcons appear to have difficulty catching food on their own. This may be the reason why few young falcons survive the winter.

Bald eagles also prey on seabirds, although they lack the specialized hunting techniques demonstrated by peregrine falcons. The eagles normally feed on fish or carrion, but on the Charlottes at least half their diet consists of seabirds. Bald eagles have been observed walking through an old forest, apparently searching for stunned or disoriented murrelets. Studies have also shown that they have developed a taste for gulls, shearwaters, fulmars and even abalone. In winter, eagles regularly eat diving ducks such as scaups and scoters.

Despite the abundance of avian predators, the sheer size of the population of seabirds ensures that more than enough survive to maintain their numbers. A far greater threat comes from other quarters: humans, fire, oil spills, logging, rats and raccoons seriously affect seabird populations. For these reasons, an island in Lepas Bay, the Anthony Islets, and Copper, Jeffrey, Rankine and Kerouard islands have all been designated ecological reserves, or have special designation to protect nesting birds. You will need a permit to go ashore on these islands at any time.

Following a few simple rules will minimize human impact on other colonies. One person walking through a colony of cormorants or gulls is enough to cause a major disruption. Gulls, in particular, will attack and kill chicks that cross invisible territorial boundaries. Cormorants will flush from nests when disturbed, leaving their eggs to be devoured by gulls and crows,

Silhouettes of peregrine falcons. Males are smaller than females, which have a wingspan of 34 to 36 centimetres.

or their young to bake in the sun. Islands that have nesting gulls and cormorants should be viewed only from the water.

Nocturnal seabird colonies appear abandoned during the day—you can be in the middle of one without knowing it. During the breeding season, nightfall brings thousands of adults crashing through the trees and undergrowth. This seemingly chaotic arrival is followed by a mad dash for the burrow.

The threat to existence comes in many guises. Domestic cats and dogs can create havoc, catching and killing adults before they locate their mates. Beach fires disorient flying birds, and if they are left burning, may advance into the forest. A large oil spill, or logging near a seabird colony, can wipe out entire populations.

For trips to any wilderness island, leave all pets on the boat (or at home), walk around the island only in daylight and do not light fires anywhere. Every island visitor has a responsibility to make sure that millions of seabirds continue to be an integral part of Haida Gwaii.

MARINE MAMMALS AND REPTILES
OF HAIDA GWAII

The cool waters that surround Haida Gwaii are part of the most favoured habitat in the Pacific for marine mammals. The Alaska current sweeps along the west coast, blending tidal currents, river runoff and areas of upwelling into a nutrient-rich solution. Plankton, fish and marine invertebrates thrive in this environment. In all, 23 species of marine mammals and one reptile have also been attracted to these islands.

Marine mammals are usually large, spending most of their life in the ocean. In the waters surrounding the Charlottes you may spot whales, dolphins, porpoises, seals, sea lions and sea otters. Of the 23 recorded species, 6 either breed or spend a significant portion of their time in nearshore waters, 10 are occasionally spotted near islands and coastlines, and 9 stay well offshore.

Of the cetaceans (whales, porpoises and dolphins), the gray whale is the most common and predictable. These large and unassuming mammals pass through inshore waters biannually, travelling between their Arctic summering areas and Baja breeding lagoons. This 20,000-kilometre journey is the longest undertaken by any mammal. Alone or in small groups, the whales travel day and night, seldom even stopping to eat. Energy is supplied by fat reserves accumulated before the journey begins.

Because they lack teeth, gray whales obtain food primarily by sucking mud from the seabed. A baleen filter in their mouth screens bottom-dwelling crustaceans from the mud and water. Naturally, these whales prefer shallow, fine-sediment areas for feeding. They also feed on floating and swimming organisms and may even consume eelgrass and kelp.

GRAY WHALES OF HAIDA GWAII

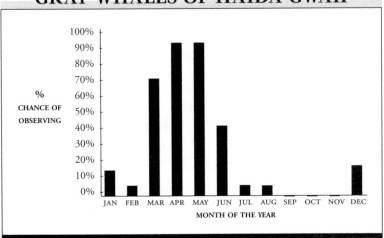

Gray whales migrate north along these shores in April and May, returning south again in very late fall. Watch for their smooth grey backs, ending in a row of knuckles just in front of the tail. Skidegate Inlet (see "Around Skidegate Inlet"), along the coast between Skidegate and Tlell, and Rose Spit are all excellent observation posts.

A second group of cetaceans possesses teeth capable of seizing fish, squid, birds, seals and sea lions. Prey is swallowed whole or in chunks; these animals can rip, but not chew, flesh. Eleven species occur here, but only four can be expected near shore.

The smallest are blunt-nosed harbor porpoises. These shy mammals prefer sheltered shorelines and waterways, such as Skidegate and Cumshewa inlets. True to their disposition, they usually travel alone or in groups of two or three. Most people glimpse only a small fin disappearing beneath the surface, as these mammals vanish when approached or disturbed.

Dall's porpoises are the exact opposite. These sleek, thick-bodied creatures are full of spirited curiosity and are reputed to be the fastest marine mammal. Their bold black-and-white forms zip through the water, sometimes creating sudden rooster tails of spray. To the delight of boaters, Dall's porpoises love to chase a fast craft and will sometimes ride bow waves. They'll zig, zag and zip across in front of a boat's prow, but will quickly vanish if you slow down for a better look.

Pacific white-sided dolphins sometimes venture into nearshore waters. Unlike Dall's porpoises, white-sided dolphins may be in groups of 50 to 100 or more. They are playful and sociable, but will probably stay well away from kayaks or larger craft.

The excitement created by porpoises and dolphins is second only to the appearance of *Orcinus orca*, the killer whale. Sighting their tall dorsal fins slicing the water's surface is simultaneously frightening and intriguing. The personality and habits of these graceful marine hunters contradict their reputation as indiscriminate monsters. A 20-year study, initiated by the late Dr. Michael Bigg, made enormous strides in furthering our understanding of these mammals. For years it was believed killer whales ate anything that moved—a belief that suggested humans were also fair game. However, logs from thousands of hours of observing these whales show that there is not one valid account of aggressive behaviour toward humans in B.C. There is only one single record of a provoked attack, and that was against a boat.

Dr. Bigg and his colleagues also identified three distinct groups of killer whales around the Charlottes. One group, referred to as *residents,* usually herds in pods of 10 to 25 animals and eats only fish. The second group,

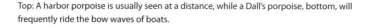

Top: A harbor porpoise is usually seen at a distance, while a Dall's porpoise, bottom, will frequently ride the bow waves of boats.

transients, usually moves in pods of 2 to 5 whales and eats only marine mammals. Recently a third group, provisionally designated as *offshores*, has been recognized. Much less is known about this latter group, although most of the sightings have occurred off the Charlottes and Vancouver Island.

If you travel long enough with a pod of transients, you may witness an attack on a harbor seal (their most common prey), or a northern sea lion. These pinnipeds, or fin-footed mammals, are common residents throughout the islands. They have hairy coats and love to "haul out" on beaches or rocky islets. They're tolerant, sometimes allowing close approach, but it's advisable to stay at least 100 metres away, even if the sea lions appear accustomed to human presence.

Sea lions habitually congregate on isolated islets, where you can sometimes witness their spectacular behaviour. Occasionally exceeding one tonne in weight, these brown beasts may seem ponderous on land, but they are truly graceful when plunging headlong into foaming surf or when swimming. We have seen kayakers paddle over their massive forms, but it is more prudent to keep a comfortable distance, as they could easily upset a small craft. At any time, but particularly during the winter months, they haul out at Rose Spit, Skedans Rocks and Reef Island.

Sea lions also congregate throughout the year at southerly Cape St. James. In the summer, more than 1,100 sea lions return to this remote tip to breed, making it the largest rookery on the

A killer whale spyhopping near Hlk'yah. Was it looking at us or was it searching for seals? Some pods of orcas, known as transients, prefer to eat marine mammals such as seals and porpoises.

Northern sea lions breed at Cape St. James. They haul out on rocky promontories all around the islands. Approach them slowly and stay at least 100 metres away.

B.C. coast. Males begin arriving on these wave-washed rocks in May, immediately establishing and defending a territory. Females and other immature animals arrive a few weeks later.

Pregnant females give birth to a single pup soon after arriving. Within the next two weeks, while they nurse their newborn and perhaps also a yearling, they mate with one of the territorial males. The females then settle into a routine of feeding well away from the colony before returning to nurse their pups. By late August this social fabric breaks apart, as most males scatter along B.C.'s coast in smaller groups. Females and pups may overwinter near the rookery or perhaps spread out along the coast. Regardless of how far they travel, they usually let the males manage on their own.

Sea lions tend to upset commercial fishers, who blame them for depleting salmon stocks and destroying fishing gear (which they sometimes do). Pressure is constantly applied to fisheries officials to shoot sea lions, and at one time this was done. Studies prove, however, that sea lions are opportunistic feeders, dining on whatever fish are most plentiful. They do not particularly favour salmon.

Harbor seals are likewise blamed for gorging on salmon: their habit of raiding spawning streams has given them a bad reputation. Despite this, they, too, are opportunists, catching whatever takes the least amount of energy. This fits their lifestyle well. They spend a lot of time hauled out and resting with others of their kind.

They can, however, be spontaneous and energetic. On one occasion we were startled by a loud splash and turned to see a fleeting shape disappearing into a kelp bed. Suddenly, a round head appeared and curious eyes examined us. After deciding we were harmless, the young seal playfully chomped on a large kelp frond, then dove after an imaginary companion.

Harbor seals seem to spend equal amounts of time on land and in the water; they rest, mate, give birth and moult on shore and at sea. You will see harbor seals on or around many sheltered rocks or islets throughout the Charlottes. Look for them specifically off Rose Spit, and within Masset, Skidegate and Cumshewa inlets. Throughout South Moresby, watch for their mottled forms along the east coast of Lyell Island, at Marco Island and in other protected areas.

Sea otters were once as plentiful as harbor seals. The smallest of all marine mammals, they were highly valued for their fur: British, American and Russian traders were ruthless in their quest for these dark pelts which fetched a fabulous price in China. So intense was their desire for wealth that greedy sailors literally traded the shirts off their backs. The Haida were willing accomplices, and they vigorously traded the skins for the wonderful goods the purchasers offered. Only remnant otter populations in Alaska and California survived the slaughter. In the past two decades there have been two substantiated sightings in the Charlottes. (Otters sighted in these parts are most likely to be the river otter. These are numerous throughout the Charlottes and are frequently seen in salt water.)

Despite their near annihilation, sea otter populations have increased dramatically in California and Alaska. In 1911, when they were first protected by law, their numbers were so far down they were facing extinction. Current studies indicate a total population of well over 30,000. On the west coast of Vancouver Island, a sea otter population was reintroduced in 1969 and 1970 and is now increasing by about 19 percent per year. More than 2,000 have been counted, and a second group of 400 is resident near Goose Island. If these two groups continue to flourish, perhaps sea otters will make their way back to Haida Gwaii and once again flourish along its western shores.

In addition to the fascinating array of mammals, the largest species of turtle in the world has been seen (and captured by fishermen) off the Charlottes. The leatherback is the only reptile found on the Charlottes. Documented sightings have come from Masset, Skidegate Inlet and the South Moresby region. Only a few sightings have occurred over the years, however, since these marine turtles tend to stay in warmer waters far to the south.

Thankfully attitudes toward all marine animals have changed. Whereas humans once killed them on sight, studying wildlife is now a major recreational activity. As more people experience the thrill of seeing these animals in their natural habitat, our sense of kinship with them, albeit poorly developed, seems to grow. Their intelligence, curiosity, care of offspring and playfulness are qualities we share. It is our hope that personal experiences will blend with respect and lead to greater understanding of these remarkable creatures.

6

LAND MAMMALS AND AMPHIBIANS
OF HAIDA GWAII

During the last Ice Age, immense sheets of ice covered these islands. However thick this ice may have been, many scientists believe there were parts of the archipelago that remained ice-free. Some speculate that these pockets, or *refugia*, may have been large enough to allow some mammals to survive. Other species arrived on the islands after the ice melted, but only 11 species were present on Haida Gwaii when the first Europeans arrived. Unfortunately, the intruders' infested ships brought rats and mice, which were previously unknown along the B.C. coast. The accidental importation of these four-legged foreigners marked the beginning of a rash of species' introductions, so that, today, there are almost an equal number of native and foreign species on the islands.

Refugia and Hecate Strait have proved to be effective barriers to mammal dispersal. When animals remain isolated for a long period of time, they begin to differ from their relatives in larger breeding populations. These differences include size and colour variations, and habitat selection. Most native mammals on Haida Gwaii exhibit such characteristics. For example, the black bear here is the largest of its kind in North America. The marten is one of the largest on the continent and is a lighter colour, with an orange tinge to its undercoat. The ermine and river otter are also subspecies unique to these islands.

There are exceptions, however, that encourage debate of refugia. One subspecies of dusky shrew, for example, seems to resemble its mainland cousins. Could it have arrived on the islands in a Haida canoe, or clinging to some floating debris? Such examples are intriguing and fuel speculation among genetic researchers.

Drivers between Masset and Tlell should be very cautious in low-light conditions. Up to 50 deer may be grazing along the right-of-way.

Bats differ from all other Haida Gwaii mammals in their ability to fly. They may fly as far as the mainland, but more research is needed to be certain. Four species inhabit these islands. One of only two known colonies of Keen's long-eared myotis in B.C. was found on G̲andll K'in in Gwaayaay (Hotspring Island). Curiously, these bats, along with some little brown myotis, roost in rocky cracks and crevices below high tide.

Originally the caribou was the only ungulate mammal on Haida Gwaii. Unfortunately, little is known about the local species: the last one to be seen was shot in 1908. It apparently fitted the pattern of mammals on isolated islands, being smaller than mainland caribou. The females may have differed from their mainland relatives by not growing antlers. These caribou appear to have maintained a tenuous existence in the bogs on Graham Island. Possibly competition from introduced deer, as well as from hunting, contributed to their demise. Accounts of searching for the last of these animals are documented in Charles Sheldon's book *The Wilderness of the North Pacific Coast Islands*.

Amphibians are another story. The western toad is the only amphibian native to the islands, and the Pacific treefrog has recently been introduced. Both are widely distributed and can be found in fields, meadows and forests. Since toads probably did not swim across Hecate Strait, they may have survived in a glacial refugia or crossed the water as stowaways.

The islands' biological balance has been altered drastically by introduced animals. The black rat may well have arrived on sailing ships, since captains had no way of ridding their vessels of these vermin. This was not the case with other introductions. By 1901 several attempts to populate the islands with deer had failed, before two subsequent introductions proved successful. Red deer from New Zealand were also released. The introduction of squirrels, beaver, elk, raccoons and mule (Sitka) deer also took place.

Some of the consequences are severe. An absence of predators and abundant food caused a population explosion among the Sitka deer. Competition among them has resulted in a change of diet to *cedar à la bush*. Much to the chagrin of foresters, these small deer eat cedar seedlings faster than they can be planted. Researchers have partially protected plantings by placing transparent cones over the seedlings, but this adds substantial cost to tree farming.

Two other non-native mammals have also become nuisances. Raccoons have a reputation for devouring the eggs of ground-nesting birds. Since these aggressive animals are able swimmers, isolated nesting islets are well within their reach. Seabird colonies have no defence against such marauders and could be decimated by this animal's omnivorous appetite.

The beaver's habit of building dams poses another kind of threat. The lowlands on Graham Island are dotted by countless lakes and ponds. Many of these were completely isolated and contained their own distinct subspecies of stickleback. These minnow-sized fish are of great scientific interest due to their genetic differences. The beaver dams raised the water levels, however, linking the freshwater oases and allowing the sticklebacks to interbreed. This may seem trivial, but to biologists these fish offer important evolutionary clues. Sticklebacks have developed special characteristics that ensure their survival in each lake's particular environment. Beavers are destroying a rare opportunity for the study of adaptation.

It is impossible to predict the behaviour of an animal when it is introduced into a new environment. There is even great danger in the escape of pets and livestock. Domestic goats once roamed at will on Ramsay Island and could have destroyed the vegetation if their populations had expanded. We have also heard rumours of thoughtless people releasing snakes, ferrets and mink.

Visitors must keep their pets leashed, particularly in wild areas. Given the knowledge of what has happened, and the uncertainty of what could happen, it would be an act of selfishness and indifference to introduce any more species to Haida Gwaii.

PART THREE

WHERE TO GO

This section will help you find a locality or special place you may want to seek out and explore. We have highlighted the main recreational spots. These locales showcase the islands' unique Native history, European settlement, geology, geography and natural history.

We begin by crossing Hecate Strait, one of the most interesting waterways along B.C.'s coastline. The next few chapters highlight southern Graham Island, then we guide you northward through Tlell, Port Clements and on to Masset. Graham Island's undisputed "top spot" is Naikoon Provincial Park. Every first-time visitor to Haida Gwaii should spend a few days exploring the beaches and trails within the park boundaries.

Southern Haida Gwaii is equally exciting to visit. Unfortunately, access to most places south of Moresby Camp are limited to boats or aircraft. Louise Island, K̲'uuna (Skedans) and all areas to the south within Gwaii Haanas National Park Reserve and Haida Heritage Site are like nowhere else in the world. SG̲ang Gwaay has been ranked as one of the world's most significant cultural sites. If you have time and the means, don't pass up an opportunity to visit this exceptional area.

A particularly nice aspect of Haida Gwaii is that you don't need a bulging budget to have a memorable experience. Beach and forest walks—all free—have been as wonderful as our more expensive boating ventures. No doubt you, like us, will find a few spots that might have been included in this guidebook. Keep them as your secret—they should be your own special memory.

7

SOUTHERN GRAHAM ISLAND

CROSSING HECATE STRAIT

Upon arriving at Prince Rupert, put your problems in your pocket and make way for thrills and adventure. A six- to eight-hour ocean cruise to the famous Misty Isles lies ahead. The ferry ride across Hecate Strait is one of the longest and most interesting ferry rides across open water in Canada. Once aboard, claim a couch near the large windows, keep binoculars handy and settle in for the crossing.

In summer, Hecate Strait is usually calm. But even when the swells grow, the clouds move in and spray sweeps the decks, you can appreciate the rougher side of its personality. For the first hour you travel through the busy waters of Chatham Sound. This sheltered waterway is part of the Inside Passage, a marine route between Alaska and Vancouver Island. Watch for other passenger liners, freighters, tugs, yachts, fishboats and pleasure craft travelling in all directions.

After the ferry reaches Edye Pass, the Hecate crossing begins.

You might expect this broad expanse of water to be deep. In fact, for most of its 200-kilometre length, Hecate Strait averages only 17 fathoms. At the northern end, depths are as shallow as 7 fathoms. The strait links Dixon Entrance, to the north, with Queen Charlotte Sound, to the south.

To understand why the basin is so shallow, you have to look to geological time. On several occasions over the last million years, sheets of ice covered both Haida Gwaii and the mainland. The ice, carrying large quantities of rock and sediment, moved slowly from the mountains to the sea, where it either floated away as icebergs or melted. Debris carried by the ice accumulated in Hecate Strait. Exploratory offshore drilling by oil companies has revealed more than 3 kilometres of sediment on the seabed.

Shallow water like this can produce rapid changes in marine conditions. The strait amplifies tidal flows: when the winds are strong, huge waves can suddenly appear. With very little warning, calm water can erupt into a frenzy. Hecate Strait is reputed to be one of the roughest stretches of water on the Pacific Ocean. During gales, Hecate's fury is so great that ferries have little choice but to wait out rough weather at dockside—departures may be postponed for 48 hours or more. "If you want a real pounding, you need to cross in the winter," said Second Officer David Parry when he was quizzed about the rough seas.

In his book, *In the Wake of the War Canoe*, Rev. William Collison, the first missionary on the Charlottes, recounts crossing Hecate Strait for the first time:

> As the wind increased, the sea arose and threatened to engulf our frail bark in its yawning depths. In six hours we had lost all sight of land, and even the mountain tops had disappeared. None of us were able to retain our seats on the thwarts, nor would it have been well to have done so, as they are only sewn to the sides of the canoe with thongs of cedar withes, and might easily have given way under the increased strain. In addition, she rode better with the ballast low down, consequently all save the steersman had to remain huddled up in the bottom of the canoe. An occasional wave broke over us, which kept us all on the alert, and soon all four of our young sailors were seized with that dread ailment mal de mer. I, together with my steersman and bowman, remained unaffected, for which I felt thankful, as it required all our efforts to keep our frail craft afloat ...
>
> Just as we were congratulating ourselves on our success, we sighted a dark ridge or wall of water rushing up rapidly towards us from the south. Apprehensive of being swamped or capsized, we furled sail, and, grasping our paddles, headed our canoe around to meet the approaching danger. It proved to be

but the turn of the incoming tide, which rushes shoreward from the ocean at this point with great force.

After thirteen hours at sea, the exhausted crew staggered ashore at Rose Spit.

The waters of Hecate Strait are as rich in fish as they are in history. At one time Prince Rupert was known as the halibut capital of the world, but overfishing has severely reduced the region's catch. Commercial fishers still seek delicious halibut and smaller groundfish, and crab pots are also set in the tens of thousands. In summer you may notice the fluorescent orange floats marking the ends of their lines. Hecate Strait is also fished heavily by salmon trollers. These smaller boats drag lures from lines attached to poles that lean out from the hull, catching fish on individual hooks. Other salmon boats use seine or gill nets.

Besides fish, a large number and variety of seabirds spend the summer in the strait. Shearwaters are easily recognized by their habit of skimming

GETTING THERE

Most people cross Hecate Strait by boat. BC Ferries' *Queen of Prince Rupert* has scheduled crossings between Prince Rupert on the mainland and Skidegate Landing on Haida Gwaii. This vessel can accommodate all types of RVs, cars, bicycles and walk-on passengers. You can even carry on your kayaks. The upper decks have several lounges, a restaurant and overnight berths. One lounge becomes an informal sleeping area after 10 p.m.

Scheduled flights via smaller airlines cross Hecate Strait from Prince Rupert to Sandspit, the Village of Queen Charlotte and Masset.

For more, see the Transportation and Travel section of "Planning Your Trip."

Original oil by Gordon Miller.

The canoe pictured here was carved on Haida Gwaii prior to 1883. It is 19.5 metres long and in the collection of the American Museum of Natural History.

MV *Queen of Prince Rupert* transports passengers and cargo safely across Hecate Strait. Reservations are highly recommended, especially for over-height or over-length vehicles.

low over the waves. Their sabre-like wings sometimes appear to shear the swells, hence their name. Shearwaters, usually seen in open water, return south before winter storms begin. Stay close to a window to observe them, or better still, stand outside on the forward deck. Of four species recorded in Hecate Strait, sooty shearwaters are the most numerous. Watch for their dark bodies gliding effortlessly over the waves or sitting duck-like in groups of 15 to 20. Sometimes they mass in flocks of more than 100,000, and sightings of a quarter-million have been documented here.

Shearwaters are not alone in their preference for seas where squid and small oceanic fish are plentiful. The gull-like fulmar and the larger black-footed albatross also depend on this special diet. Since both these species are uncommon here, it is all the more thrilling when you do spot one. Bird enthusiasts will sometimes go to a lot of expense chartering vessels in the hope of seeing such species. With many pelagic birds spending up to five months in Hecate Strait, the ferry is still your best bet for some inexpensive birding.

Birdwatchers will notice the bird fauna change as the low-lying land of Haida Gwaii appears. The number of shearwaters tapers off as they are replaced by grebes, pigeon guillemots and scoters. Approaching Lawn Hill along the coast of Graham Island, the ferry makes a sharp turn and follows an ocean trench visible only by depth sounder. Soon you'll pass the Native community of Skidegate, then Torrens and Jewell islands, before easing into the dock at Skidegate Landing. You have now entered Skidegate Inlet.

AROUND SKIDEGATE INLET

For many visitors, Skidegate Inlet provides the first close-up view of Haida Gwaii. This marine channel separates Graham Island, to the north, and Moresby, to the south, the largest islands in the chain. More than 12 kilometres wide at its eastern mouth, Skidegate Inlet winds between islands and mountains for 30 kilometres before it becomes Skidegate Channel, which connects to the west coast. These waterways provide terrific opportunities to explore homesteads and old Haida village sites, to watch seabirds and marine mammals, to find fossils and examine intertidal life or to fish for salmon. Skidegate Inlet lends itself nicely to exploration by either boat or car, as described below.

GETTING THERE

The *Queen of Prince Rupert* ferry unloads vehicles and passengers within the inlet in a cove on Graham Island. Amphibious aircraft and helicopters can arrive at a concrete ramp close to the Village of Queen Charlotte or at Sandspit Airport on Moresby Island. Small boats enter Skidegate Inlet from Hecate Strait, or from the west via narrow Skidegate Channel.

If you drive through the Village of Queen Charlotte and travel 1.8 km past the elementary/secondary school you'll reach Haydn Turner Campsite. At this Lions Club park there are 12 large campsites with tables, firepits, tent areas and nearby pit toilets. Fresh water is available from a tap, but we recommend filling your drinking-water containers in the Village of Queen Charlotte.

Travel 3.4 km farther to reach the Kagan Bay Campsite. This has six sites and pit toilets. There is also private camping near the Village of Queen Charlotte. The nearest RV park with full hook-ups is across the inlet in Sandspit.

SKIDEGATE INLET

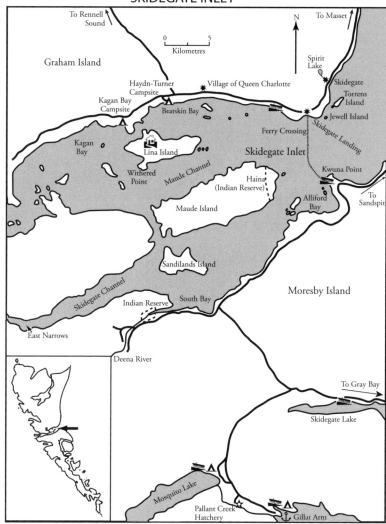

MAP LEGEND

✳ Community	⚑ Viewing tower	⬛ Watchmen site	– – – Park boundary
☆ Site of interest	Warden station	⚓ Anchorage	·········· Trail
Ⓟ Parking	⚲ Picnic sites	⛵ Boat ramp	– – – Indian reserve
Homestead	Park hiking shelter	▲ Hill/mountain	Ecological reserve
Divesite	▲ Camping	⚘ Bog	Ferry crossing
Sand dunes	Fresh water from a pipe		– – – – Gravel road

EXPLORING BY BOAT

You can begin a circle trip around the inlet at the cement airplane ramp located between Skidegate Landing and the Village of Queen Charlotte, where there is plenty of parking and a phone booth. Unfortunately, strong westerly winds can make launching troublesome at times. With permission from ferry personnel, you may also launch at Skidegate Landing. In adverse conditions you may opt to take the shuttle ferry MV *Kwuna* across to Moresby Island. On the Moresby side, you can slide your boat in at Alliford Bay (the ferry landing), Sandspit Harbour or the government dock in Sandspit. Small boats navigate easily throughout the inlet, but a chart is essential as numerous rocks and shallows make boating hazardous for those new to the area.

If you begin your trip at the airplane ramp, take a moment to examine some of the boulders along the beach. Ammonites (extinct, coiled marine shells) and clams almost pop from the rocks, their black fossils contrasting sharply with the sandstone that imprisons them. Many fossil sites have been discovered in Skidegate Inlet, imprints of creatures that lived here between 65 million and 140 million years ago. Such fossils are invaluable to scientists attempting to learn more about ancient animal and plant species.

Once underway, head toward the Village of Queen Charlotte. You'll pass exquisite sand beaches on Maple, Gooden and Roderick islands. Modern homesteads have been built on some of these islands—please respect private property.

One of the larger islands, Lina, shows evidence of numerous previous inhabitants. The Haida dwelt in at least three places around Lina's perimeter. On the extreme east end, several tiny islets shelter a clearing that was once the site of Lina Village. Depressions in the tall grass are now the only trace of the former houses.

During pioneering days, eight White families homesteaded elsewhere on the island. Their buildings have vanished as well, a common occurrence on the Charlottes. Farmers have come and gone, but their gardens remain. If you search carefully along the south shore you should find gnarled apple trees, an oversized holly tree and several flowering shrubs. Tall stems of foxglove, an introduced flower, often mark these former cultivations, which are dotted throughout the islands.

This ammonite, *Dubariceras freboldi*, from Maude Island is a very important fossil in the Jurassic paleontology of North America. Related to the modern nautilus, this marine mollusc lived here about 195 million years ago.

After rounding Withered Point on Lina Island, you'll find yourself in Kagan Bay. Also known as Waterfowl Bay, this shallow basin lives up to its name. In midsummer, we once recorded 10 bird species jammed together on one small rock. Thousands of scoters and grebes pause here during their migration. Numerous rocks, islets and extensive mud flats guarantee hours of good birdwatching. Kagan Bay and connecting Maude Channel are also pleasant places to canoe or kayak. Tidal currents swirl past the tips of some islands, creating eddies and small whirlpools.

Depending on the amount of time available, you have two options while in Maude Channel. A shortcut between Maude and Graham Island leads west via Skidegate Channel. Kayakers, in particular, will enjoy the East and West narrows, since the flood tide coming from Hecate Strait has a range roughly twice that coming from the Pacific side. This can create a maelstrom of eddies, currents, standing waves and whirlpools.

Since many boats find these channels tricky to negotiate, we recommend passage only at slack water. To reach the open Pacific you'll have to paddle or motor more than 30 kilometres.

If, on the other hand, you turn east past Sandilands Island, you can explore the south side of Maude Island. This sausage-shaped island bears the scars of successive logging operations. Lush spruce and hemlock now cover the wounds. Boats can usually motor right next to the sheer cliffs along this side. At low tide you'll be treated to a spectacular array of intertidal life. Thousands of brown or white anemones dangle from the cliff face like dripping wax. Water normally supports their characteristic barrel shape, but their muscles stretch as the tide drops. Fossils discovered along this shoreline have made Maude Island famous within the geological community. Each layer of rock has such exquisite specimens that these fossils have become the comparative base for others of this time period throughout the world.

At the extreme east end of Maude Island, look for the grass-covered point and a tiny island. Haina Village, or Sunshine-Town, was once located here. When west coast villages were decimated by disease in the late 1800s, survivors moved to this village site. Haida homes and totems were raised alongside a Methodist church. By 1893, however, the residents had moved on to form the larger community of Skidegate Mission. Because this is a Native reserve, you need permission to explore it.

With Maude Island behind you, head for the islets near Kwuna Point. Three seabird species nest on these tiny islets. Watch for pigeon guillemots with black bodies and white wing patches. As they scoot across the water or squat on a favourite rock, their brilliant red legs leave no doubt as to their identity. Often gathering near kelp beds, they dive in search of skinny, eel-like fish called blennies. They can hold several fish in their bills as they return to nests under logs or in rock crevices.

Glaucous-winged gulls also feed and nest here. Unlike guillemots, they build exposed nests on islets that have little or no vegetation. In June and early July the small islets appear snowy as parents incubate their speckled eggs. Once hatched, the scruffy grey chicks scamper from the nest, and by summer's end they're large enough to fend for themselves.

The other nesting seabird may be harder to find. Almost the size of gulls, black oystercatchers are the buffoons of the inlet. Like a clown with an exaggerated appendage, this absurd, red-billed shorebird balances its chunky body on elongated pink legs. A golden eye rimmed in red completes the costume. With such brilliant coloration the oystercatcher might seem an easy bird to spot. However, they prefer secluded islets where they lay their eggs just above the high-tide line. Look for the adults resting on boulders or flying together offshore. Their loud, monotonous "queep" carries halfway across the inlet.

In September, anglers easily outnumber bird species around these islets. They are attracted by the coho salmon, which seem to like the deep, clear waters around Maude Island and nearby Kwuna Point. For years the popular local technique was drift fishing with buzz bombs or similar lures. Fishermen now take a creative approach, spin-casting lures and spoons over ledges and near submerged rocks. Trollers prefer flashers and hoochies, guarding their colours like a best-kept secret. We trolled a flasher with a broken back and a green hoochie at 30-minute intervals. During line checks, a few ounces of weight were added if nothing touched the lure. These fish feed primarily near the surface.

Another popular fishing method involves criss-crossing the shoals near Sandspit. Although these shallow waters are exposed to the seas of Hecate Strait, local anglers love to spend the long summer evenings out here, fantasizing about bent rods and whirling reels. During June and July, coho weighing about 2 kilograms feed in water up to 30 metres deep. We enjoyed being out in the open, but our timing was off—only a small pink salmon took our hoochie. We would have done better here in the fall. Skidegate's fishing really heats up in late September and remains productive throughout October. Good catches at that time of the year reach 7 kilograms, but winners in the annual coho derby usually weigh in at 9 kilograms—beauties.

Whether your pleasure be fishing, boating, birding or exploring, eventually you'll have to head in. Leave Alliford Bay, pass Maude Island and cross Bearskin Bay. A visit to Torrens and Jewell islands is a delightful detour in fair weather. A pebble beach on Torrens Island makes for easy landing, where you can enjoy a picnic amid the driftwood or go searching for deer in the undergrowth. Make your way back to the boat ramp by following the shoreline into Skidegate Inlet.

EXPLORING BY CAR

Begin your road trip by driving to Skidegate Village. Opposite the George Brown Recreation Centre is a parking lot and the trailhead for Spirit Lake. This 3-kilometre trail system is suitable for most hikers. The trails have several loops, allowing hikers to return within two hours or to stay longer, picnicking at tables near the lake. Unfortunately, there are no toilets. The trail passes through a second-growth forest, then enters an old-growth stand. Several large cedars have been culturally modified: the Haida obviously used this area for harvesting cedars and, undoubtedly, other forest plants.

If you end your Spirit Lake hike before noon, there is still plenty of time to cross Skidegate Inlet and visit Moresby Island. The shuttle ferry MV *Kwuna* transports vehicles and passengers from Skidegate Landing to Alliford Bay across the inlet. The 20-minute ride is a must, especially if you don't have the opportunity to tour the inlet in your own craft. A small lounge provides protected viewing during rain, but on nice days, outside on deck is the place to be. We've seen storm-petrels in spring, porpoises in the summer and hundreds of migrating birds in the fall. And keep a sharp lookout for whales.

As mentioned earlier, gray whales pass by here twice each year, migrating to and from the Arctic. These whales are primarily bottom feeders, which helps explain why they linger around the shallow areas within this inlet. Grays position their jaws sideways, very close to the sandy bottom. By folding their lips outwards and quickly retracting their tongue, they can suck in large amounts of sand and living

Spirit Lake is a nice beginning to an exploration of the Skidegate area. The 3-kilometre network of gravelled trails can be used by hikers of all ages.

organisms. Their baleen plate filters unwanted sand and water, retaining thousands of tiny, 2- or 3-centimetre-long amphipods and other small organisms. Between each feed they usually surface to breathe. Watch for a 2-metre, lollipop-shaped spout or a smooth, mottled grey back with a series of bumps or "knuckles" located near the tail.

This gazebo located along the Onward Point Trail provides welcome shelter on wet days. Whales, porpoises and seabirds can all be watched from this prominent headland.

After disembarking from the ferry, drive toward Sandspit. You will soon reach the Onward Point trailhead on the seaward side of the road. This short trail is manageable for families with small children. A gazebo, perched on a rocky bluff, makes an excellent whale-viewing spot, particularly in wet weather.

Beach Road follows the shoreline right to bustling Sandspit Airport. Many private homes and small businesses front this 14.6-kilometre paved road. Heading south from Sandspit, Copper Bay Road will take you to Gray Bay, Skidegate Lake, Pallant Creek and Cumshewa Inlet. Maintained logging roads allow you to travel in a circle, beginning and ending at the Alliford Bay ferry. Many people drive this loop for a day's outing (see "Gray Bay").

A walk out on the spit is a pleasant alternative to driving the back roads. A well-worn trail through the beach grass begins at the government dock. Extensive offshore shallows attract all kinds of birds. During migration, shorebirds rest and regroup along the beaches. Farther out, thousands of scoters may cover the water like a black sheet. Their spring arrival coincides with the spawning of Pacific herring. If a mischievous eagle or an overzealous boater puts them to flight, their wings produce a high-pitched, tremulous whistle.

Anglers enjoy the spit as much as birdwatchers do. On an incoming tide, winds and currents may combine to form large eddies within casting distance of shore. Buzz bombs or krocodiles cast into the swirling water hook many a coho salmon.

We also recommend visiting Sandspit Airport. Photo displays in the main foyer highlight Native and aerial history. Parks Canada also has an information centre here, open from May through September.

Don't forget your ferry return to Graham Island; sailing times are posted at both docks. On several occasions we have missed the boat due to a long line of cars. Arrive half an hour before departure to ensure your vehicle gets on board. You can spend the waiting time beachcombing nearby.

RENNELL SOUND

Within an hour's drive of the Village of Queen Charlotte, you'll reach a modest viewpoint overlooking Rennell Sound. On a bright day, the aquamarine swells below shimmer with the promise of discoveries. The sound is 15 kilometres across in places, and cuts 30 kilometres deep into Graham Island. It offers wonderful beaches, hidden coves, a diversity of wildlife and good camping sites, as well as excellent fishing and boating—altogether an ideal combination for experiencing the power, beauty and excitement of the open ocean.

At the base of the steep hill, you will reach a T intersection. The left turn leads to private property; turn right and within a minute you'll arrive at Rennell Sound Recreation Site. We recommend starting your exploration here.

The BC Forest Service cleared seven places large enough for tents or trailers, and small boats can be launched at this spot. A sign indicates public roads, beach trails and a scuba-diving area. Farther along the road there are three more campsites at Cone Head Recreation Site (between Bonanza and Gregory beaches). Both recreation sites have tables, firepits and outhouses. Allow at least a day to explore these west-coast beaches.

The first trail begins near the dryland log sorting area, which can't be missed as you continue 3 kilometres past the campsite. The road splits here. Take the left fork through the sorting area and watch for the sign indicating Five Mile Beach. From here it's a two-minute walk to the water's edge. At low tide, an isthmus connects with a tiny island. Sharp rocks splashed by Pacific swells support a healthy range of intertidal life. Look for shells of abalone and turban snails on the rocks. If you're lucky, you may discover *Dentalium*, the "money-tusk" shell, on the beach. These pencil-shaped shells were once a form of currency, their value being partly determined by length. Shells of more than 7 centimetres were so valuable that only wealthy Haida chiefs owned them.

The best beaches, Gregory and Bonanza, are farther along. To reach them, drive 3 to 5 kilometres past the Riley Creek bridge. Orange fluorescent markers or brown posts indicate vehicle pull-outs and trailheads. Short, well-maintained trails suitable for small children lead directly to sand and surf.

Rocky outcrops at both ends of these beaches enclose the soft sand, but heavy surf often breaks against them with tremendous force. Only creatures that can withstand the impact of tonnes of water live on such exposed places. Chalky white gooseneck barnacles and large California mussels are permanent residents of this violent world. The barnacles cement themselves to rocks via a tough, leathery neck. California mussels use fibrous strands as anchors on hard surfaces. Rough-skinned sea stars, such as *Pisaster,* move slowly over beds of mussels and barnacles. Their thousands of tube feet serve two important functions. They hold the sea stars firmly against the rocks when waves smash upon them, and they assist when the sea stars feed. The tube feet pry mussel shells apart, then the sea stars inserts its stomach into the shell and digests its contents. What a way to go!

At low tide, the exposed headlands abound with intertidal life. But as the tide turns and the channels begin to fill, you can easily shift your attention to wave watching. The rising water soon forces a retreat to higher ground, as breaking waves race up the channels to explode in a seething froth. This titanic force is spellbinding.

Pacific swells often deposit unusual articles on shore, such as tropical plants, bits of sea life and international garbage from ships. Interest in their mysterious origins is surpassed only by the captivating nature of waves. Rollers that have the strength and fury to smash logs into oblivion can possess, at the same time, the agility to carry delicate light bulbs and Japanese glass fishing floats and gently deposit them, intact, amid the stones.

RENNELL SOUND

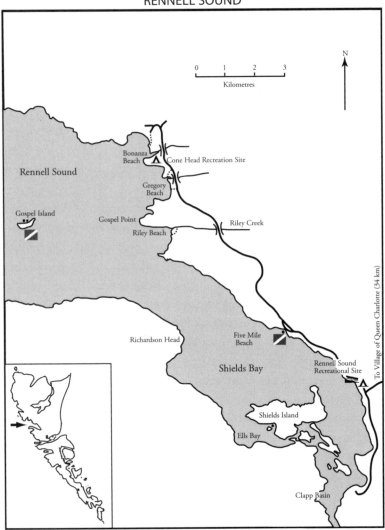

MAP LEGEND

✳	Community	⚒	Viewing tower	🏛	Watchmen site	– – – Park boundary
☆	Site of interest	⚲	Warden station	⚓	Anchorage	·········· Trail
Ⓟ	Parking	⚵	Picnic sites	⛵	Boat ramp	– – – – Indian reserve
🏠	Homestead	☗	Park hiking shelter	▲	Hill/mountain	······· Ecological reserve
◩	Divesite	⚐	Camping	⚶	Bog	Ferry crossing
Λ Λ	Sand dunes	⛲	Fresh water from a pipe			– – – – – Gravel road

GETTING THERE

Rennell Sound is located on the west coast of Graham Island and can be reached easily by road, or in a more roundabout way by boat. Gravel roads leading to the sound begin at the Village of Queen Charlotte and Port Clements. Logging trucks often travel these roads from 7:00 a.m. to 5:30 p.m. daily. Contact the Western Forest Products office (phone: 250-557-6825) to obtain permission to use the road and for the latest road report.

From the Village of Queen Charlotte, drive west to the end of pavement. The road to Rennell Sound runs north for 22.5 km to the Rennell turnoff. An alternative route leads from Port Clements southward through the interior for about 51 km, until meeting the same turnoff to Rennell. As you near the coast the terrain steepens, and after 12 km of turns and switchbacks, the sound comes into view. A steep hill with a 24 percent grade separates this viewpoint from the ocean below. The hill may appear forbidding, but small RVs have made it down and back. If you have a heavy trailer, there is an area near the top where you can leave it temporarily. Inspect the 1-km grade before towing a load down.

We recommend filling drinking water containers in the Village of Queen Charlotte.

For more, see the Transportation and Travel section of "Planning Your Trip."

Treasures from all over the Pacific Ocean are washed ashore on the Charlottes. Beaches at Rennell Sound are the easiest to access on the west coast of Haida Gwaii.

Rennell Sound offers beachcombing, rustic camping, fishing and thundering surf. At times the Pacific is flat calm, but come prepared for wind and wild weather.

To view these beaches from the water, return to the Rennell Sound Recreation Site. Launch your boat directly from there. A group of five islands and several islets resembles a peninsula from shore. These islands form a protected harbour that will accommodate smaller boats. Shallower water between the islands hides numerous rocks and shoals. With a chart in hand, it's safe to meander among them in a canoe or small craft.

These islands host a tremendous variety of intertidal life. Living organisms cover virtually every square centimetre of rock. Blue mussels are so numerous they sometimes envelop the rocks that support them. Within the length of your boat, you can see hundreds of sea stars. As you stare into the clear depths, rock scallops' orange lips will grin back, and silver will flash from schools of needlefish as they flee for cover. Check tide tables for low tides (about one hour before Prince Rupert—Pacific Daylight Saving Time).

In suitable weather, cruise out past these islands. Bald eagles seem to escort you toward the horizon. The mountains behind you form the northern Queen Charlotte Range. On a calm day, the reflected vistas beg to be photographed. Anglers search out the 20-fathom zone to jig for cod and halibut. If you're searching for salmon, troll the shoreline. To round out the day, head for the quiet retreat of Gospel Island. A sheltered, sun-splashed beach awaits you, and you may discover sea lions and seals basking on its western edge.

The west coast of Haida Gwaii has a deserved reputation for being wild and unpredictable. Thundering waves and howling winds delight some people, while others prefer a calm sea with gentle breezes. Rennell Sound has all these attributes and much more. A day or two camping at Rennell Sound will give you a good taste of the open Pacific's formidable personality.

8

MID GRAHAM ISLAND

OF CANOES AND CULTURE

All tribes of the Pacific Northwest built dugout canoes. These craft set the standard for transportation, trade, hunting and fishing, and for conducting raids. Haida canoes, however, were prized up and down the coast for their craftsmanship, size and seaworthiness. The moist climate of Haida Gwaii produced superior cedar for building the largest canoes, and the Haida's seamanship in open water gave them dominance over rival tribes. Other tribes were unwilling to attack them in their homeland because the Haida were renowned for their ferocity and were well protected by the difficult crossing. The very sight of their war canoes approaching struck terror into tribes as far south as Puget Sound. The Haida also had a deserved reputation as shrewd traders, and they carved canoes for barter as well as for their own use.

Until recently, the last big canoe carved on Haida Gwaii was commissioned in 1909, when Alfred and Robert Davidson undertook to build one 17 metres long for the Alaska–Yukon–Pacific Exposition in Seattle, Washington. That giant eventually sold to the National Museum of Canada in Ottawa, Ontario, and was on display in the Canadian Pavilion during Expo '86 in Vancouver, B.C.

Such a canoe could carry 4.5 tonnes of cargo. In his 1872 travelogue, Francis Poole recounts a trip from the Charlottes to Victoria in a canoe containing three dozen people. *Queen Charlotte Islands: A Narrative of Discovery and Adventure in the North Pacific* describes a three-week journey during which Native paddlers demonstrated phenomenal stamina and skill. That story, and similar accounts by Rev. William Collison of crossing Hecate Strait in severe weather, will convince even the hardiest river canoeists that whitewater paddling is mere child's play. For a Haida, every oceanic trip posed a life-threatening risk.

At one time, the carving of canoes was an important occupation. The Haida made a variety during the winter months, then paddled them to the mainland each spring for trade. As has already been noted, their success in this commerce was due in part to the size and quality of the cedars that grow in these temperate rainforests. The Haida made virtually everything from this soft, straight-grained conifer. Hilary Stewart, in her book *Cedar*, aptly calls it the "tree of life" and explains how the Natives

GETTING THERE

The two canoes discussed in this chapter are found in separate locations—you'll find them more interesting if you visit them in the sequence described.

The oldest Haida canoe on Haida Gwaii is located between Port Clements and Juskatla (Western Forest Products' headquarters on the Charlottes). Abandoned before completion, this canoe remains only partly shaped from a huge red cedar. To see this one, drive 14.8 km toward Juskatla from the museum in Port. A sign 0.7 km past the Ferguson Bay junction indicates the side road that leads to the canoe. Although the trailhead lies 0.3 km farther on, turning space there is limited, so we'd advise parking soon after turning onto this side road. This is particularly important for large RVs. (Vehicles hauling trailers should not enter the side road.) At the trailhead you may notice two logs lying on the ground that appear to have been shaped into the formative stages of canoes. A five-minute walk via the crushed rock trail leads to the best canoe. This one can be compared with another, the historic *Loo Taas*, that's stored in a building adjacent to the Haida Gwaii Museum at Skidegate. If you're really keen, it is possible for groups to arrange to paddle a replica of this 18-metre canoe. For more information about this, inquire at the Gwaalagaa Naay Corporation office, located next door to the museum.

Examining the bow of a canoe that never made it to the water. For unknown reasons, this canoe and at least three others were abandoned in the forest near Juskatla.

selected, cut and shaped the trunks into canoes.

Evidence of this activity is visible all over the islands. One important location was Masset Inlet on Graham Island. Villagers from Old Massett went there in January to fall trees, as the wood contains little sap at that season. Old cedars frequently rot, so the Natives sounded the trunks by pounding on them to discover whether they were suited for canoe or house construction. Once a suitable candidate was selected, they would usually cut a test hole into the heartwood to confirm its soundness. If found to be solid, the tree would be felled after an appropriate ceremony. Logs destined to become canoes would be rough-shaped on site before being dragged or towed back to the village.

The arrival of Europeans, with their manufactured boats and unknown diseases that ravaged entire villages, soon spelled the end for such physically demanding labours. Brush eventually concealed all evidence of the old logging. In recent decades, hikers and loggers have encountered stumps, treetops and even blanks (unfinished canoes) forgotten in the woods. Several such blanks can be seen in Masset Inlet, but the most accessible is in an old clear-cut near Port Clements. The bow of that unfinished canoe faces the stump from which it was felled, fully 3 kilometres from the nearest beach. The job of dragging the cured and hollowed hull through the forest would be done by slaves and hired men who specialized in canoe carving. The final shaping, steam-spreading and painting would take place back at the village.

Scores of dugouts were once drawn up on the beach below Skidegate Village. At low tide, canoe runs are still visible on the southern edge of the beach. These are paths perpendicular to the shore where beach stones were cleared to allow canoes to land and launch without damage to the hull.

Almost a century went by before craftsmen once again took up the challenge of constructing a canoe. When the Bank of British Columbia commissioned one for exhibition at Expo '86, the designer and construction foreman was acclaimed Haida artist Bill Reid, whose hometown was Skidegate. The completion of his 18-metre craft is chronicled in a video display in the Haida Gwaii Museum. Rediscovery of forgotten techniques was crucial to execute this immense project. The Haida are justifiably proud of this canoe, named *Loo Taas*, which means Wave Eater. It is symbolic of their renewed tribal vigour.

On July 11, 1987, *Loo Taas* arrived in Skidegate after several crews spent three weeks paddling it north from Vancouver. Two thousand people crowded the beach as *Loo Taas* swept toward its ancestral home. The sun was bright that memorable day. While still a long way from shore, the flash of synchronous paddles signalled the canoe's progress. As it came on, 10 bare-chested men could be seen driving pointed paddles forward and back to the beat of a tambourine drum. *Loo Taas* spat an impressive bow wake. The paddlers' deep "oooh-ah" chant resonated across the water. Bill Reid sat in the stern ahead of the steersman, a blue fedora shielding his proud face. How his heart must have throbbed to that chorus!

That night, a thousand guests were invited to a Skidegate potlatch. The feasting, singing, dancing, oratory and gift giving made that evening the event of the decade on the islands. The ceremony will be a lifelong memory for everyone who attended.

That such canoes are worthy of regional and national recognition indicates the value of Haida heritage to all Canadians. We hope *Loo Taas* will gnash these waters for years to come.

NADU—TRAILS TO TRIBULATION

At the end of Nadu Road, on Masset Sound, two short walks graphically illustrate the broken dreams found in so many places on these islands. Here moulder the remnants of a homestead and a failed business enterprise. Overgrown pioneer settlements and abandoned industrial sites throughout the Charlottes are the major landmarks left by White people. Easy access to two such ventures at Nadu allows you to get a feel for many others in just a couple of hours.

The side road into Nadu was originally built during the 1920s to supply inland subsistence farmers from the water's edge. The highway did not exist then, so transportation was by steamship. The road's slope near the sound was logged in the 1970s and presents an opportunity for those who haven't travelled the back roads to see what was once a clear-cut. Hemlock and alder trees are growing rapidly to cover this scar. Their vigorous growth has already concealed evidence of the tribulations to which civilization subjected this landscape.

You'll reach a rock breakwater at the former homestead by following the shoreline south from the old dock. For easiest walking, begin your journey about two hours after high tide and return before it comes in. (Add two hours to the Prince Rupert tide tables for accurate timing since you're on enclosed Masset Inlet.) Overhanging vegetation makes the shoreline traverse very difficult during high tide.

The unmortared breakwater, built of beach cobbles, is only 1 kilometre away. The even sides and attention to design are marks of a skilled stonemason. After seven decades only a small portion has collapsed. This labour of love is rarely seen among modern homesteaders and is an indication of the care put into all the construction at this site.

Follow a trail up the embankment behind the dilapidated boathouse. This leads through the cedars to a clearing with a "fruitless" apple orchard. In 1911 the promising new home of the Edward Evans family stood here. The three huge rhododendron bushes are evidence of Mrs. Evans' efforts to domesticate the wilderness. These transplanted southern shrubs have grown to 6 metres tall and display gorgeous blooms during the first week of July.

The smooth adze marks on the collapsed house beams and the even joints speak to the skills of an artist. We immediately suspected a Scandinavian influence. Later we read in Dalzell's *The Queen Charlotte Islands, 1774–1966* that "master axemen" Ole Anderson and Alec Johnson were hired by Evans to build this substantial house. The craftsmanship and aesthetic touches evident in this homestead only serve to enhance the sense of despair that pervades the place—so much for naught.

NADU

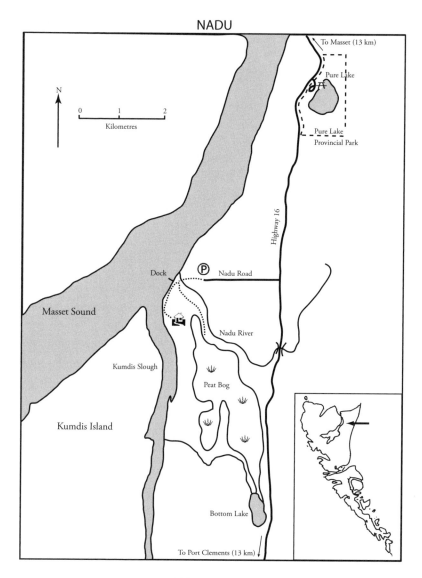

MAP LEGEND

✳	Community	⊼	Viewing tower	🏛	Watchmen site	‒ ‒ ‒	Park boundary
☆	Site of interest	⋮	Warden station	⌁	Anchorage	··········	Trail
Ⓟ	Parking	⚘	Picnic sites	⇌	Boat ramp	‑ ‑ ‑	Indian reserve
🏠	Homestead	⬥	Park hiking shelter	▲	Hill/mountain	·‑··‑··	Ecological reserve
◪	Divesite	▲	Camping	⚘	Bog	··········	Ferry crossing
⋀⋀	Sand dunes	🚰	Fresh water from a pipe			‑ ‑ ‑ ‑	Gravel road

It must have been devastating to leave these dreams and dollars behind, a story typical of farming on the Charlottes. Encouraged by exaggerated agricultural claims and government land giveaways, many pioneers devoted everything they had to their farms. Today, no one on the islands earns a living solely from crops or cattle.

Oddly, many back-to-the-landers ignored the lessons of the past when they immigrated to the Charlottes in the late '60s and '70s. These latter-day pioneers not only had a weak sense of history, but also lacked the strong work ethic of their forebears. Most were squatters, holding no property title, and sought only to eke out a meagre living. It still wasn't enough. Like Nadu, virtually all their communities, some on remote islands, have been abandoned. A creeping layer of green overtakes them all.

In 1967 another enterprise started at Nadu with the same high hopes that had inspired previous pioneers. Bering Industries of Victoria, B.C., spent $1 million constructing a peat moss plant to process a nearby bog into a horticultural product. The moss was extracted by draining the bog, allowing the dry top layer of moss to be suctioned off.

Ironically, the very qualities that render peat useless for farming are excellent attributes when the moss is added to proper soil. Its sterility, lightness, compressibility, absorbent nature and organic composition make it easy to work and valuable for gardening and other uses.

GETTING THERE

Nadu Road is marked on the Yellowhead Highway about 19 km north of Port Clements, roughly halfway to Masset. From the highway, this gravel road runs 2 km and ends at a small slide. (Due to the limited turning area and close-growing alders, vehicles with trailers, and large RVs, should not attempt to go down this road.) A trail below the slide leads to an old dock on the shore of Masset Sound, a walk that shouldn't take more than 10 minutes. Time your visit for a falling tide. Visitors with a pioneering spirit should be able to brush aside the burgeoning alders to find both the sites detailed in this chapter.

Note: Gumboots are mandatory footgear for both Nadu locations.

Stone breakwater and boat ramp at Nadu. This homestead is remarkable for the quality of construction, still evident even though the buildings have collapsed. Most homesteads were eventually abandoned.

From the dock you can follow an alder-grown road up a gentle incline to the bog workings about 1.6 kilometres away. The walk passes through a mixed wood to a bench above Nadu River. There are no views until the trees give way at the edge of the bog. Little remains at the extraction site, but if you haven't visited a bog before, seize the opportunity to look around.

The reason for the business failure is unclear, although the distance to markets must have been a factor. Peat-harvesting operations in the lower Fraser Valley would have prevented serious competition. Evidently, only one shipment was ever made from the Nadu plant. The foundations of the buildings and a slowly rotting dock are all that remain of this venture.

Of all the efforts to earn a living attempted on these islands, only fishing and logging have met with continued success. As we learn more about the importance of careful management of our so-called renewable resources, however, even their future seems uncertain. In the midst of all this, a new economic opportunity is beginning to pay off on Haida Gwaii: tourism. With international attention focused on the richly rewarding adventure of touring these beautiful islands, there is the potential for even greater economic benefit to flow from the area's stunning natural attributes. Here, at last, is an enterprise that can maintain and enhance the independent lifestyle so cherished by islanders. We hope this industry will continue to be successful.

NORTHERN GRAHAM ISLAND

LANGARA ISLAND VICINITY

Called North Island by some, Langara is a forested, low-profile rocky isle of about 25 square kilometres. Lying off the northwestern tip of Graham Island, it is fully exposed to the pounding Pacific. Wind, waves and a serrated shore give it a frightening sort of beauty. The scenery is memorable, but you should come well prepared.

This location, too remote for drop-in visitors, has attracted every sort of inhabitant over the years: Haida villagers, trading sailors, fishermen, environmental students, lightkeepers and biologists. Originally the Haida lived around the island in several villages, the largest being Kiusta on nearby Graham Island. This site was abandoned in about 1850 when most of the residents migrated to the Alaskan panhandle and eastward toward Masset. Kiusta has been used only seasonally since.

Native use of this area is long-standing. In 1986, archaeologists from the Haida Gwaii Museum uncovered campfire charcoal dating back 10,400 years. Subject to further verification, this will go down as one of the oldest known sites of human activity in British Columbia. Such ancient Aboriginal colonization lends perspective to "discovery" of Haida Gwaii by European navigators.

In 1787, English fur trader George Dixon was the first European to circumnavigate this archipelago. As well as naming the group of islands after Queen Charlotte (wife of George III of England), he named Langara "North Island" and also came up with the appellation Cloak Bay following this profitable exchange: "There were 10 canoes about the ship, which

LANGARA ISLAND

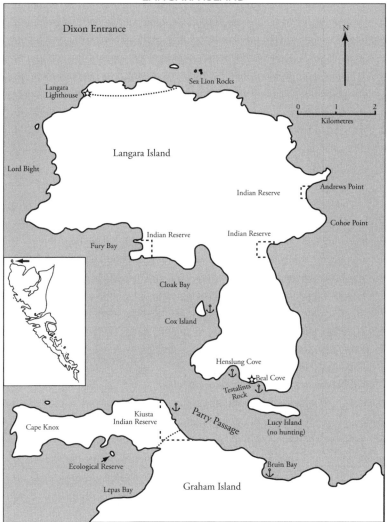

MAP LEGEND

✳ Community	🗼 Viewing tower	🏛 Watchmen site	– – – Park boundary
☆ Site of interest	👤 Warden station	⚓ Anchorage	·········· Trail
Ⓟ Parking	⊼ Picnic sites	🛶 Boat ramp	– – – – Indian reserve
🏠 Homestead	🏚 Park hiking shelter	▲ Hill/mountain	······· Ecological reserve
◩ Divesite	▲ Camping	🌿 Bog	········· Ferry crossing
ʌʌ Sand dunes	🚰 Fresh water from a pipe		– – – – – Gravel road

contained, as nearly as I could estimate, 120 people; many of these brought most beautiful beaver cloaks, others excellent skins, and, in short, none came empty handed, and the rapidity with which they sold them was a circumstance additionally pleasing; they fairly quarreled with each other about which should sell his cloak first ..." These were the glory days of the infamous sea otter trade.

In contrast to the sea otter's fate, fish still thrive around Langara Island. The commercial fleet has been enjoying superlative salmon catches in this vicinity for years. Now the lucrative sport-fishing industry has discovered the area as well.

In recent years a floating lodge was anchored in Henslung Cove to cater to fly-in clients. One patron declared the experience "the best fishing I've had in 30 years on the B.C. coast." Weight records at Langara Lodge exceed 50 kilograms for halibut, 34 kilograms for spring salmon and 10 kilograms for the largest coho salmon ever landed. Large ling cod and chum salmon supplement the take. The lodge has gained a worldwide reputation and capacity bookings as a result of such tremendous catches.

Several other floating resorts have since sprung up in the area. All these operations are relatively expensive and open to reserved guests only. (For more, see "Overnighting on Haida Gwaii" and "Planning Your Trip.")

Meanwhile, adolescents who participate in a program called "Rediscovery" forgo such luxurious accommodation and live close to the land. These island teens use the rustic cabins at Lepas Bay as their base. Every summer, consecutive two-week programs provide hands-

GETTING THERE

Though the location is remote, it's possible for the venturesome to organize their own travel and camp at Langara Island. Floatplanes and fishing boats can be chartered out of Masset. Camping locations are at Cape Knox, Lepas Bay and Pillar Bay, all on Graham Island. (Note: Native reserves border these sites—obtain permission before camping on any Native land.) Mooring buoys for yachters are located in Pillar Bay, Bruin Bay, Henslung Cove, Beal Cove, Cloak Bay and in front of Kiusta village.

on learning in environmental awareness, outdoor skills and respect for traditional Haida culture. Rediscovery has been so successful that the program's originators have given training workshops to instructors in the United States.

The lightkeepers at Langara are the only people who live on the island year-round. Langara lighthouse is notoriously difficult for boat landings because there's no moorage. Most people come and go by helicopter. These lightkeepers are Canada's most westerly residents. They serve us all by operating directional beacons and taking weather and seismograph (earthquake) readings. Since submarine earthquakes sometimes generate tsunamis (destructive waves), this lighthouse is the vanguard of the Canadian early warning system. The station was established in 1913 at the same time as its companion on the southern tip of this island chain—Cape St. James.

Like their rocky counterpart to the south, Cape Knox and Lepas Bay on Graham Island are completely exposed, and both provide plenty of rugged scenery. Cape Knox also offers the possibility of cave exploration. Out from Pillar Bay's beach, facing Dixon Entrance, towers a 29-metre column of conglomerate rock and sandstone. There are similar, though smaller, features in Cloak Bay: one called Porthole Rock has a 2-metre hole through it.

Another geological oddity is Plum Pudding Rock, or Testatlints, in Parry Passage. This enormous boulder, accessible at low tide, is topped by a thicket of trees and sits on the shore of Langara Island. Recognized by geologists as an erratic feature, it was deposited by glaciers during the Ice Age. A shaman whose grave lies on its summit gave the stone its Haida name.

Walking about on land is the best way to really appreciate these locations. Just within the trees at Kiusta, a row of depressions outlines what were once houses in the former village. Only a few corner posts remain upright to mark their perimeter. Roof beams covered in moss lie across the pits, and the rainforest crowds close—a scene typical of abandoned Haida villages. Unusual here is the three-pole mortuary, which once supported the remains of a Haida chief. Called the Edenshaw pole, this triple totem is the only one of its kind in existence. At the far end of the beach behind it, faces stare from rocks at the tide line. Although ground out by Haida, the meaning and function of such petroglyphs remain a mystery.

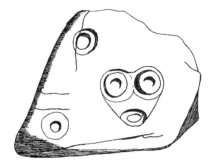

Petroglyphs on a beach boulder at Kiusta. The age and purpose of such rock carvings are unknown. Three-dimensional petroglyphs are not the same as pictographs or rock paintings. The latter are not found on the Charlottes.

A trail leads across the wooded peninsula from Kiusta to the famous crescent beach at Lepas Bay. A spectacular 55-kilometre coastal hike begins here. The route south takes you to caves and misty rainforest, beachcombing treasures and freshwater fishing. Sea-run cutthroat trout can attain sporting size in the deeper coastal creeks.

A visit to Langara Island would not be complete without seeing its peregrine falcons. These streamlined hunters are admired the world over for their speed and finesse in flight. At one time the population here was phenomenally dense: up to 20 pairs nested on the cliffs. Since 1968, only five to seven nests have been active. Some scientists believe their decline is due to the falling numbers of ancient murrelets, a major food source.

Murrelets once numbered more than 20,000 pairs, making Langara Island the site of the world's largest ancient murrelet colony (along with other burrow-nesting seabirds). Unfortunately, Norway rats were introduced to the island and wreaked havoc with the vulnerable nesting birds. The result: only a very small number of ancient murrelets survived the rat attack. All other species were wiped out.

In an effort to restore the island's nesting seabirds, the Canadian Wildlife Service established a rat removal program. Beginning in 1995 and continuing for several years, a systematic poisoning and trapping program successfully purged the island of the vermin. In 2004, researchers returned to determine if the rat extermination had been beneficial to the birds. The results were heartening.

Estimates of nesting ancient murrelets indicate that the breeding population has doubled in size from about 6,000 pairs in 1999 to over 12,000 pairs five years later. Also, a small pocket of nesting Cassin's auklets was discovered on the north shore. Both of these very positive signs suggest seabird nesting success has increased and the colony is in much better health.

Despite the remoteness of Langara, civilization has upset its cultural and biological balance. Much was lost before we were able to fully understand and appreciate this place. Langara Island still offers us its beauty, resources and spirit. Knowing now the island's fragility, we must act responsibly to preserve and, where possible, restore the natural attributes we damaged in our carelessness.

DELKATLA WILDLIFE SANCTUARY

Every spring, millions of shorebirds and waterfowl leave their wintering areas and fly north to nesting grounds in the Arctic. One migration route lies along the western edge of North America—the Pacific Flyway. Birds can't make this trip without stopping for rest, shelter and food, and favourite locations spaced along their flyways supply these requirements. Delkatla slough is one such habitat and is one of the best places on Haida Gwaii to see birds during spring migration and in the fall when they return south.

GETTING THERE

This 553-hectare lowland refuge lies adjacent to the Village of Masset. Delkatla is accessible by car and trail, and has three viewing towers. For a visit, follow Tow Hill Road east past Masset, turn left onto Cemetery Road, and drive 1.7 km to a gravel parking lot. Begin your walk at this location or along the dike, 300 m farther on. A new Delkata Wildlife Sanctuary Interpretive Centre has been built along the edge of the sanctuary on Trumpeter Drive.

There is an RV park and campground across from the refuge, between the bridge and Cemetery Road. Partial hookups, a wash house, showers and a kitchen shelter are available. The Visitor Centre near the bridge has a free sani-station and coin-operated car wash.

DELKATLA WILDLIFE SANCTUARY

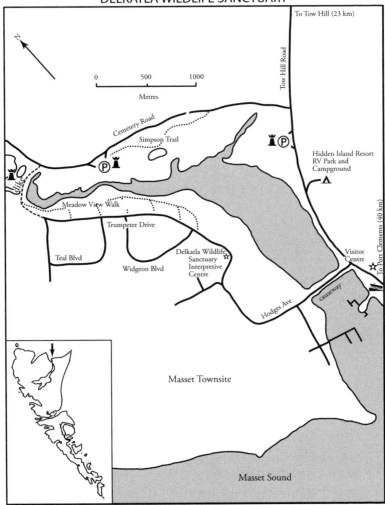

MAP LEGEND

✳	Community	ⵂ	Viewing tower	🏛	Watchmen site	– – – Park boundary
☆	Site of interest	ⵗ	Warden station	⚓	Anchorage	········· Trail
Ⓟ	Parking	⋔	Picnic sites	⛴	Boat ramp	– – – – Indian reserve
	Homestead	▸	Park hiking shelter	▲	Hill/mountain	⋯⋯ Ecological reserve
◿	Divesite	▲	Camping	⚘	Bog	⸺⸺ Ferry crossing
⋀	Sand dunes		Fresh water from a pipe			– – – – Gravel road

A border of dense conifers, several roads and Masset townsite rim the sanctuary's marsh. Ponds of varying sizes, separated by ditches and dikes, cover most of the sanctuary. In 1977 a tidal gate was installed, which allows seawater to flood the largest basin. The present bridge, finished in 1995, allows normal tidal action within the sanctuary. Water levels on the largest pond fluctuate four times a day, revealing extensive mud flats at low tide. Above the water line, lush grass, wildflowers and small trees grow in the dark soil. Birds use all these habitats.

A short trail from the parking area along Cemetery Road leads to a viewing tower. This is an excellent vantage point for scanning the entire marsh with binoculars, but the best birding begins as you return to ground level. Three trails lead to the waterways.

Simpson Trail, marked by a driftwood sign at the Cemetery Road parking lot, winds pleasantly along the treed side of the sanctuary. Rustic benches provide an opportunity to sit quietly listening for calls. Through the dark foliage you may glimpse a shy varied thrush or a chatty winter wren, a Steller's jay or a hairy woodpecker. Particular subspecies of these birds are endemic to these islands.

At several spots the trail emerges at meadows and ponds. Skulk along the edge of a ditch, staying alert for waterfowl. A fanfare of discordant trumpets will announce the arrival of the largest species—swans and geese. Mallards, American widgeons and teal may be feeding with their tails turned up in the shallows. They can execute a near-vertical takeoff, which allows them into confined ponds and ditches. If a bald eagle or peregrine falcon suddenly appears, these smaller birds will scatter. An alarmed common snipe may burst out, while Lincoln's sparrows furtively flit between the grass hummocks.

You can take a second route along a dike that bisects the marsh. It begins 300 metres past the first parking lot on Cemetery Road. Midway along, a second viewing tower provides a platform to set up a spotting scope and observe distant waterfowl. Wade through thigh-high grass near the ponds. This open portion of Delkatla is the best area to see sandhill cranes performing their spring courtship dance. You'll need patience and stealth to sight these elegant birds as they leap repeatedly skyward, then drop awkwardly to earth, all the while flapping, trumpeting and bowing.

Male northern pintail ducks (*Anas acuta*). These are non-diving ducks, so the shallow waters within Delkatla provide habitat. These ducks breed and reside here year-round.

A dowitcher uses its bill to probe the bottom like a sewing machine, feeding on small invertebrates. Short-billed dowitchers breed in the Delkatla marsh.

Sandhill cranes are but one of more than 130 species of birds recorded at Delkatla. The high number of sightings is mainly due to the dedication and commitment of local naturalist Margo Hearne (see profile in "Their Place To Be"). For 14 years she has recorded migration patterns and numbers, details that are vital to research on species breeding. Recent studies focused on the least sandpiper, a tiny shorebird that normally breeds on the Arctic barrens. For unknown reasons, up to 90 pairs have nested at Delkatla, the highest breeding density in North America. In 1987, adults and downy young were colour banded. By late summer, only the immatures remained. Their parents had left for Central America, leaving the juveniles to find their own way south.

Unfortunately, these and other ground-nesting birds have to contend with obnoxious neighbours. Hereford cattle graze within the sanctuary because border fences are not maintained. These lumbering beasts create havoc by disturbing incubating adults and squashing ground nests. Since Delkatla is only a municipal sanctuary, it has no environmental protection.

From Trumpeter Drive at the eastern edge of Masset, Meadow View Walk offers unobstructed views over the open water. In late April and early May, chocolate-coloured dowitchers probe the muck, black-banded killdeer cry plaintively and flocks of tiny shorebirds zoom over the water's edge like jets in formation. More than 20 species of shorebirds have been recorded here.

Most birds that stop at Delkatla are common along the Pacific Flyway. Rare species, however, do drop in from distant locales. A warm-weather cattle egret was spotted during one Christmas bird count. Marbled godwits, which rarely stray east of the Rockies, have also made a surprise appearance. Wood sandpipers and ruffs, which regularly migrate beyond the outer Aleutian Islands, caused quite a sensation when they appeared in Delkatla. All these birds are rare in B.C.

Since it's on a major migration route, Delkatla will always be a good place for birders to visit. Spring and fall are the best times, but a storm may yield a few surprises. Who knows? You might spot a transient from Siberia, or witness the spectacular dive of a peregrine falcon.

INTRODUCTION TO NAIKOON PROVINCIAL PARK

If you've ever stood in wonder before the monumental *Raven and the First Men* at the Museum of Anthropology at the University of British Columbia in Vancouver, you've been touched by Naikoon. This world-famous cedar carving by Haida artist Bill Reid interprets the myth describing the creation of humans at Rose Spit in Naikoon Provincial Park. That such artistry was inspired here is indicative of the special nature of this landscape.

Within the boundaries of Naikoon Park lie 72,600 hectares of beaches, sand dunes, bogs and lakes. With the exception of two bedrock outcrops, more than 100 kilometres of unbroken beach form its oceanic perimeter. Extensive sand deposits are continuously blown into shifting dunes behind the driftwood. The park's interior is largely a boggy lowland interspersed with a few lakes. This is the Argonaut Plain, a landform created by glacial action thousands of years ago. Some significant geological discoveries have been made here, but they have little commercial value.

Amazingly, the provincial government promoted development of this plain in the early 1900s by issuing homestead permits. Although none of these settlers managed to establish a permanent residence, private property still exists within today's park boundaries. Modern homes along the northern beaches and the Tlell River have replaced some old homesteads.

The B.C. government made a wiser land-use decision in 1973 when it declared Naikoon a provincial park, an excellent choice for the preservation of landforms and lowland typical of B.C.'s coast. A park also served to protect the habitat of some unusual plants, birds and the 5-centimetre-long three-spine stickleback mentioned in "Land Mammals And Amphibians Of Haida Gwaii," which has evolved into specialized subspecies in some of the park's lakes. Three Provincial Ecological Reserves near the park boundaries protect additional areas with environmental significance.

Seasonal visitors can enjoy a wide range of recreational opportunities that the park has to offer. Naikoon has something for everyone—from four-wheeling on the beach to quiet contemplation of nature. It has a coastal trek for experienced backpackers, forest trails for families and limitless beachcombing. The fishing is a big draw for anglers, particularly

NAIKOON PROVINCIAL PARK

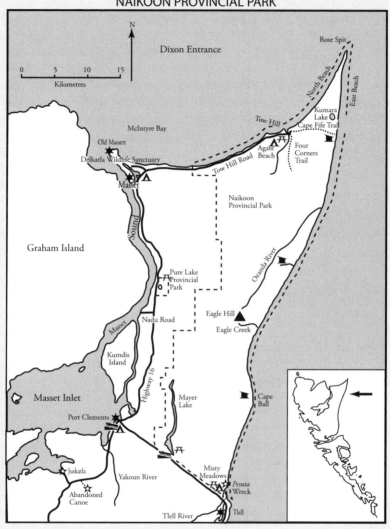

MAP LEGEND

✳ Community	🏛 Viewing tower	🏛 Watchmen site	– – – Park boundary
☆ Site of interest	Warden station	⚓ Anchorage	·········· Trail
Ⓟ Parking	⚘ Picnic sites	Boat ramp	– – – – Indian reserve
Homestead	Park hiking shelter	▲ Hill/mountain	Ecological reserve
Divesite	▲ Camping	✿ Bog	Ferry crossing
⋀ Sand dunes	Fresh water from a pipe		– – – – Gravel road

in the fall, when salmon and steelhead enter the park's rivers. Both sea-run and resident cutthroat trout can be fished in the Tlell and Sangan rivers, as well as in Mayer Lake, which is great for canoeing and has a launching ramp for boats.

The park's headquarters is located on the Yellowhead Highway just south of the Tlell River. Facilities include Agate Beach and Misty Meadows, serviced campgrounds at the north and south ends of the park. Neither of these campgrounds has hot water, hookups or sani-dumps, and the campsites are available on a first-come, first-served basis. A fee is charged from May 15 to September 15.

There are picnic areas in a satellite provincial park called Pure Lake, and at Tow Hill, Mayer Lake, Tlell River and Misty Meadows, all within Naikoon. Most stores and commercial services are in the nearby villages of Masset or Port Clements. A regular provincial fishing licence is required for anglers within B.C. provincial parks. Hunting is permitted within Naikoon Provincial Park. See the Hunting section of "Planning Your Trip" for more details.

For brochures and current information, contact the supervisor at:
Naikoon Provincial Park,
Box 19, Tlell, BC V0T 1Y0
Phone (250) 557-4390
Website: <www.env.gov.bc.ca/bcparks/>

TOW HILL AREA

The rounded dome of Tow Hill is the dominant landmark and a must-see for visitors to Naikoon Park. There are picnic facilities at the hill, a short trail to its summit and a grand view of Dixon Entrance. From its base, anglers may cast into a river or the sea, jig offshore for halibut or catch crab beyond the surf. Hiking routes lead inland in both directions along the extensive beaches. This is a pleasant place to picnic for a few hours or to linger for several days of camping, fishing, crabbing and exploration.

Agate Beach is named for the translucent stones found all along this shore. They're a form of quartz, washed from glacial deposits by the waves and tumbled in the saltwater swash until they gleam. They aren't precious stones, but don't try telling this to a child—for young castaways these are diamonds from a pirate's booty.

The pebble beach gives way to soft sand at low tide. If the surf is down, inflatable boats can be launched from the beach. The water averages 4 to 10 fathoms offshore, ideal for jigging bottom fish. Buzz bombs, cod jigs or baited hooks are popular for halibut. If you don't have a boat, try bait-casting

GETTING THERE

From Masset, a narrow but well-travelled gravel road leads east past the old Canadian Forces base toward Naikoon Provincial Park. It passes beachfront homes and an ecological reserve before reaching Agate Beach Campground at 25 km. This campground is open year-round and has 32 RV spots, 11 tent pads, a kitchen shelter, pit toilets and tap water. An overnight fee applies May through September. Arrive early to secure a space, as the closest alternative is the Hidden Island Resort RV Park and Campground in Masset.

Beyond the campground the road rounds Tow Hill and within 2 km reaches the access to North Beach. A small parking lot has nearby picnic tables and fire rings meant for day use. (A campground is currently in the planning stages.) Trailers are best parked at the Agate Beach campground because there is limited turning space at the Tow Hill parking lot.

for groundfish from the base of Tow Hill. The Hiellen River also supports cutthroat trout and Dolly Varden, and commercial fishers work offshore for Dungeness crab, which are abundant. You can set out crab traps as well if you have a boat and the surf stays calm for a few hours.

A more popular method of crab fishing is to wade through the surf at low tide. You will, however, need a net and chestwaders. Hardy (or hungry) souls sometimes brave the cold water and wade out in only their bathing suits. You need a licence to harvest crab: be sure to check the

TOW HILL

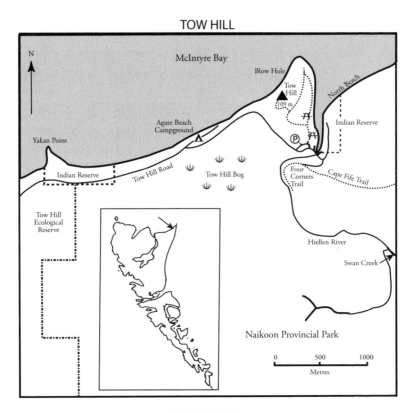

MAP LEGEND

✳ Community	🏛 Viewing tower	🏛 Watchmen site	– – – Park boundary
☆ Site of interest	╽ Warden station	⚓ Anchorage	········ Trail
Ⓟ Parking	⚲ Picnic sites	➤ Boat ramp	– – – – Indian reserve
🏠 Homestead	▪ Park hiking shelter	▲ Hill/mountain	······· Ecological reserve
◣ Divesite	▲ Camping	☙ Bog	▬▬▬ Ferry crossing
⋏ Sand dunes	⛲ Fresh water from a pipe		– – – – Gravel road

saltwater fishing regulations for sizes and limits.

From the campground, Tow Hill is a 15-minute walk along the beach, or a 2-kilometre ride along the road. From its ocean side, the distinctive character of Tow Hill can be examined. The cliff is composed of hexagonal columns of rock that fit together like six-sided cells of honeycomb. This is basalt: an igneous (fire-formed) stone that long ago flowed into cracks of sandstone that were already in place here. When the molten basalt cooled, it cracked into metre-wide columns.

Part of being touched by Naikoon is collecting shells. Each tide renews the beach, so there's always the possibility of finding something new.

Tow Hill was further sculpted by glaciers during the last Ice Age. Viewed from North Beach, the gradual, inland slope of the hill lies in contrast to its fluted face. A wall of ice pushed down from the Queen

It's chilly, but wading in the surf is one way to catch crabs. A forked stick or dip net will lift the crabs off the bottom.

Charlotte Mountains, depositing gravel against the back side of the hill before rising over it and moving out to sea. On the seaward side, bedrock was plucked away. This left an excellent example of a landform known as a *roche moutonnée*.

The Haida have a wonderful legend interpreting the creation of several rock formations here. The legend—involving an eagle, a whale and an angry ogre named Tow—is recounted in considerable detail by Kathleen E. (Betty) Dalzell in her authoritative history *The Queen Charlotte Islands, Book 2: Of Places and Names.*

From the parking lot at the base of Tow Hill, a trail meanders along the Hiellen River, passing picnic tables on the way to a rocky point beneath the cliff. A boardwalk branches from the picnic site and rises to the 109-metre summit. On a clear day, islands in the Alaskan panhandle can be seen to the north, 72 kilometres away across Dixon Entrance. Sickle-shaped North Beach slices the surf on the right. To the left, the campsite is visible and in the distance beyond is the ridge of the Queen Charlotte Mountains. Directly below the lookout the cliff drops to a rocky point, where pelagic cormorants sometimes gather before roosting overnight on the cliff face. This edge is concealed—*do not leave the established trail.*

After taking in the vistas and crashing surf around the hill, you may want to investigate the forests behind it. Here, the pale beauty of a single

delight flower and the whistle of a shy varied thrush are contrasting pleasures on a micro scale. Among these trees, a general store, a post office and a clam cannery once operated. A rusting boiler and concrete foundations in the trees downstream from the bridge are all that remain. This property belongs

Fishing in the Hiellen River can be good when the tide drops. Dolly Varden and cutthroat trout are caught in summer, and there is a small coho run in the fall.

to the Old Masset Village Council. If you wish to camp in the trees, be sure to obtain permission from the band office in Old Massett.

In the early 1900s an ill-informed government in Victoria promoted vast tracts of Graham Island for agricultural settlement. Immigrants found themselves trying to locate unsurveyed land that had no access. Later they discovered there was no export market for the produce they grew. At first only a few determined settlers used the beach as their road, but by 1912 there were about a hundred people dealing at the Tow Hill store. World War I and the subsequent Depression ended their efforts. Today their wagon routes are walking trails from Tow Hill to East Beach and the park's interior. To explore them is to gain an appreciation of the work ethic of these pioneers.

FOUR CORNERS AND CAPE FIFE TRAILS

The departure point for both the Four Corners and Cape Fife trails is on a marked side road on the immediate east side of the Hiellen River. Vehicles are best left nearby at the Tow Hill parking lot. Both trails are suitable for small children along the initial portions.

The Four Corners Trail originally led south for nearly five kilometres. Today, only the northern end can be easily walked or ridden. A massive blowdown, rotten bridges and heavy overgrowth make it very difficult to reach the interior. Anyone wishing to follow this settler route to its extremity should be equipped with waterproof boots, GPS, a 1:50,000 topographic map and an excellent sense of direction!

The first part of the trail, however, makes a short, pleasant walk. The mossy road is now fringed with tall trees and edged in some places with drainage ditches—all dug with pick and spade. For those who carried out this backbreaking labour, the eventual abandonment of the trail must have been heart-wrenching. Apart from the road, a few fence posts and the old bridge, all other signs of human habitation have been either overgrown with moss or rotted away into the humus.

Take the time, though, to investigate the bogs alongside the road. Here you might surprise a cock-eared deer or, if you're lucky, some sandhill cranes, which nest in such places. Occasionally they will be heard overhead, calling with a guttural, vibrating "gar-oo-oo-oo." Judging from the names Swan Creek and Cygnet Lake, trumpeter swans may have once nested nearby. Determined birders may want to consider trying to find definitive evidence of nesting, as this would be a significant provincial record.

The Cape Fife Trail leads to East Beach (see "East Beach"), winding 10 kilometres through rainforest and open woods before reaching sand dunes just south of Kumara Lake. The route is level and in good condition, with cedar timbers spanning the wet and muddy portions. At about the halfway point, the dark woods are left behind as open marshes and meadows appear. About five kilometres in there is a wilderness campsite and trailside bench. A poorly flagged route forks over to Mica Lake from here, but there is no suitable ground for tenting at this location. Allow 15 minutes to reach the lake, and watch carefully for faded flagging tape.

A new Haida-style hiking shelter marks the eastern end of the trail. You can complete a circle trip by following East and North Beach back to Tow Hill, but this makes for an exceedingly long day. Try to have a vehicle pick you up at North Beach, or camp overnight to make this an easier option.

From a base at Agate Beach, anyone curious about the natural environment or seeking some quiet relaxation can happily spend three or four days in the Tow Hill vicinity.

TOW HILL BOG

Bog communities have their own beauty and points of ecological interest, but the landscape, and sometimes the name, can put people off. "Who wants to stomp about in a sodden swamp?" some may think, but those who venture farther will be well rewarded.

Bogs are a major feature of B.C.'s coast, and Canada has more bogs than any other country. Preserving this bog on the Argonaut Plain was a major reason for the park's creation, and an ecological reserve has been created nearby to give this vegetative resource additional protection for research purposes.

This peaty plain was formed, and is maintained, by high rainfall and poor drainage. The water table is close to the surface, indicated by the numerous small pools. Few plants can tolerate such a root-soaking habitat. Stunted conifers, sphagnum moss and evergreen shrubs, such as salal, are dominant and easily recognizable. Ten species of sphagnum, which forms peat moss, have been identified here.

The solid strata of moss, capable of filling shallow bodies of water, functions much like a sponge—and indeed feels like one underfoot. Inhibiting the water's flow and preventing oxygenation, the moss also turns it acidic by releasing tannin, a natural plant by-product. This chemical accounts for Naikoon's brownish streams. Tannin is also a component of tea; you might imagine you're walking across a gigantic tea bag!

These chemical conditions are typical of peat bogs and necessary for their development. A bog is defined as a deposit of partially decomposed organic matter. The sphagnum moss and other plants that grow here are not broken down into soil when they die, as happens in most plant decay. Bacteria and microscopic organisms that normally carry out the task of decomposition are deficient in bogs due to the acid and lack of oxygen. Thus each year's growth is established on layers of previous plants.

Bogs often evolve to many metres deep and can date back to the end of the Ice Age. Although their lowermost layers become black and oozy, laboratory analysis will reveal woody pieces and microscopic pollen grains released by flowers each spring. Most pollen is scattered on the ground, so peat bogs function like a bank, containing extensive deposits undamaged by decay. Since each species' pollen looks different, scientists can tell what plants once grew in this vicinity.

Researchers recently discovered a species of fir tree that grew here 30,000 years ago. Even more remarkable is the fact that no firs grow

GETTING THERE

Follow the road from Masset to Naikoon Park (about 25 km). Across the road from Agate Beach Campground, look for the deer trails that lead up onto a typical peat bog. Gumboots are advised. A two-minute stroll will take you into this interesting environment. The summit of Tow Hill (see preceding section) is a good place to get an overall view of this bog.

A flying insect attracted by a round-leafed sundew's flower-like leaf has been caught on the glandular hairs. The insect's protein will be dissolved to provide the plant with nitrogen it cannot obtain from its impoverished habitat.

naturally on the Charlottes today. They were evidently removed by the ice sheets and have not returned, although this conifer is found in abundance on the adjacent northern mainland. In other instances, some plants that grow on these islands are found nowhere else in B.C., or have their closest counterparts in Asia. Such unusual distributions, and the changes to the earth's climate they imply, are the subject of considerable debate among scientists.

Additional discoveries in ancient deposits at Cape Ball on East Beach provided some of the evidence for refugia in the Charlottes. For years, geologists have refuted suggestions that pockets of green would have survived at low elevations during the Ice Age. Botanists and zoologists have argued otherwise because the odd distribution of plants and distinctive subspecies of animals found on the Charlottes are best explained by uninterrupted evolution within a refugium.

If the depths of a bog are so revealing, the surface can hardly be dull. A quick examination on your knees soon demonstrates this. If you visit Tow Hill Bog in early July you'll find two inconspicuous

Dwarf shrubs of the bog include Labrador tea (*Ledum groenlandicum*) and western swamp kalmia (*Kalmia microphylla*). Labrador tea has dense clusters of white flowers, while the kalmia's are pink. Both plants have rolled leaf edges.

Western swamp laurel. (*Kalmia microphylla*)

(Drawings by Sheila Douglas)

plants in bloom. Even if they're not flowering, the adaptations of the round-leafed sundew and the common butterwort will boggle your mind.

These plants are insectivorous—they supplement their nutrition by capturing and digesting insects. They do this because their habitat is deficient in minerals and nitrogen. Both have mechanisms for capturing small prey on their glandular leaves. Once trapped by sticky hairs, bugs are dissolved by enzymes and absorbed. It's challenging to capture this detail on film but a good close-up will amaze those who believe such oddities grow only in tropical jungles.

After walking around a bit you'll discover there are wetter and drier areas within the bog, and that plants tend to favour particular micro-habitats—localized conditions beneficial to a particular plant's needs. Along with the insect-digesters found in wet areas are beauties such as cotton grass and tall shooting star. Even without a field guide, their descriptive names should help you identify these white and pink species.

Around the perimeter of the bog, the peat moss forms hummocks. On this drier ground grow several species of the heather family. Look for bog cranberry (like a miniature shooting star), Labrador tea (with fuzzy rusty underleaves) and swamp laurel (bright pink flowers). Here, too, survive stunted shore pines and dwarf juniper. They look like bonsai, the dwarfed, potted art trees of Japan. It may have taken them several hundred years to reach this size under such difficult growing conditions.

While searching for these plants, don't be surprised to see small frogs leaping away from just in front of your feet. Pacific treefrogs have sticky pads on their toes, enabling them to climb shrubs and trees. For the most part, they are content to clamber in the moss and low bushes. Like many land creatures on these islands, this frog was introduced. Fortunately, they have not become a problem like other non-native creatures.

For simple majesty, Tow Hill Bog can't compete with the coastal features of Naikoon Park. It requires greater effort to learn its intricacies and to appreciate its many unique and fascinating features. All of this, however, is within easy grasp of anyone willing to spend an hour looking more closely at its natural history.

"Islands of the people" is the meaning of Haida Gwaii, but many residents refer to their home as "The Misty Isles"—a fitting description.

Old Sitka spruce grow to an average of 60 metres high and 2 metres in diameter.

Many Haida buildings feature ornately painted designs such as these on Looking Around and Blinking House.

Traditional Haida button blankets are donned for special events.

Loo Tass, the late Bill Reid's canoe, was launched in 1986.

Haida chiefs wear their impressive ceremonial attire to celebrate a potlatch.

Tow Hill, a prominent landmark shown here at sunset, is an outcrop of basalt columns about 100 metres high in Naikoon Provincial Park. An elaborate and memorable Haida myth explains the formation of the columns, tidal potholes, loose boulders, large rock, spouting blowhole and booming sound.

This idyllic view of Skincuttle Inlet from Jedway is typical of the scenery in Gwaii Haanas National Park Reserve and Haida Heritage Site.

Haida Gwaii is rich in fauna: sea lions, colourful sun stars and red rock crabs are common sights. Below, northern sea lions haul out on wave-washed Cape St. James.

Naikoon's Agate Beach is named for the translucent stones found all along this shore. A form of quartz, they were washed from glacial deposits by the waves.

The balance rock, just north of Skidegate, looks like it could fall over at any moment. It is a glacial erratic deposited by receding glaciers thousands of years ago.

Orcas swimming close to shore provide an exciting photo op.

Piercing the silence with its creaky stutter, the bald eagle is the most noticeable aerial predator on Gwaii Haanas.

The black oystercatcher (top) and common loon (bottom) frequent rocky headlands and sheltered inlets.

Deer thrive on these islands. Watch for them along roadsides and in meadows and estuaries.

Mortuary poles (top left, right) still stand in two ancient villages. Memorial poles (bottom left) were measures of wealth and prestige.

Growing throughout the islands, salmonberries bloom in May and yield edible fruit in early summer.

Raccoons may seem cute, but their behaviour is not: they eat the eggs and young of nesting seabirds.

Immense patches of lupine cover Rose Spit and border many beaches in Haida Gwaii.

NORTH BEACH

North Beach is one of the most popular attractions on the Charlottes. Its strand is remarkably wide, firm and beautiful. This expanse of sand stretches 15 kilometres from the Hiellen River to the base of Rose Spit. It's a great place to enjoy the surf and sand, ride along the beach, beachcomb, dig for clams or catch crabs.

The extensive beaches on the Charlottes owe their existence to glacial and water action. Sheets of ice hundreds of metres deep once slid from the Queen Charlotte Mountains carrying millions of tonnes of sand, gravel and rock. This ice melted slowly, depositing its cargo over what are now the lowlands of Graham Island and the surrounding sea.

Since the Ice Age ended, Hecate Strait and Dixon Entrance have had a dramatic effect on these glacial deposits. Nearshore currents and waves in Hecate Strait wash northward, eroding the deposits along East Beach. Similar patterns circulate the fine material in Dixon Entrance. All these materials move eastward toward Rose Spit. Ocean currents, combined with onshore wind and waves, transport this sand onto the gentle slope of North Beach. In places the beach is more than 200 metres wide.

GETTING THERE

North Beach stretches along the northeastern edge of Graham Island from the village of Old Massett to Rose Spit. It is accessible from various unmarked side roads along its entire length. This section covers only the portion east of Tow Hill that lies within Naikoon Park. A 25-km gravel road from Masset ends just after crossing the Hiellen River. Here, 4 x 4 vehicles can be driven directly onto the hard-packed beach sand. All drivers must keep their motorized vehicles between the orange markers and the high-tide line. It is permissible, however, to cross from North Beach to East Beach via a connector road across the base of Rose Spit. Driving on the dunes is strictly prohibited.

Caution: Crossing Rose Spit or following East Beach is not recommended for inexperienced off-road drivers.

Think twice before giving in to temptation and driving your vehicle straight onto the beach. The tide can come in with deceptive speed. Tom discovered this the hard way. In 1982, as he was photographing his new truck on the beach, the incoming waves began to lick the tires. Before you could say "pass the towrope," the sand softened and the vehicle settled into the beach like a nesting duck. There was no choice but to abandon the truck, head for higher ground and watch in horror as the incoming surf turned it turtle, filled the cab with sand then flattened the vehicle into the beach.

Anyone without four-wheel drive would be well advised to walk or to ride a mountain bike here. We found that bicycles are by far the best way to explore the beach. A leisurely round trip along the beach can be completed in half a day. Afterwards, thoroughly wash your bike to prevent corrosion. Since there are no dependable streams along the beach, it is best to clean it later at the campground.

North Beach bounty! A bucket of Dungeness crabs and some razor clams make a great meal.

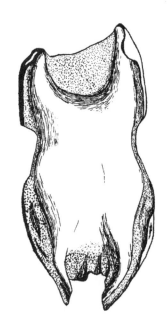

The egg case of a big skate (*Raja binoculata*) can be 22.5 centimetres long. This skate grows to 2.4 metres, is common over muddy bottoms and is taken commercially.

If you have a 4 x 4, the ride along the beach from the Hiellen River to the spit takes about 30 minutes. As you cruise along the beach, keep an eye open for drift logs, kelp and other hazards. It will take a further 15 minutes to cross Rose Spit and, if conditions allow, to continue down East Beach. Watch for a large park sign marking the access road.

By car or bicycle, plan to start your beach explorations on a falling tide. This will allow ample time to stop and beachcomb. After every tide the beach looks different. On occasion it will be washed clean. At other times you will have to navigate through every sort of international flotsam imaginable. After most storms, serious beachcombers race along the tide line seeking their most cherished prize—spherical glass fishing floats. These balls, which can be as large as basketballs, break away from Japanese fishing nets.

Other interesting debris includes sponges, jellyfish, shells and unusual fish. Even a great white shark has cast up on this beach. Once we found a large skate. On another visit we discovered a peculiar leathery pouch within a tangle of kelp. It was later identified as a mermaid's purse. This pouch protects the skate's embryo until it is strong enough to swim free.

Besides beachcombing, there are lots of other activities to occupy your time at North Beach. The shallow water offshore makes first-class habitat for Dungeness crab. Bright orange floats mark crab traps set by commercial boats from Masset. As the tide falls, a quick dig in the sand may expose equally delectable razor clams. In B.C., these olive-coloured shellfish occur only here and at Long Beach on Vancouver Island. According to fisheries officials, razor clams seldom accumulate dangerous levels of red-tide toxins, which contaminate other bivalves in the Charlottes.

Razor clams are concentrated along the low-tide line. They bury themselves 15 to 20 centimetres beneath the sand. A shallow dimple marks their "show." The ideal tool for digging them is a narrow-bladed shovel called a "clam gun." Various techniques are effective, but all require speed and care because the clams can move quickly and fracture easily. You must have a tidal-waters licence to dig for them; check the saltwater fishing regulations for bag limits.

Sea spume and surf, Naikoon Provincial Park.

Between 1923 and 1931, a cannery on the Hiellen River processed the razor clams harvested at North Beach. You can find an old boiler and concrete foundations from this cannery hidden in undergrowth on the east bank. After the cannery closed, the clams were taken to Masset for processing.

Summertime is not the only time to have fun on these beaches. For many years, kayakers have launched their small craft from the beach and frolicked in the large winter waves. Recently, the northern beaches have also been discovered by surfing enthusiasts eager to catch a wave, even if it means having to don a dry suit and hood. Midway between Masset and Tow Hill, and off the mouth of the Hiellen River have become favourite spots. Surf's up!

Experiencing North Beach will be a highlight of any visit to Haida Gwaii. It's a place to walk alone when the surf is pounding and the salt spray stiffens your hair, a place to build castles of sand on sunny days, to relax around an evening campfire sharing tall tales or to cruise along the hard sand in a dune buggy. It's hard to imagine anyone not enjoying this special environment.

ROSE SPIT

Back at the beginning of time, when the water that once covered the earth subsided, only a raven survived. In his loneliness the bird combed the islands that broke the surface of the great sea, seeking companionship. Finally, while soaring over a long sandy beach, he heard faint cries emanating from a clamshell that had washed up on the shore. The raven swooped down and pried the shell open. To his great wonder, the sounds grew louder and louder, and the startled bird watched in amazement as several men clambered out.

This Haida myth of human creation has been retold for centuries and has parallels with the Biblical story of the ark on Mount Ararat. The Charlottes event occurred at Nai-Kun, the long nose of Nai, which today is known as Rose Spit. Natives and visitors hold the spit in high esteem as one of the most interesting places in Haida Gwaii.

The spit has undergone several name changes over the last 200 years. The present title gives undeserved recognition to a British politician who never visited this place. Fortunately, the original name

GETTING THERE

Rose Spit extends into Dixon Entrance from the extreme northeastern corner of Graham Island. The quickest approach is via Masset, or alternatively, East Beach. From Masset drive the 25-km gravel road to Tow Hill. From here it's a 15-km hike, bicycle ride or drive along North Beach to where the trees end at the base of the spit. The land portion of the spit extends another 3 km. Vehicles must stay on the road and are prohibited in all other areas of the reserve.

NORTH BEACH AND ROSE SPIT

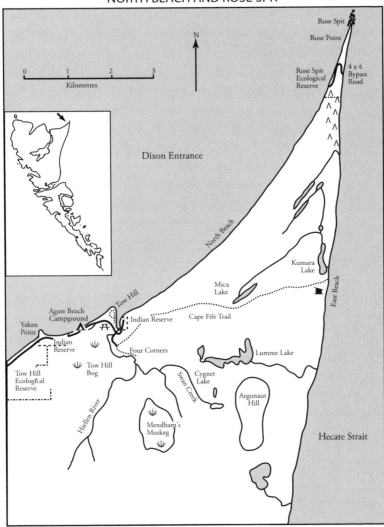

MAP LEGEND

✳	Community	🗼	Viewing tower	🏛	Watchmen site	− − −	Park boundary
☆	Site of interest	▪	Warden station	⚓	Anchorage	········	Trail
Ⓟ	Parking	⚶	Picnic sites	⤳	Boat ramp	− − − −	Indian reserve
🏠	Homestead	▪	Park hiking shelter	▲	Hill/mountain	−·−·−·	Ecological reserve
◣	Divesite	▲	Camping	�	Bog	··············	Ferry crossing
∧∧	Sand dunes	🚰	Fresh water from a pipe			− − − − −	Gravel road

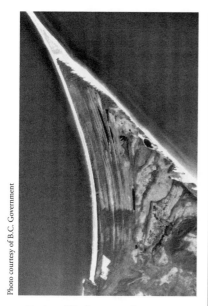

Northward-flowing currents have extended Rose Spit several kilometres to the sea. The ridges paralleling North Beach are old shorelines formed at times of higher sea levels following the last Ice Age.

is preserved by adjacent Naikoon Provincial Park, for it's more fitting than any bestowed by European navigators.

Rose Spit is located at the junction of North and East beaches. Waves and currents that move along these shorelines have built an elongated neck of sand and gravel. The base is 1 kilometre wide at the forest edge, and the spit hooks 3 kilometres out to sea. An additional 3-kilometre bar continues beneath the water's surface. Portions of this submarine section are sometimes visible as offshore sandbars. This is the largest such formation in the province.

The best overview of the spit is gained from atop the sand dunes at the forest edge. Prevailing winds from the southeast have shaped sand into dunes exceeding 10 metres in height. In the process, large trees have been partially buried. Many plants that grow here have thick waxy leaves or special root systems. Both represent adaptations to the brutal conditions—plants are washed by salt spray, dried by the sun, pelted by drifting sand and blown by wind. (See "Tlell River and Sand Dunes" for more about the difficult plant colonization of dunes.)

From this vantage, other features of the spit are also visible. Rose Spit is bordered on both sides by compacted driftwood. The amount of wood appears to be increasing, as photos from 1960 show considerably fewer logs. In places it is possible to walk across the mass of tangled wood for 50 metres before touching the shore.

Between the lines of logs the spit is covered by a lush meadow. Botanists have recognized three distinct plant communities containing rare species. One, sea mertensia, is found nowhere else in B.C. Others, such as bighead sedge and western dune tansy, are found only on shore sand. Flowering patches of yellow paintbrush and blue lupines are so fragrant that you might smell them downwind.

Plants are but one of many specialties of the spit. Upwelling currents concentrate plankton and fish near the surface, attracting many birds: more than 100 species have been recorded here. Expect to see shearwaters, ducks, sandhill cranes and many species of gulls. During migration, the area is also a haven for shorebirds, which stop here to rest and feed. Occasionally,

Bighead sedge (*Carex macrocephyla*) is an important pioneer of plant colonization on dunes. It's one of the few that can establish roots in the shifting sand.

a peregrine falcon will ambush migrating peeps and plovers.

While keeping a constant watch for wildlife, a walk to the tip of the spit is a must. The merging of Hecate Strait and Dixon Entrance creates spectacular displays. When the surf is up and the tides are changing, opposing waves smash against each other in a spuming wall of water. Turning your back to the waves creates an exhilarating sensation. The boiling sea wraps around you on three sides, leaving only a narrow line of retreat.

The erratic water movements have formed an offshore sandbar that is a favourite haul-out for both seals and sea lions. If you have binoculars, you should be able to spot their large brown and grey shapes on the lee side. As an added bonus, a walk out the spit may yield a glimpse of either gray or killer whales.

Although Rose Spit is a mecca for wildlife and recreationists, it can be a death trap for mariners. Boats are advised to stay well out from this menacing crooked finger. Those who are unfortunate enough to be swept into the grasp of the vicious currents that swirl around the spit often capsize. Over the years, many lives have been lost. In some cases, even those who were lucky enough to reach the beach still died of exposure.

In 1971 the unique features of the spit were protected by the B.C. government under the Ecological Reserves Act. The purpose of the act is to secure such places for scientific research. Visitors are welcome, but should be aware that it is illegal to camp, have a fire, hunt or otherwise disturb or remove plants and animals. Hikers and motorized vehicles are directed to stay on designated roads or beaches in this area.

When you stand alone at the very tip of Rose Spit, you feel like the first person on earth. One experiences what it might have been like stepping out of the clamshell after the Great Flood. The immense power of the sea wrapping around you is simultaneously humbling and rejuvenating. Behind lies a whole new world. You return to it with renewed appreciation and a sense of having been touched by the spirit of Nai-Kun.

EAST BEACH

At 70 kilometres, East Beach is one of the longest beaches in North America. A four- to seven-day trek along its length has been gaining popularity ever since the park was created. Though the route is flat, it can still be a challenge to backpackers. The trek offers that wonderful sense of shoreline solitude that humans find so soothing to their psyche. Many hikers, familiar with more rugged terrain, have proclaimed this a highlight of their outdoor experiences. The beach is also travelled in more leisurely style by people in four-wheel-drive vehicles.

The trail begins at the Tlell River bridge just north of Misty Meadows Campground. From the picnic site at the bridge, a 2-kilometre trail follows the river through the forest to the beach. A faster route is to follow Beitush Road along the river's edge, then wade the river at low tide. It's only knee-deep at a stony ford. By walking northward from this point, you keep the prevailing wind, rain and sun at your back.

Before heading out on this adventure you should prepare for all kinds of weather—even in summer there can be fog, rain and cool temperatures. It's also essential to carry a watch and up-to-date tide table. You'll need these to time your crossing of unbridged tidal rivers.

From the mouth of the Tlell River the beach is beautiful. To seaward, an unbroken but ever-changing expanse of cloud and waves stretches from horizon to horizon. In the foreground, semipalmated plovers scurry down the beach, which fades to infinity. On the left stretches a continuous line of sand cliffs or dunes, topped by spruce forest. A few days of such spectacular scenic monotony satisfies some; others take 10 delightful days to reach the end of this magnificent trip.

Four kilometres from the picnic site is the bow remnant of the 1928 shipwreck *Pesuta*. This wooden barge was under tow in Hecate Strait when its line parted in a winter storm. The barge and its cargo of logs became driftwood. When looking at the millions of drift logs on these islands, note how few are of natural origin. Virtually all have sprung loose from log booms over the past five or six decades. Driftwood, at least on the Charlottes, is largely a human-made phenomenon.

A couple of hours' walk north of the wreck will bring you to Cape Ball River, a good overnight location. Please respect the private property here and pitch tents near the hiking shelter. Private holdings, such as lots 1357 and 1358, still exist within the park and are noted on topographic maps of 1:50,000 scale.

The tide floods the mouth of this river, as well as the others along this route. Fresh water and a crossing can be gained only at low tide. You

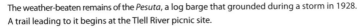

The weather-beaten remains of the *Pesuta*, a log barge that grounded during a storm in 1928. A trail leading to it begins at the Tlell River picnic site.

also need a receding tide to pass under the 60-metre sand cliffs at Cape Ball. The trek north around this headland to Eagle Hill may take as long as five hours. Eagle Creek is the only break in this wall that will allow a retreat from incoming waves.

Recently, some exciting research on these cliffs and on the plain beyond resulted in discoveries that are altering our perception of geologic events in British Columbia. Other fields of research are now reforming their theories based on the biological, climatic and cultural history of the Charlottes.

This site was chosen for investigation because the uncompressed sediments were deposited in chronological order during and after the Ice Age. Researchers have determined that melting of the provincial ice cap throughout most of B.C. began about 10,000 years ago. However, geologist John Clague of the Geological Survey of Canada and biologist Rolf Mathewes of Simon Fraser University have discovered plant remains in these cliffs dating back 16,000 years.

There were actually trees and peat bogs here when continental Canada was still as stiff as an icicle. This evidence strengthens the theory that there

was an oasis or refugium during the last big chill. If all these features were in place, could there have been animals or people present? Stay tuned to the Charlottes as the leading edge of science probes these possibilities.

Moving north along the beach, there are good camping spots at Eagle Creek, Lot 114 A (where there is another shelter), the Oeanda River mouth and

Hiking around the cliffs at Cape Ball. The layers of sand were laid down by a silt-laden river flowing from a melting glacier. The occasional boulder between the layers fell from drifting ice floes.

Kumara Lake. The availability of fresh water determines where you camp each night. Rivers are either tidal, of periodic flow or enter the ocean beneath the beach, making it difficult to obtain drinking water. Topographic maps will help you locate the streams on this featureless coast.

In a pinch, you can take water from ponds behind the beach. All surface water in the park is tea-coloured, having drained through peat. The Scots may claim it makes better whisky, but we advise boiling or otherwise purifying this water before drinking it. Flavoured juice crystals make it more palatable. Alternatively, a plastic tarp can serve as both a cooking shelter and water-catcher. It will funnel rain into a water bottle when used as a flysheet or when spread across a sandy depression overnight.

Nearing Kumara Lake, sand dunes become prominent. Look for places where sand-buried trees have been uncovered by high waves during recent storms. In other areas you can find marine shells embedded in the mud banks above sea level. Obviously, this land has not always been the way it appears today. The landscape is in a constant state of transformation.

Dune formation and erosion are natural processes, but they are accelerated by the removal of stabilizing plants (see "Tlell River and Sand Dunes"). Regrettably, in places around Rose Spit, 4 x 4s have damaged plants and their supporting dunes. According to the park master plan of 1983, these "infernal combustion" machines are supposed to be prohibited

GETTING THERE

East Beach in Naikoon Park stretches continuously from the Tlell River in the south to Rose Spit on the northeast tip of Graham Island. You can hike it from the north, but it is best begun at Tlell. Get advice and information on current conditions from the park headquarters located here. Refer also to the sections on Rose Spit, North Beach and Tow Hill to complete your picture of this 90-km hike. (Relevant topographic maps are listed at the end of this section.)

Beware! This is an unpatrolled wilderness. You cannot be assured of a speedy rescue if you run into trouble.

Three shelters along East Beach provide protection from wind and rain. The newest, built in a traditional Haida design, is at Cape Fife.

from this wild beach. For a time they were, but politicians reversed this policy under local pressure.

There is a third hiking shelter at Cape Fife, where a trail leads past the southern end of Kumara Lake directly to Tow Hill (see "Tow Hill Area"). This inland route will cut 10 kilometres off the trek via North Beach. But since you would miss beautiful Rose Spit to the north, we recommend the trail option only if time is short. Hikers exiting via Cape Fife will have to visit the spit on another day or be forever sorry.

TOPOGRAPHIC MAPS

The following topographic maps (NTS 1:50,000 scale) cover the entire hike and may be purchased at the government agent's office in the Village of Queen Charlotte or mail-ordered from:

Map and Air Photo Sales, Surveys and Resource Mapping Branch
Ministry of Crown Lands, Parliament Buildings, Victoria, BC V8V lX5

103 G/12 West Tlell	103 G/13 West Eagle Hill
103 G/13 East Eagle Hill	103 J/4 West Tow Hill
103 J/4 East Tow Hill	

Tide tables for the islands are found in
Canadian Tide and Current Tables, Volume 6: Barkley Sound and Discovery Passage to Dixon Entrance.
See the Navigation and Safety section of "Planning Your Trip" for ordering information.

SAND DUNES, TLELL RIVER AND VICINITY

THE SAND DUNES

Before heading to the dunes, check the information shelter outside park headquarters. An interpretive plaque shows the flowers you can expect to see on the dunes. The shelter also details local facilities and services. The nearest campground is Misty Meadows, only half a kilometre down the road. This park facility has 40 sites, a kitchen shelter, pit toilets and taps for drinking water. The campground is serviced daily and open year-round, and a fee is charged May through September.

A return walk to the dunes begins from the campground and can be comfortably completed in two hours. Start on the trail at the parking/picnic area that leads to the beach. Once through the trees, take note of some landmarks—many people miss the exit from the beach on their return. Head south (to your right) and follow the forest edge along the coast. Within 15 minutes you'll come to the first dunes. If you feel the wind on your face, it is probably coming from the southeast. Sou'easterlies are the most prevalent and strongest winds in the Charlottes. Without them there would be no dunes.

Along this section of Graham Island's coast, massive sand deposits are being eroded and re-deposited onto the beaches. Where the ground behind the beach is low-lying, windblown sand forms dunes. These moving mounds often reach an impressive size. Active dunes are sparsely vegetated.

When you arrive where the dunes are advancing, note the parallel zones that characterize this area. At the front is the surf zone, whose limit is defined by fresh drift logs. Behind them is a narrow zone of older driftwood, often partially buried. Behind that is a transition zone. This is an ecological no man's land where sand dunes and plant life fight one another for supremacy. The final zone is the fringing forest. This is the plants' ultimate defence in stopping the dunes' advance.

Take a careful walk across these zones and you'll witness the force that moves this sand. On the windward side of old fence posts, the blasting and chiselling action of windblown sand has raised the grain. In the transition zone you might find a ventifact. This is a stone with glossy surfaces and sharp ridges that have been sandblasted by the wind. Finally, on the dunes, you will see dead trees. Large branches protruding from trunks at ground level show that some have been smothered by sand to depths of 10 metres.

These dunes actually start at the driftwood. Sand picked up here by the wind shifts until it meets an obstruction. In this way, small dunes accumulate around rocks, driftwood or even plants. As the dune grows it acts as a windbreak. The sand rolls up the windward slope, then drops over the lee side. By tiny granular increments, the dune continues to grow as it is pushed before the wind. Small dunes travel faster than large ones, so they ultimately merge with others. You will notice that the landscape features here are all aligned in the direction of the prevailing wind.

As dunes travel across the transition zone, plants attempt to cover them. Grasses and sedges are particularly suited to this type of colonization. As sand piles around their stems, they send up new leaf shoots. They can grow rhizomes (horizontal subterranean stems) very quickly, and green leaves pop up all along this system. In this shifting environment, this method of rapid reproduction is much more effective than the annual setting of seeds. You might recognize species such as bighead sedge or wild strawberry.

These plants are pioneers, trying to stabilize the dune with their rhizomes and runners. If they succeed, other plants like dune tansy and beach lupine can get a start. If they fail, the wind may resume the dune's progress, or a blowout, an erosional hollow blown out of a disturbed dune, may occur. This happens when root systems are damaged by drought, grazing cattle, beach

This massive blowout in a dune has eroded right down to a former beach. Such erosion is very difficult to stop, and the sand can move on to bury good pasture land or forest trees.

buggies or human trampling. Each plant is important. Walk carefully and avoid crushing plants or making a rut.

Generally, dunes at the forest edge are fully vegetated. The trees prevent further progress. On the forest side of these dunes, mosses and shrubs have formed a stable plant community. At the southernmost end of the walk, note how grasses have successfully covered the dunes.

About an hour after starting out, you will see hydroelectric poles above the beach. From here you may choose to return along the highway to see the dunes from their lee side. The distance is about the same as returning along the beach.

TLELL RIVER

The other walk from the campground takes you in the opposite direction. If you're an angler, you probably headed this way first—never mind the sand dunes. The Tlell River bridge is just a short walk along the highway north of the campground. There are good access points to the river's lower reaches from Beitush Road, which parallels the east bank. Many people head for the section downstream from the bridge in order to cast first at the fish swimming with the flood tides.

Living on a sand dune is tough! Beach silver-top (*Glehnia littoralis*) has developed numerous specializations to adapt to extreme desiccation, salt spray and soft sand. The plant has deep roots, a water-storing taproot and extraordinarily thick and leathery leaves.

The main species of interest here is coho salmon, which run from the first week of September to mid-October. Timing is dependent on fall rains; the fish mass offshore until river levels are high enough for successful spawning. They peak midway between these times, with fish ranging from 5 to 9 kilograms. Green krocodile lures are a favourite.

The Tlell River is also known for steelhead, although this run isn't as good as it used to be. These seagoing trout grow to 4.6 kilograms and enter the river from early February through April. Fishing is good on both the upper and lower sections.

If you miss these runs, take heart. The Tlell also offers good cutthroat trout fishing in the spring and early summer. These fish go to sea and are caught on their return. Dolly Varden weighing up to 2 kilograms can also be caught in midsummer. Be certain to check the tidal and non-tidal fishing regulations, as they change from year to year. Fishing licences are not available from park staff, but a nearby lodge and the gas station in Port Clements sell licences and tackle.

Continue your walk along the east bank past the trees at the end of Beitush Road. Notice how the river heads north, paralleling the beach. The north-flowing ocean currents that created Rose Spit have also formed a small spit here.

On the open dunes you can view the remains of two teepee-like structures. These are Haida fishing stations that were apparently still active

GETTING THERE

Tlell is an unincorporated hamlet scattered around the southern edge of Naikoon Park. Here the Yellowhead Highway crosses the Tlell River via a wooden bridge. Tlell is 42 km north of the Skidegate Landing ferry dock and 21 km south of Port Clements. The park headquarters and Misty Meadows Campground are about 1 km south of the river. The Tlell area, with the most extensive sand dunes in B.C., is a great place to walk. The river is also known internationally for its salmon fishing. There are two walks that explore these attractions as well as a nearby forest trail. Carry this guide along to identify features en route.

in 1884 when Captain Newton Chittenden explored this area. The wreck of the *Pesuta* is visible in the distance (see "East Beach"). If you return to the campground via the beach, allow three hours for the round trip.

TLELL ANVIL TRAIL

If you have had enough of beach, surf and sand, then the prospect of a pleasant forest walk awaits you a few kilometres south of the Misty Meadows campground.

The Anvil Trail loops through a typical island forest. You'll walk beneath towering spruce, hemlock and cedar. Trees such as these are among the most massive living things on earth. By contrast, delicate single white blossoms poke shyly out from just above the forest floor. In spring, fairy slipper orchids add splashes of soft mauve to the green of prolific mosses and ferns. While walking near the river, you may see salmon spawning in late summer or early September. Allow two hours to fully enjoy the cool air, solitude and soft sounds.

A squall off the mouth of the Tlell River.

10

NORTH MORESBY ISLAND

GRAY BAY

Alders and hemlock overhang the bumpy, one-lane Spur 20, which you drive along after turning off Copper Bay Road. A small bridge crossing Gray Bay Creek marks your entry to Gray Bay and a BC Forest recreation site. Twenty-four campsites have been cleared along the road paralleling the beach. All the sites have tables and nearby pit toilets. Site #1 has three shelters, while site #9 has a shelter designed for larger groups. Within a few paces of each site lies one of the best beaches on the islands. Soft grey sand arcs around a gentle bay reminiscent of a tropical paradise. Low tide exposes sand flats stretching well out from shore. Throw off your shoes and titillate your toes in the bubbling surf.

When you're ready to explore beyond the beach, there are three hiking options nearby. The shortest trail begins about 100 metres back

When visiting Gray Bay, take time to walk the beaches and soak in the solitude. Most campsites are well spaced and all have access to the beach.

GRAY BAY TO CUMSHEWA HEAD

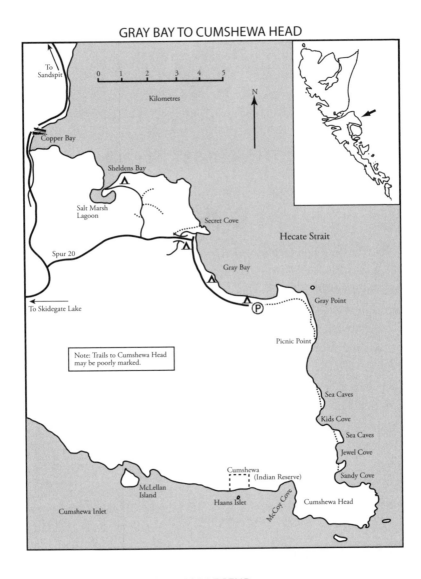

To Sandspit

0 1 2 3 4 5

Kilometres

N

Copper Bay

Sheldens Bay

Salt Marsh
Lagoon

Secret Cove

Hecate Strait

Spur 20

Gray Bay

To Skidegate Lake

Gray Point

Picnic Point

Note: Trails to Cumshewa Head
may be poorly marked.

Sea Caves

Kids Cove

Sea Caves

Jewel Cove

Cumshewa
(Indian Reserve)

Sandy Cove

McLellan
Island

Haans Islet

McCoy Cove

Cumshewa Head

Cumshewa Inlet

MAP LEGEND

✳	Community	⚊	Viewing tower	⛪	Watchmen site	– – –	Park boundary
☆	Site of interest	⚊	Warden station	⚓	Anchorage	⋯⋯	Trail
Ⓟ	Parking	⚘	Picnic sites	⛴	Boat ramp	– – – –	Indian reserve
🏠	Homestead	☗	Park hiking shelter	▲	Hill/mountain	⋯⋯⋯	Ecological reserve
◪	Divesite	⚊	Camping	⚘	Bog	⋯⋯⋯	Ferry crossing
Λ	Sand dunes	⛲	Fresh water from a pipe			– – – – –	Gravel road

from Gray Bay Creek. A 15-minute walk on a sandy path through the trees ends at Secret Cove. In this quiet spot, cast your worries out with the receding tide. Let your eyes wander the expanse of Hecate Strait and allow the music of songbirds to soothe muscle and mind.

You'll need more time to walk or cycle the road that runs along Gray Bay. The road south ends abruptly at a small turnaround where a footbridge allows easy crossing of a salmon-bearing creek. A trail continues on the other side and soon ends at the foundations of an old LORAN (LOng RAnge Navigation) station. Global Positioning System (GPS), a navigational method using satellites, has made such land-based structures obsolete.

Trails lead from there to Gray Point and south to Cumshewa Head. The trip to Cumshewa Head and back involves at least a full day's hike.

GETTING THERE

The 4-km crescent beach at Gray Bay is located south of Sandspit on the northeast side of Moresby Island. From Sandspit, it takes about an hour to get there via Copper Bay Road. This partially paved road heads south, passing the airport and numerous shacks at Copper Bay. After 19 km, turn left off Copper Bay Road onto Spur 20, which leads east for an additional 7 km to Gray Bay.

A much longer alternative route from Alliford Bay also leads to Gray Bay, but you have to travel entirely on private gravel roads that are open to the public. Logging trucks travel from various locations along these roads at unscheduled intervals. During working hours on weekdays, visitors should stop at the Teal-Jones Group office in Sandspit for information on current logging activity (see the Transportation and Travel section of "Planning Your Trip" for contacts). Watch for signs on the logging roads and follow their directions.

Note: The campsite at Gray Bay lacks clear drinking water. The Sandspit Inn allows tourists to fill portable water containers from an outside tap.

Flooding sea cave on the coastal hike between Gray Point and Cumshewa Head. This rugged 10-kilometre walk is recommended only for fit scramblers.

For the first portion, a minimal trail parallels the beach. Families with small children might find this to be a long walk. Beyond that point, the trail deteriorates into a flagged route along beaches, deer trails and awkward rocky scrambles.

Keen hikers may wish to tackle this trail during the long days of summer—this latitude enjoys 17 hours of light at the solstice. A round trip to the Head takes 12 to 14 hours. Plan to leave Gray Point just after a high tide to avoid being caught by water. Sea caves, rocky outcrops and tidepools are the main attractions. Also watch for seals and river otters in the surf. Take a marine chart and topographic map to track your progress, as well as plenty of snacks and drinking water. This is one of the few hikes mentioned in this book where hiking boots have a definite advantage over gumboots.

If Cumshewa Head is beyond your ability, try hiking, cycling or driving to Sheldens Bay. From the bridge at Gray Bay Creek, travel back toward Sandspit 3.4 kilometres. A spur to the right leads to Sheldens Bay, 7.6 kilometres farther on. Ambitious mountain bikers may wish to cycle this bumpy, hilly, gravel road.

About midway along, the road climbs a small hill overlooking a lake and most of Hecate Strait. The road then descends to a picnic area with tables, four campsites and pit toilets. There is room for parking, but people with motorhomes or trailers are advised to leave them at Gray Bay. An additional road leads from the picnic area to Dogfish Bay. This road is best walked or cycled. Allow about 30 minutes walking one way.

Several homesteaders lived in the Sheldens Bay area in the early 1900s. Now it is a haven for deer and migrating waterfowl. Look for dabbling ducks, shorebirds and great blue herons. You may be lucky and spot trumpeter swans or sandhill cranes.

Gray Bay is typical of the Charlottes: many of the islands' best qualities are found here. Sandy beaches are sheltered by rough volcanic headlands. Scattered beneath giant spruce and hemlock, the rustic campsites ensure privacy, yet link to nearby roads and trails. Relaxing, walking, wave watching or birding will easily fill your time for several days. You'll find Gray Bay to be a pleasant introduction to the Charlottes.

LOUISE ISLAND CIRCUMNAVIGATION

Louise Island is the third-largest island in the Charlottes. If your time is limited, the circuit around it will provide a taste of the wild archipelago farther south. Louise Island has ancient archaeology, recent relics and natural history, and gives you the opportunity to see the Moresby region from its maritime aspect. We have divided the trip into two sections: Cumshewa Inlet and K̲'uuna llnagaay (Skedans) through to Louise Narrows.

For anyone wanting to spend several days fishing and camping in the inlet, a BC Forest recreation site in the trees at Moresby Camp provides rudimentary facilities. A similar campsite with 11 spaces and a picnic shelter has been built at nearby Mosquito Lake.

Waterways around Louise Island are generally protected, but some open directly onto Hecate Strait. Small boats and kayaks do venture out that far, though they need to beware of the wind and waves. The exposed waters can be rough. On one occasion we waited five hours for a northeaster to calm down enough to allow us around Skedans Point.

SANDSPIT TO LOUISE ISLAND

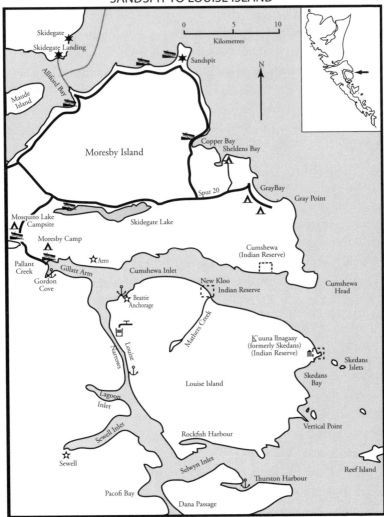

Skidegate
Skidegate Landing
Alliford Bay
Maude Island
Sandspit

0   5   10
Kilometres

N

Moresby Island

Copper Bay
Sheldens Bay

Spur 20
GrayBay
Gray Point

Mosquito Lake
Campsite
Moresby Camp
Skidegate Lake

Cumshewa
(Indian Reserve)

Pallant
Creek
Gordon
Cove
Gillatt Arm
Aero
Cumshewa Inlet

New Kloo
Indian Reserve

Cumshewa
Head

Beattie
Anchorage

Mathers Creek

K'uuna llnagaay
(formerly Skedans)
(Indian Reserve)

Skedans
Islets

Louise

Narrows

Louise Island

Skedans
Bay

Lagoon
Inlet

Sewell Inlet

Rockfish Harbour

Vertical Point

Reef Island

Sewell

Selwyn Inlet

Thurston Harbour

Pacofi Bay

Dana Passage

MAP LEGEND

✹ Community	🗼 Viewing tower	🏛 Watchmen site	– – – Park boundary
☆ Site of interest	⚒ Warden station	⚓ Anchorage	········· Trail
Ⓟ Parking	⚘ Picnic sites	⛴ Boat ramp	– – – – Indian reserve
🏠 Homestead	⬛ Park hiking shelter	▲ Hill/mountain	·······- Ecological reserve
◩ Divesite	⚤ Camping	🌾 Bog	·········· Ferry crossing
ᴧᴧ Sand dunes	Fresh water from a pipe		– – – – Gravel road

Our inflatable made the trip successfully, but as we rounded the point we couldn't help but notice a double kayak drawn up on a boulder-strewn beach with everything laid out to dry.

Craft heading south from Moresby Camp can fill up with fresh water in Carmichael Passage, just north of Louise Narrows. A sign indicates the plastic water pipe on a log float.

CUMSHEWA INLET

Cumshewa Inlet, a deep channel with Moresby Camp at its head, is the launching point for boaters heading to the southern islands and passages. From here, Cumshewa Inlet can be explored by motor boat in one day. There is a small dock and a gravel boat ramp. A 4 x 4 is recommended—more than one visitor whose vehicle didn't measure up has become stuck on the beach.

GETTING THERE

Louise Island and Cumshewa Inlet, located in the North Moresby region, are accessible by boat, helicopter and floatplane. Trailered boats are best launched at the gravel ramp at Moresby Camp. This is a former logging encampment on Gillatt Arm of Cumshewa Inlet. It can be reached by gravel roads leading from the ferry dock at Alliford Bay on Skidegate Inlet, or from Sandspit. The route is marked, but may have active logging. Check at the Teal-Jones Group office in Sandspit or call before driving (see the Transportation and Travel section in "Planning Your Trip" for contacts). Shuttle service for kayakers without a vehicle is available in Sandspit, but people with plenty of time and energy have paddled into this area right from the ferry dock at Skidegate Landing.

Note: Orientation and registration are required for independent travellers to K̲'uuna llnagaay (Skedans) (see the Orientation and Reservations section in "Planning Your Trip").

There is still active logging on the south shore of the inlet, and some visitors find the resulting clear-cuts a detracting eyesore. It's hard to argue with that sentiment, but those of us who use paper and live in wood-frame houses may want to weigh our opinions carefully. Moresby Island residents are understandably touchy about criticism of their livelihood. Logging has gone on here for decades, and most cut areas are regenerating nicely. We've walked in forests that at first looked virgin, only to be surprised later by stumps. Nature knows its business!

During the Second World War, as many as 10 logging camps existed on this inlet. Crews bundled logs into heavy rafts, known as Davis rafts, that were towed south to mainland mills at a speed of two or three knots. There was enough wood in some rafts to cut more than 2 million board feet of lumber. (A board foot is a plank one inch thick by one foot square.) Such huge rafts were expensive to move, but saved the high log losses associated with unbundled booms. Today's self-loading, self-dumping, self-propelled log barges are some of the more interesting vessels plying these inlets.

The biggest logging operation in this area was Aero, named for the airplane (Sitka) spruce. Aero had the only logging railroad on the Charlottes, and track ran from the ocean over the hill to Skidegate Lake. Steep hills required the use of geared-drive locomotives that sounded

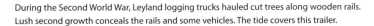

During the Second World War, Leyland logging trucks hauled cut trees along wooden rails. Lush second growth conceals the rails and some vehicles. The tide covers this trailer.

like they were going 90, but actually crawled up the steep grades with massive loads—sometimes only one log to a car. In the bush at Aero lie the remains of several such flatcars and a locomotive. The old roadbeds have grown up with emerald grass to form cultivated paths through tunnels of second-growth alders. Spikes of flowered foxglove and lupine are healing the embankments, but the feeling here is peculiar. Today it's hard to imagine the steaming shriek of the locos and the roar of the two-man chainsaws that were used here in 1945.

Invisible from the water is a monstrous fuel storage tank that rises to the height of the forest canopy. Finding it standing within this forest is like discovering a piece of civilization out of context, reminiscent of the technological monolith built in the Amazon jungle by the eccentric inventor in Paul Theroux's book *The Mosquito Coast*. Aero is one of the more interesting abandoned European sites to explore in the Charlottes because its ruins are widely distributed, not extensively overgrown and easily accessible.

A very different kind of logging activity can be found at Mathers Creek, farther east and across the inlet from Aero. This site is also known as Church Creek, after the place of worship that once stood here. This watershed was also first logged during the war years, but hauling here was done on ingenious log roads. Trucks with hard rubber tires ran on flattened log "rails." A number of these vehicles remain in the second growth a few minutes' walk west of the creek. The lack of light, and the dense tree trunks, make them a challenge to photograph. Old machinery also lies within the tidal zone, so boaters should use extreme caution when approaching the beach.

Mathers Creek was the location of the former village of New Kloo (also spelled Clew). This short-lived Native settlement was built in 1887 in contemporary style. People came here from T'aanuu llnagaay (formerly Tanu) after that village deteriorated due to contact with a European culture counter to its own. Reverend Thomas Crosby helped build the new town, including a plant for extracting oil from dogfish livers. The oil was sold for lubricating machinery and burning in lamps.

Despite the brave effort, New Kloo was abandoned in 1897 in favour of Skidegate. The concentration of community facilities at the

Several books have been written about abandoned Haida villages. They are useful in the field to identify totems and understand this complex society. Similar books have been written for children.

latter location made it sensible for scattered villages to amalgamate. The experience humiliated the survivors of T'aanuu llnagaay. Only 20 years earlier their original village held 547 people, one of the largest populations in this archipelago. Their headstones along Mathers Creek bear many familiar surnames—Clew, Ninstence and Skdance. Over the years, some of these graves have been robbed, a most despicable act.

Moving down the inlet toward Hecate Strait, don't be surprised to encounter porpoises. Of the two species common in the Charlottes, harbor porpoises are most likely to be seen within such fjords. They are shy and will not tolerate pursuit. Be on the lookout for their grey backs and triangular dorsal fins disappearing into the distance. Occasionally porpoises are caught in gillnets, especially when commercial boats are going after the enhanced stocks of salmon that return to spawn in Pallant and Mathers creeks.

Cumshewa Inlet and Gillatt Arm are popular for sport fishing, too, as anglers try for coho salmon between mid-August and September. Several ships have anchored here to serve as floating lodges for well-heeled clients. They troll herring, a very effective bait, but the locals like green buzz bombs and pink hoochies. Try your luck. Good fishing is almost assured in these waters because the salmon are concentrated as they pass up the narrow inlet.

The steep sides and plunging depths of this marine valley are characteristic of routes once gouged by glaciers. All along British Columbia's coast there are fjords like this, which were enlarged during the last Ice Age. B.C. geologist A. Sutherland Brown has found evidence to suggest that this area was covered by 1,000 metres of ice. This frozen flow originated in the mountains to the west and ground slowly toward Hecate Strait. Imagine it as Nature's earth mover, scraping soil from the hills and pushing a ridge of rubble before it. When the ice melted, it left a mound across the mouth of this inlet. Marine charts label this Fairburn Shoals, and it marks the terminus of the former ice front.

Upright timbers at the former village of Cumshewa. These cedar posts likely flanked a central totem at the gable end of a house.

Fairburn Shoals is covered by a huge bed of bull kelp, which can be a significant barrier to navigation, especially at low tide. When the tide is high, you might find a narrow passage along the shoreline. This route saved our skins one day when a heavy swell, topped by whitecaps, made the inlet dangerous. Sneaking our inflatable into the lee of the kelp, we found calmer water.

Near here is the village from which the inlet draws its name. Very little remains at Cumshewa. However, it still has a pleasant, serene atmosphere. Several totems and some leaning house planks have been all but overtaken by the trees. At low tide you can walk out to Haans Islet, a former burial site in front of the village.

Photo courtesy of Royal British Columbia Museum

Those born at K̲'uuna left or died long ago. Their remarkable poles gradually leaned and fell. Of these two poles, only the left—an eagle mortuary—remains upright.

K̲'uuna llnagaay (Skedans), on Louise Island, is probably the most famous abandoned village on the Charlottes. In 1878 the Canadian geologist George Dawson photographed 56 totems standing here before a row of 27 houses. A more recent book, *Those Born at Koona*, by John and Carolyn Smyly, describes these totems in detail and is a useful on-site guide.

Sadly, most of the totems here have succumbed to rot and gravity. We've noted the inevitable deterioration, even over the past few years, in those still standing. How inspiring it would have been to have visited here with painter Emily Carr in 1912, before the superior totems rotted or were collected by museums.

Today, one remarkable specimen is nearly indistinguishable from a rotting log. Beside a path at the western edge of the village sits the carved figure of a wolf. It crouches horizontally, a memorial to a deceased authority. A large tree now grows from its back, and moss obscures the figure's minor defining lines. When you suddenly recognize its form, the feeling of surprise is akin to being startled by a live beast in the grass. More than a century has passed since this carving was released from its bondage in a cedar log. Now it is returning to the earth that claimed its carver and his village. This wolf's supernatural ability to snap our vision is not unlike the Haida belief in transformations. It demonstrates the power in Native art and is indicative of Haida kinship with nature.

Landing at K̲'uuna llnagaay is best accomplished from the south side. A sandy, sheltered beach and small float offer easy landing for small craft. Skedans Bay, located to the southwest of Skedans Point, offers temporary anchorage for larger craft. A small creek and visible waterfall enter this bay.

K'UUNA LLNAGAAY THROUGH TO LOUISE NARROWS

From the village of <u>K</u>'uuna llnagaay a collection of smaller islands, including Reef and Skedans, can be seen. The far side of these islands is frequented by northern sea lions. As many as a hundred of these animals can be seen here, although their numbers have declined—despite being protected since 1970 under the federal Fisheries Act. Haida were known to kill these marine behemoths. The figures of sea lions appeared on totems that once stood in the village of <u>K</u>'uuna llnagaay.

Head south for Limestone Islands and Vertical Point. The Haida once had a small village at Vertical Point, but no evidence of it remains today. In wet weather, paddlers will be pleased to come upon a tiny cabin here. It was the studio of a New York artist in summers past. Vertical draws its name from the upturned limestone beds at the point.

You can pass a quiet evening in Rockfish Harbour on the southwest corner of Louise Island. It didn't live up to the angling expectations awakened by its name, but the bay does offer fair-weather anchorage and fresh water for campers. From Rockfish Harbour, you may wish to explore three sites adjacent to Louise Island—Pacofi Bay, Sewell Inlet and Lagoon Inlet. Like us, you may find these two industrial settlements and the tidal rapids almost as interesting as old Haida villages.

Pacofi is an acronym for the Pacific Coast Fisheries plant that began operation in 1910 in the bay of the same name. Many rusty remnants are still visible. Over the years a packing plant, a saltery, an oil and fertilizer reduction plant and a plant for making potash from kelp operated here periodically. BC Packers demolished most of the buildings in 1949, but machinery still remains in the woods and on the beach. Use caution when landing because submerged concrete blocks and metal are scattered along the shoreline.

Like the Native villages, this place, too, is fast disappearing beneath the encroaching rainforest. In the next millennium, archaeologists may be unearthing places such as Pacofi to reveal clues as to why White, Asian and Native men worked in the same building, but resided in separate quarters.

In nearby Sewell Inlet, Western Forest Products Ltd. once ran a small company town. Visiting this town was like taking a walk back

Rusting boilers in Pacofi Bay are breaking down rapidly in the saltchuck. Few of the many packing operations attempted here over a 40-year period were financially successful. Most fish plants are now located in larger mainland cities.

in time. In its heyday, 52 families lived here. They made good use of a driving range, tennis courts, bowling alley, post office and pub—the Full Boar Inn. Today only four families live here; workers now fly in for short stays. The hustle and bustle of this lively coastal community is long gone. The sound of a generator provides the only clue that a few people still work here. Eventually, all of the remaining buildings will be moved or demolished.

The demise of such towns is perhaps inevitable as cutblocks for logging are withdrawn or reduced. Some blame forest companies for overcutting, but residents point directly to the formation of the national park reserve for their lost livelihood. Soon after the park boundaries were announced, one very frustrated longtime resident declared: "I wouldn't want to be an environmentalist in there [the pub] on Friday night. That's what you'd call livin' dangerously."

If the suggestion of bottled fluid and suds is appealing, you may want to make Lagoon Inlet one of your last stops. Here, a bedrock bottleneck squeezes the foaming tide in and out of a shallow basin. Levels between the inlet and lagoon may vary by a metre, creating lots of froth as the water races to catch up. River otters often play in the reversing rapids, and deer and bear graze along the estuary. Camping is good inside the "bottle," but plan your departure so you're not left high and dry when its contents drain.

Return to Moresby Camp via Louise Narrows, a dredged channel. It provides easy passage on a rising tide between Louise and Moresby Islands. Moving through during tidal changes is similar to running a river. Paddlers will be challenged to make progress "upstream." Prior to their excavation in 1967, these narrows resembled the more southerly Burnaby Narrows, where the flushing action draws an abundant supply of nutrients for marine organisms.

GWAII HAANAS NATIONAL PARK RESERVE
AND HAIDA HERITAGE SITE

Many thousands of years ago, a small but determined group of travellers somehow crossed what is now Hecate Strait and made their way through a tangle of densely forested islands, past shimmering mountains and cascading streams. They may have been following a run of fish, tracking a wounded whale or searching for fresh crabapples or berries; or they may have been looking for a home. Whether by chance or by purpose, they reached what is arguably one of the continent's great places of natural beauty. Gwaii Haanas—"a place of beauty"—is a world like no other.

The Haida have always recognized the beauty and rich nature of these islands. So, too, have the timber companies. For over 50 years, they logged magnificent stands of spruce, red cedar and hemlock for the sole purpose of feeding a hungry lumber market. As more trees fell and clear-cuts increased, many people both on and off the islands began to oppose this seemingly uncontrolled resource extraction. Regrettably, however, it took some time for our governments to realize that a problem of seismic proportions was about to erupt. As a result, ever-increasing tensions between the Haida and the logging companies culminated in a dramatic standoff on Lyell Island. This drew international attention that forced government, along with the logging companies, to begin serious discussions with the Haida in an effort to find solutions.

As a result, a unique partnership evolved. Representatives of the Council of the Haida Nation and the government of Canada cooperatively manage Gwaii Haanas. Administering a park with so many interests at stake has been challenging, but has yielded excellent results.

GWAII HAANAS NATIONAL PARK RESERVE AND HAIDA HERITAGE SITE

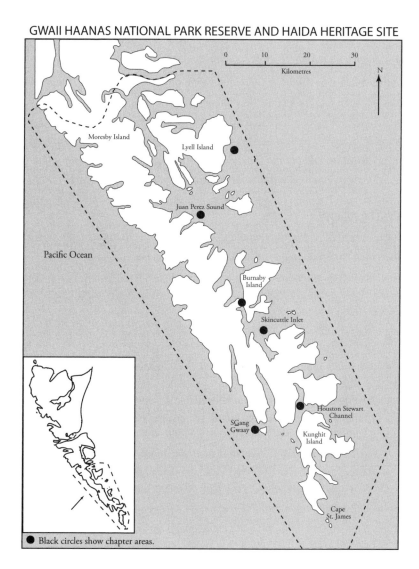

● Black circles show chapter areas.

MAP LEGEND

✳ Community	Ï Viewing tower	🏛 Watchmen site	- - - Park boundary
☆ Site of interest	∮ Warden station	⚓ Anchorage	·········· Trail
℗ Parking	⋔ Picnic sites	⛴ Boat ramp	- - - - Indian reserve
🏠 Homestead	⬟ Park hiking shelter	▲ Hill/mountain	·-·-·- Ecological reserve
◪ Divesite	△ Camping	🌿 Bog	Ferry crossing
Λ Sand dunes	⛲ Fresh water from a pipe		- - - - Gravel road

In its July/August 2005 issue, *National Geographic Traveler* magazine awarded Gwaii Haanas the highest overall rating of any park in North America, with the panellists specifically pinpointing the area's "high cultural integrity." Authenticity was also highlighted: "Archaeological and historic artifacts are left to their natural processes as per Haida tradition, which surprises visitors who expect 'preservation.'" Needless to say, the natural beauty, serenity and abundant wildlife also made a resounding impression on the panel.

We are certain the 3,000 or so annual visitors would agree.

VISITING GWAII HAANAS

Gwaii Haanas' northern boundary crosses Tasu Sound on Moresby Island, the ridge of the Tangil Peninsula, and extends out to sea far enough so that all outer islands south to Cape St. James are included. The park encompasses about 15 percent of the land in the island archipelago.

NAME CHANGES

Agreeing on names for Haida heritage villages was one of many challenges facing the joint management of Gwaii Haanas. Since it will likely take years for maps to reflect these name changes, here is a quick guide to the most frequently visited sites. The unique appearance of these Haida names are the result of an oral language being written using the Roman alphabet. There may be more name changes in the future.

Former Name	Haida Name
Skedans	K̲'uuna Llnagaay
Tanu	T'aanuu Llnagaay
Windy Bay area	Hlk'yah G̲aawG̲a
Village at Windy Bay	Hlk'yah llnagaay
Hotspring Island	G̲andll K'in Gwaayaay
Anthony Island	SG̲ang Gwaay
Ninstints	SG̲ang Gwaay llnagaay

There are no maintained roads, trails or public developments in Gwaii Haanas: access is by air or from the water. When planning your trip, keep in mind that there are no public services south of Sandspit. A few people, however, do live legally within the park boundaries. Families at Rose Harbour operate bed-and-breakfast facilities, and seasonal watchmen live at K̲'uuna llnagaay (Skedans), T'aanuu llnagaay (Tanu), Hlk'yah G̲aawG̲a (Windy Bay), G̲andll K'in Gwaayaay (Hotspring Island) and SG̲ang Gwaay llnagaay (Ninstints). Parks Canada operates two warden stations: one is located at the south end of Huxley Island in Juan Perez Sound, the other is on Ellen Island in Houston Stewart Channel.

Recreationists organizing their own tour must contact the Gwaii Haanas office well in advance of their departure date to book their time. Budget your travel time, as you must attend an orientation session prior to entering the park reserve. Fees also apply to both individuals and tour groups. (See the Orientation and Reservations section in "Planning Your Trip").

If you are kayaking, you should allow two weeks to go from Moresby Camp (see "Louise Island Circumnavigation") to SG̲ang Gwaay. That's a lot of paddling. Since the inlets of northern Moresby Island may have less appeal, we recommend that you charter a plane or boat to take you to the village of T'aanuu, within Juan Perez Sound, or to Rose Harbour (see the Chartering and Tours section in "Planning Your Trip").

Motorized pleasure craft can launch at Moresby Camp and within a day can be as far south as Lyell Island. Weather permitting, inflatable and small hard-hulled boats can go almost anywhere, providing you carry enough gas to make the return trip. Inflatables have several advantages—they are generally more seaworthy, can carry substantial amounts of gear and can still be loaded into aircraft or towed behind yachts. On one of our trips, we chartered a vessel south to Rose Harbour, then returned at a leisurely pace in our own inflatable.

If you are a novice at these types of boating, we recommend signing up with a tour company. Several companies lead trips between May and September. Some of them often feature acclaimed specialists as guides. The Village of Queen Charlotte Visitor Centre, the Gwaii Haanas office, travel agents, outdoor periodicals or even retail stores specializing in outdoor recreation should be able to provide contacts. The Visitor Centre website also lists on-island tour operators.

Most visitors to Gwaii Haanas tend to head for the main attractions—ancient village sites and Hotspring Island. We chose to highlight six areas worthy of exploration that include these, plus numerous lesser-known sites. No doubt you will find additional favourites of your own!

Many people pack along a fishing rod with the idea of supplementing their meals with fresh salmon, cod or other favourite finfish. Be aware that fishing closures for some species are in effect in specific locations. (See the Fishing section in "Planning your Trip" for more information on where you can drop your line.)

One final note. Notwithstanding the beauty and the cultural and natural diversity of Gwaii Haanas, the park reserve is not a pristine wilderness. Several places along the east coast show signs of previous non-Native habitation or of industry that began within the 20th century. We found some of these sites compelling, others much less so. Nevertheless, they are part of Gwaii Haanas' rich historical heritage.

For further information, contact:
The Superintendent,
Gwaii Haanas National Park Reserve and Haida Heritage Site
Box 37, Village of Queen Charlotte, BC V0T 1S0
Phone: 250-559-8818/Fax: 250-559-8366
Email: gwaii.haanas@pc.gc.ca
Website: <www.pc.gc.ca/gwaiihaanas>
or:
Village of Queen Charlotte Visitor Centre
P.O. Box 819, 3220 Wharf St.
Village of Queen Charlotte, BC V0T 1S0
Phone: 250-559-8316
Fax: 250-559-8952
Email: info@qcinfo.ca
Website: <www.qcinfo.ca>

JUAN PEREZ AND DARWIN SOUNDS

Juan Perez Sound is a wide body of water lying east of Moresby Island and south of Lyell Island. This sound and its protected passage, Darwin Sound, are probably the busiest waters in the South Moresby region. From March through September, numerous commercial and recreational boats visit the area. A stop at Gandll K'in Gwaayaay (Hotspring Island) is a must—these natural hot springs are a perfect place to begin or end your visit to this region.

GETTING THERE

This widespread area is accessible to aircraft and boats. Yachters approaching from the north can moor in the small cove on the west side of Hoya Passage, in a tiny cove within the Bischof Islands (fair weather only), on the north side of Murchison Island and on the north side of Ramsey Island. If you are approaching from the south, Section Cove on the northwest corner of Burnaby Island or Skaat Harbour offer good moorage in most weather conditions.

Haida Gwaii watchmen have a house on Gandll K'in Gwaayaay (Hotspring Island), but overnighting here or on nearby House and Little House Island is not permitted. Call ahead on VHF channel 6 before you go to shore on Gandll K'in Gwaayaay.

Parks Canada has a warden field station at the south end of Huxley Island. In an emergency, they can be reached on VHF channel 16, or by satellite phone at 1-877-852-3100.

Potable water from a pipe attached to a substantial float is available in a small cove on Moresby Island opposite Shuttle Island. Water is also available at the warden station on Huxley Island.

Pets are prohibited on Gandll K'in Gwaayaay.

A portion of the northwest shore of Ramsay Island is closed from April 1 through June 30 due to sensitive ancient murrelet nesting colonies.

DARWIN SOUND TO JUAN PEREZ SOUND

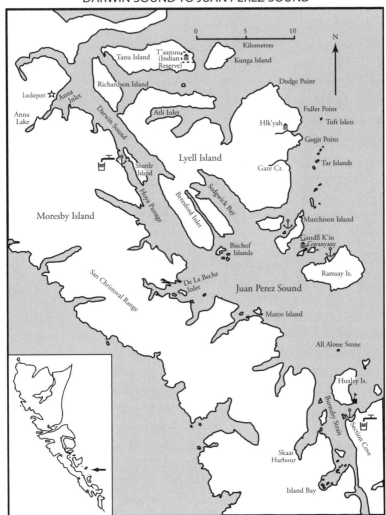

0   5   10
Kilometres

N

Tanu Island
T'aanuu (Indian Reserve)
Kunga Island

Richardson Island
Dodge Point

Lockeport
Anna Inlet
Fuller Point
Tuft Islets

Anna Lake
Atli Inlet
Hlk'yah
Gogit Point

Darwin Sound
Lyell Island
Gate Cr.
Tar Islands

Shuttle Island

Hoya Passage
Beresford Inlet
Sedgwick Bay

Moresby Island
Murchison Island

Gandll K'in Gwaayaay

Bischof Islands
Ramsay Is.

San Christoval Range
De La Beche Inlet
Juan Perez Sound

Marco Island

All Alone Stone

Huxley Is.

Burnaby Strait

Section Cove

Skaat Harbour

Island Bay

MAP LEGEND

✳ Community	🏺 Viewing tower	🏛 Watchmen site	- - - Park boundary
☆ Site of interest	⚲ Warden station	⚓ Anchorage	········· Trail
Ⓟ Parking	⚵ Picnic sites	⛴ Boat ramp	- - - - Indian reserve
🏠 Homestead	🏚 Park hiking shelter	▲ Hill/mountain	-··-··- Ecological reserve
◪ Divesite	▲ Camping	🌱 Bog	··········· Ferry crossing
⋀⋀ Sand dunes	🚰 Fresh water from a pipe		- - - - - Gravel road

The shores of the sounds and their mountain backdrops are very rugged. The infinite combinations of landforms and perspectives create some of the most pleasing scenery in Gwaii Haanas. Even when the view becomes monochromatic on rainy days, it's still striking. With the confusion of colour removed, you can better observe the subtle qualities of line and texture.

One such "Misty Isles" day we drove into Anna Inlet at the north end of Darwin Sound. Clouds all but obscured the 1,020-metre summits around us. One could easily imagine Valkyries living among the shrouded crags above. The peace of the inlet was calming, the surface of the water dimpled only here and there by diving. Ashore, the former mining community of Lockeport lay surrounded by grassy meadows, with a pretty alder forest for a backdrop. Anna Creek tumbled down like wine spilled by the Norse gods; its crisp, cold water tasted divine.

Other than the convenient camping at Lockeport, you'll be hard-pressed to find suitable spots in Darwin Sound. Bedrock lines most of the shore, and the bush has few clearings and plenty of bugs. The cove on Shuttle Island can serve as a camp in a pinch. In the opposite bay on Moresby Island, water gushes from a plastic pipe tied to a substantial float. Yachters should top up their water tanks here, since the only other source of reliable piped water is at Huxley Island warden station, or much further south, in Louscoone Inlet.

George Dawson, an extraordinary Canadian with a formidable reputation in geology, first surveyed this area in 1878. His writings are still standard references for researchers. The names applied to features in this region—Darwin, Lyell, Ramsay, Murchison, Faraday, Sedgwick, Richardson and Bischof—are tributes to geologists or other scientists whom he admired.

The tiny islands named after K.G. Bischof, a German geochemist, are clustered in an open circle at the north end of Juan Perez Sound. Rugged and attractive, they provide temporary shelter for boats waiting to cross the sound. This is a popular spot for camping, but unfortunately it lacks fresh water. If you're just waiting for the winds to subside, pull your kayak out on the 200-metre-long, Y-shaped islet in the southwest corner and enjoy the fine vistas of Juan Perez Sound.

Immediately north of the Bischofs lies Beresford Inlet. This long narrow inlet is the result of a geological fault running along its entire length. Fresh water is available from creeks at its head if you happen to run short while on the Bischofs. Watch out for strong tidal currents and hidden rocks in the inlet.

The name of an English geologist, de la Beche, is commemorated by both an island and a rugged inlet that cuts into the coast of Moresby Island. Behind them the San Christoval Range rises 1,800 metres to face Juan Perez Sound. These mountains are sparsely treed and their summits are close to shore. Consequently, their semi-open rock slopes make for relatively quick ascents. Even though no trails lead to the peaks, this is one of the better places to reach the high country in Gwaii Haanas.

De La Beche Inlet offers pretty boating opportunities but is unsuitable for camping, as there are no beaches. Skittagetan Lagoon has dangerous rocks, so access is limited to paddlers. Even in the very protected harbour of nearby Sac Bay, a 30-metre yacht that Tom was aboard dragged anchor while everyone slept. No one awoke until the hull bumped a rock at the bay's entrance. Strong downdrafts called "williwaws" had shifted the vessel. Fortunately, no damage was done. Faced with such unpredictable winds, yachters should always set two anchors.

For short hikes, boaters frequently go ashore to visit the unnamed lakes above Sac Bay and Haswell Bay. Pull on your gumboots, because there are no defined trails over the boggy ground. Enthusiasts will want to continue up the open rock slopes to the ridge of the San Christovals, where a fantastic view of Juan Perez Sound awaits.

Farther south, hidden behind Marco Island, a beach with a stream provides a good camping spot. If necessary, kayakers and small boaters can wait here for conditions to improve before crossing to Gandll K'in Gwaayaay. As you start out, watch for seals hauled out on rocks at the east end of Marco Island.

Gandll K'in Gwaayaay, an 8-hectare island, is home to a group of hot springs that have, rather fortuitously, come to the surface on land rather than on the seabed. They seep from the bedrock at several locations. Pool temperatures range from 52°C to 76°C and can even vary from day to day within the same pool. Drinking the highly mineralized water

Radio ahead and reserve your time at G̲andll Ḵ'in. This is a busy spot, so you might have difficulty procuring a solitary soak.

apparently yields no health benefits and is not recommended. In times past, however, this may have been different.

While reading *Queen Charlotte Islands: A Narrative of Discovery and Adventure in the North Pacific*, we noted that Francis Poole reported that Haida Chief Klue believed the hot pools were a cure for all diseases. One of Poole's own men returned from "Volcanic Island" (Hotspring Island) having remedied his rheumatic fever. Such claims about the restorative powers of hot springs are consistent with those of health spas the world over.

Most hot-spring devotees simply want a bath. A nearby shower and soap house allows you to have a scrub before entering the pools, and keeps detergents out of the natural springs. Then you need to make a choice! This seaside spa offers three pools of various sizes. The outdoor basins and rock pools look onto the superb Juan Perez vista; changing wave patterns and passing squalls, boats and birds constantly reinvent this scene. A field companion likened it to living within a Toni Onley painting. Luxuriating up to your neck in hot water as the sun slides over the San Christovals has to be the *pièce de résistance* of experiences in southern Gwaii Haanas.

With the increased tourist traffic in this area, the hot springs have understandably become busy spots. However, the Parks Canada policy of allowing only 12 visitors ashore at a time increases your chances of some solitude. Also, the Haida Gwaii watchmen live and work here, and they too require some privacy. If you're lucky you will be alone, but your relaxing moments may be cut short by the arrival of the declining daylight. You should allow enough time to be back at your campsite before dark.

As darkness descends over the steamy pools, another group of visitors—bats—arrives on the scene. Each summer, a colony of Little brown myotis and Keen's long-eared myotis return to this island to share a cave just below the high-tide level. Although Keen's long-eared myotis have been reported from other locations in the province, there are only two known maternity colonies. Hotspring Island is one, the other is at Tahsis on Vancouver Island. Both species of bats rouse at dusk to forage on the abundant moths and other insects attracted to the warm water. Accommodating the bats' feeding habits is another reason the pools remain closed to bathers in the late evening.

The pools of Gandll K'in Gwaayaay are certainly more enjoyable when fewer people are about; boats, aircraft and people coming and going can be distracting. Still, we've always managed to enjoy special moments in spite of these things. Whatever the time of day, we ease ourselves into the crystal clear pools, with the warmth of water and friendship always strong. Our conversations quickly mellow as the heat seeps through our soul. The hot springs may not cure physical ailments, but they surely restore the psyche.

EAST COAST OF LYELL ISLAND— HLK'YAH GAAWGA

Many people consider Lyell Island to be the centrepiece of the Gwaii Haanas region. It was here that the Haida made their stand to protest logging, and it was pictures of Lyell Island clear-cuts that first attracted the attention of most Canadians to the issues involved in the national-park proposal. The national media was present when the Haida were arrested in 1985 for blocking the loggers' access. Although northern and eastern portions of the island were extensively clear-cut before the protests began, the Hlk'yah GaawGa (Windy Bay area) watershed and Dodge Point were eventually saved from the saw. This part of Lyell Island and the much smaller satellite islands to the east are worthy of a day's exploration.

The entrance to this bay is exposed, and we recommend postponing your passage along the outside of Lyell Island if the weather is poor or threatening. Strong tides also run past both Gogit and Fuller points. Check your tide tables and weather channels before heading this way. If you do become stormbound here, there is good camping with fresh water from the creek. Looking Around and Blinking House, located near the campground, is a modified traditional Haida-designed structure with wooden sleeping platforms. It was officially opened in 1987. Hlk'yah llnagaay is also the site of an ancient village, and remnants of former houses can be seen on the opposite shore. Former residents had access to the stands of magnificent trees immediately behind. It was this rainforest that inspired the fight to save Gwaii Haanas: its beauty was recognized long ago. Today, a boardwalk leading to the largest trees winds through this famous forest.

GETTING THERE

Both Hlk'yah GaawGa (Windy Bay area) and Hlk'yah llnagaay (Village at Windy Bay) remained unmarked on topographic maps and marine charts. Located between Gogit Point and Fuller Point, the bay, creek and ancient village are accessible only by boat. In emergencies, you may stay in Looking Around and Blinking House but check with the Haida watchmen first.

Examining an old Haida test hole in a western red cedar (*Thuja plicata*) trunk in Hlk'yah GaawGa watershed. Trees of this size became canoes or house timbers. Evidently this specimen was unsuitable.

In 1900, biologist William Osgood spent five weeks studying the flora and fauna of these islands. In his writings about the rainforest, he said: "The spruces stand in magnificent groves, the grandeur of which is appreciated only when one gets above the tangle of underbrush and obtains an unobstructed view of the tall, straight, reddish barked trunks, column after column extending far back into the forest, until the dim light is finally obscured and individual trees can no longer be distinguished."

It sounds rather like the Parthenon, and Hlk'yah G̲aawG̲a is certainly a temple of nature. There is little undergrowth to obstruct movement, and a deep carpet of moss invites your tread across the forest floor. To step off the trail for a moment alone is humbling, yet inspiring. The trees are so big that one feels insignificant creeping over their spreading roots. The cedars in this valley rise to 70 metres. Nearing 1,000 years old, some are among the most ancient living organisms in this country.

Very little direct sunlight penetrates below the forest canopy, and sounds are muffled. Occasionally the song of some small bird faintly reaches your ear. You might recognize the muffled notes of a Townsend's warbler, a golden-crowned kinglet or a chestnut-backed chickadee. Other bird calls carry surprisingly well. The double bell tone of a common raven resonates through the trunks, "dong-dong." From the sky above, a bald eagle cries its creaky stutter. It's easy to understand why the Haida attributed supernatural qualities to these latter two birds.

The Haida came into these woods to gather plants and to cut western red cedar for medicines, clothes, canoes and building materials. Many of the huge trees show signs of Native use: some have their bark stripped off, others have been "holed" in a test for internal rot. There is no way to pinpoint the location of specific specimens, but a boardwalk trail will guide you through some of the finest examples; you may discover others if you decide to wander off the trail. If you do step away from the trail, be aware that it is very easy to become disoriented in these woods. Stay within sight of your hiking partners.

Where bark has been removed from red cedar, the resulting scar is usually easy to spot. The Haida collected the bark by making horizontal cuts, then pulling out and ripping strips up the trunk. They separated the fibres and wove them into clothing and various coverings. The soft bark was also made into rope, fishnets, baskets and numerous items of a twined or woven nature. This activity did not kill the tree. (The process of collecting bark is still done throughout Haida Gwaii.)

Cedars at Hlk'yah G̲aawG̲a were also used for construction. The men sought large, straight trees for house timbers, canoes and totem poles. Depending on its intended use, a tree would be tested for core rot. Once selected, trees were felled by chipping and/or burning. We discovered one horizontal log that had been partially cut into boards.

There is so much evidence of tree use here that this watershed could be considered a living museum. Cedar was (and still is) a multi-purpose material for the Haida, and was virtually their exclusive choice in wood. It is soft, light, straight-grained, easy to split and holds paint well. It also contains a fragrant natural oil that makes it resistant to decay, even in the sodden Northwest Coast climate.

As surely as cedar is the wood of life for the Haida, salmon is their food of life. Windy Bay Creek has the distinction of being the largest and most productive spawning stream in Gwaii Haanas. When autumn rains raise water levels, chum, pink and coho salmon return to lay eggs in the gravel where they hatched. Pinks are the most abundant: in late September they can number as many as 55,000 fish. Coho complete their life cycle from late October through November.

Five kilometres to the north, Dodge Point was the site of Gwaii Haanas's largest breeding colonies of ancient murrelets. In 1982 this colony was estimated to contain more than 10,000 nests. Today the numbers have been decimated due to rat predation. Because murrelets need the spaced trees and open floors of old-growth forests, they become grounded if obstructed by low-level vegetation. They need lots of open space to manoeuvre around tree trunks. They nest in underground burrows, hidden among the roots of mature spruce and cedar trees. In late March, adults return to the colony and select burrows within sight of the sea. After hatching, young birds leave their burrows at night, following the calls from their parents, who wait for them just offshore. Once on the water, the adults and chicks head out to sea. You may see them near Tuft Islets at the end of May or early in June.

All the islands off the east coast of Lyell are good places to see a variety of marine fauna. The Tar Islands are frequently used by seals for haul-outs. Killer whales know this and often cruise this coast for prey. We once encountered a pod of five orca at Agglomerate Island. While we stood transfixed on a ledge only a few feet above the water, the whales engaged in a seemingly spontaneous display of playful behaviour literally beneath our feet. For a full 30 minutes these magnificent marine mammals interacted with one another and with us. They swam in gentle spirals and rolls around each other, rubbed against kelp stalks and spyhopped (raised their heads straight out of the water) to check our activity on shore, all of this within six metres of where we stood. Finally, after their engaging performance was over, it seemed to be our turn, and the whales lay on the surface of the water to listen while we tried to entertain them with songs. When at last they departed, it seemed only because we had exhausted our meagre repertoire of antics. We were frustrated by our inability to communicate with these intelligent mammals. Yet there was no doubt

A giant among giants. The tall trees at Hlk'yah GaawGa are among the oldest on the islands. Some date back to the first millennium.

in our minds that they had chosen to spend time in our presence. We felt oddly grateful and privileged to witness this rare display.

We hope your time spent on the eastern coast of Lyell Island will rank as one of your best Gwaii Haanas adventures.

BURNABY NARROWS

Burnaby Strait connects the waters of Juan Perez Sound and Skincuttle Inlet. The strait tapers to a section 50 metres wide that charts and maps label Dolomite Narrows. The local name—Burnaby Narrows—is, however, widely accepted. This is a premier location for viewing intertidal life. There are also points of interest north and south of the narrows.

Burnaby Strait is widest at its northern end. On the northwest corner of Burnaby Island, Section Cove has campsites, fresh water, a sandy beach and a mooring buoy for larger craft. There may also be chained logs anchored near the shore. They are chained together to make floating pens for the Haida fishery for Pacific herring spawn. In spring, large blades of the kelp called *Macrocystis* hang from the logs. As the herring gather in huge schools, they are netted and put in these pens until they spawn on the kelp. The herring lay small white eggs directly on the kelp,

GETTING THERE

Burnaby Narrows (also called Dolomite Narrows) is accessible only to boats. At most low tides, the narrows dry and passage through them is impossible. Marine markers aid navigation at high tide, but motorized boats should proceed with caution. Large craft can find good anchorage at Section Cove (at the northwest end of Burnaby Island) or at Bag Harbour (southwest of the narrows).

Camping is no longer permitted here, although you can picnic on the grassy east side. You will find suitable campsites, some with small streams, at the entrance to Island Bay (north of the narrows) or in Bag Harbour and Tangle Cove (south of the narrows).

sometimes several layers deep. The resulting algal caviar, known as K'aaw, is a delicacy for Native people and the Japanese. K'aaw may be eaten raw, quick-fried, dipped in hot water, frozen or dried. In past years, this industry has generated more than $10 million in overseas sales.

Heading south toward the narrows you'll pass the entrance to Island Bay. Motor or paddle very slowly and keep your chart in hand, for the bay is guarded by 17 islands and at least as many rocks. All of these provide a picturesque foreground to Yatza Mountain, part of the San Christoval Range. On clear days its summit provides fine views, though no defined trails lead to the top. A cascade at the far end of Island Bay offers a refreshing drink and a place to fill water containers. In 1961 the carcass of a great white shark discovered here was the first ever recorded in the province. At least a dozen more great whites have washed ashore throughout Haida Gwaii since then.

Your trip to Burnaby Narrows needs to be carefully timed. If you plan on heading right through, do so on high slack tides. If you want to spend an hour or two viewing the profuse intertidal life, it's best to arrive just before or after low tide. You'll find it almost impossible to walk here without stepping on something alive. For this reason, Parks Canada requests visitors to drift through the area. As you float over the shallows, the crystal clear water affords excellent views of a marine ecosystem in action.

The abundance of marine life is due to the strong tidal action through the narrows, which brings a constant supply of nutrients to these creatures. Most are filter-feeders, including clams, barnacles and mussels. They strain the water they take in through special brushes called cirri, which trap minute, free-floating organisms. Equally conspicuous, sea stars blanket the bottom like a tapestry of the heavens. Each has a different colour, and when surrounded by textured algae they make terrific photographic compositions.

You may also notice curious mounds in the mud, or sandy-coloured rings resembling rubber toilet plungers. The large, spherical moon snail creates both. This carnivorous shellfish plows beneath the surface in search of clams, which it envelops with its fleshy foot. Once a clam is trapped, the snail rasps a small hole through the clamshell, allowing access to its innards. The purpose of the rubbery rings puzzles many people: in fact,

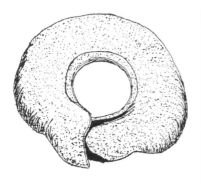

The egg case of the moon snail is a layer of eggs sandwiched between two layers of sand. Hundreds may appear in tidal areas.

they are used for reproduction. As the snails extrude their eggs in a gelatinous sheet, sand binds to the sticky mass, forming a thin collar that hardens, then splits. The grey ring of sand and eggs remains on top of the muddy ocean floor. About midsummer, this egg case breaks down, releasing thousands of free-swimming moon snail larvae.

Red rock crabs also live hereabouts. These crustaceans are smaller and have less meat than the commercially favoured Dungeness crab. Their black-tipped pincers possess considerable strength, adding new meaning to the term "armed and dangerous." Tom discovered this the hard way when demonstrating the method of capturing crabs by hand. Using an approved technique, he grasped the shell from the rear, only to find that his specimen was unusually agile, deftly pinching his index

Bat stars abound in the sheltered waters of Burnaby Narrows. They feed on seaweed, dead animals and sea urchins. Their range of colours includes red, yellow, brown, green and blue.

finger with the strength of a vice. Blood, pincer and crab flew in different directions as he recoiled in pain. Clenched teeth later gave way to a smug smile, however, as he cracked open the dismembered limbs and savoured the tasty meat of the culprit.

Be prepared to share this environment with some other wildlife. During our early-morning explorations we encountered raccoons, eagles and ravens foraging for breakfast. Black bears are also regular visitors and are one of the reasons camping is not allowed here.

Only the fast-rising tide will limit your time in this exciting area. When the water becomes too deep for viewing, set out to explore nearby bays and coves. To the immediate south, Bag Harbour is the site of a former seasonal Haida village. The remnants of several salmon weirs can be seen in the bed of the stream that enters here, and a rusted boiler and a heap of shells on the shore are vestiges of a clam cannery that operated here between 1908 and 1910.

Although this is one of the richest shellfish beds on our Pacific coast, these clams should not be eaten. Burnaby Narrows and other places around Gwaii Haanas have frequent algae blooms known as red tide, caused by tiny micro-organisms in the water. These organisms contain a toxin that is harmless to clams but potentially deadly for humans. Since regular testing for this poison does not occur, harvesting of clams (except razor clams) is permanently prohibited here and throughout the islands.

Bag Harbour is an excellent small-boat refuge. You can safely wait here for Burnaby Narrows to flood if you're travelling north. You can also anchor while you explore the surrounding forests, beaches and salmon stream.

Every visitor to this part of Gwaii Haanas should try to include at least one full day in the Burnaby Narrows area. Although intertidal life flourishes throughout the islands, the Narrows are unique. Floating over one of the richest areas of intertidal life has been a highlight of their visit for many travellers to Haida Gwaii.

SKINCUTTLE INLET

Skincuttle Inlet is a six-kilometre-wide opening that enters Hecate Strait between Burnaby and Moresby islands. Within the inlet are five scattered groups of smaller islands. Many inlets, bays and a strait divide the shoreline into attractive anchorages. Surrounding hills rise to 350 metres and form a solid wooded aspect. Low tides expose the sculpted rocks along the shoreline, on the smallest islands and above Harriet Harbour.

Anyone interested in minerals or geology will enjoy several days of exploration in Skincuttle Inlet. Mining here dates back to 1862. You'll find huge open pits, several underground tunnels, and the remains of three mining communities, a former cannery and a nearby commune.

Jedway was first established in the early 1900s, when its copper deposits attracted prospectors. Although the miners searched throughout the inlet, their home base was along the west side of Harriet Harbour. The townsite included two wharfs, a sawmill and numerous cabins. Today, the site is completely overgrown. Before this became a park reserve, diggers hunting for antique bottles scavenged the dump. Removing any items now, however, contravenes park reserve policy.

Above Harriet Harbour, waste rock forms a loose slope below an open pit. Pieces of heavy magnetite, a rich ore of iron, still litter the ground. Jedway was one of two iron-ore mines in Gwaii Haanas that shipped concentrate to Japanese steel mills (the other was at Tasu on the west coast of Moresby Island). The mine operated between 1961 and 1968, employing 130 full-time staff.

GETTING THERE

This large inlet is accessible to all aircraft and boats. Yachters will find fair weather anchorage in Harriet Harbour or a more protected mooring in Jedway Bay. Campsites abound in this area, but a few places are permanently closed. These include the isthmus between the two eastern Swan Islets, Bolkus Island, Slug Islet and East Copper Island across the middle of Skincuttle Inlet. Rankine Islands, southeast of Skincuttle Inlet, are also closed. All of these locations have sensitive seabird nesting sites.

SKINCUTTLE INLET TO HOUSTON STEWART CHANNEL

N

Burnaby Island

Island Bay

Poole Pt.

East Copper Island

George Is.

Bag Harbour

Swan Bay

Pelican Cove

Copper Islands

Bolkus Island

Skincuttle Inlet

0   5
Kilometres

Ikeda Point

Jedway Bay

Jedway

Slim Inlet

Harriet Harbour

Collinson Bay

Houston Inlet

Rankine Islands

Flamingo Inlet

Moresby Island

Carpenter Bay

Louscoone Inlet

Rose Inlet

Raspberry Cove

Ellen Js.

Private

Rose Harbour

Houston Stewart Channel

Flatrock Island

SGang Gwaay

Gordon Islands

Kunghit Island

MAP LEGEND

✳	Community	⚒	Viewing tower	🏛	Watchmen site	– – – Park boundary
☆	Site of interest	⚲	Warden station	⚓	Anchorage	·········· Trail
Ⓟ	Parking	⋒	Picnic sites	🛶	Boat ramp	– – – – Indian reserve
🏠	Homestead	⚑	Park hiking shelter	▲	Hill/mountain	–··–··– Ecological reserve
◪	Divesite	⋀	Camping	🌿	Bog	Ferry crossing
⋀	Sand dunes	⌷	Fresh water from a pipe			– – – – Gravel road

The Haida name for the island shielding this pretty bay is "Giilii Gwaay," meaning trap. This can mean a salmon trap but it can also be a trap for mariners. As mentioned, magnetite was mined here and significant amounts of it still remain. It may cause compasses to give inaccurate readings, so use caution and your GPS if you are travelling during times of limited visibility. Companies at industrial sites such as this commonly dumped their scrap metal in the sea. If you set your anchor, you could snag some of this debris. As if that weren't enough, this seemingly protected bay is prone to strong southerly downdrafts.

Harriet Island offers some protection for anchored boats should you decide to go ashore. The townsite of Jedway has been cleaned, but some tailing ponds remain. These should be avoided. The roads leading to the mines are still open for walking. The least obstructed route parallels the harbour before leading uphill. It will take slow walkers two hours to reach the ridge between Jedway and Ikeda Cove, a vantage point that offers fine sunset views of Skincuttle Inlet.

From the ridge, the road descends toward Ikeda Cove, stopping short of the water and leading to additional workings on the south slope. During construction of this road the workings of an earlier copper mine were partially obliterated. If you look along the upper side, you may spot a mine portal and the dump piles of this 1906–20 operation, which was managed by the successful Japanese businessman Arichika Ikeda.

After it was sorted by hand, ore was carted to the loading wharf on a one-metre-gauge tramway for shipping to a smelter on Vancouver Island. In the piles left at the ore bunkers you can find chalcopyrite, a brassy mineral sometimes called copper pyrite. From the road's lowest point, you can follow the rails to the old camp at the water's edge.

We were wary of the water draining from these mines and we do not recommend it for drinking. Instead, fresh water can be obtained from the streams that run into Harriet Harbour, or possibly at Jedway Bay. Boaters may be able to fill their tanks at the end of the bay; fresh water once trickled from a plastic pipe there. Parks Canada, however, does not maintain this source.

A Japanese abalone cannery also used to operate in Jedway Bay. In the woods behind the rotting buildings is a touching inscription on a

Wave action helped create this tidal cavern at Poole Point. One end opens to the sea, the other on land. Landings can be made on calm days.

wooden grave marker. The grave of Mrs. Taniyo Isozaki dates from the dark decades when the Japanese were ostracized by the White community. Sadly, we know little about her or the cannery operation.

A fellow by the name of Francis Poole was the first European resident in Skincuttle Inlet. This English engineer prospected for copper here in 1862–63 and later published an account of his explorations in *Queen Charlotte Islands: A Narrative of Discovery and Adventure in the North Pacific.* Poole's venture failed, his miners mutinied and his life was threatened several times. Remarkably, he still wrote appreciatively of the area: "I stood by the beach for fully half an hour, thinking how difficult it would be to find a sweeter spot in all the world, and how at no distant date that very beach would assuredly give way to the wharves and landing-places of a flourishing commercial town. Harriet Harbour has only to be known in order to be seized upon in the interests of trade and colonization."

Poole never realized his own vision, however, since he was unsuccessful in his quest for copper. His mines were located in the limestone on Copper Island and at Pelican Cove on Burnaby Island. Old shafts and camp remains are still visible at the sites where he laboured.

Poole Point on Burnaby Island is named after him, but some of the holes here are from erosion, not mining. This point is subject to strong winds, and it is difficult to land on its stony beaches. Those who do make it ashore will be fascinated by the cave. Heavy seas have carved the granite rocks into a horseshoe-shaped cavern that has two openings on the same shore. The major opening gapes ten by six metres. The adjacent hole has a partially collapsed ceiling, creating a separated arch. At low tide you can kayak into the flooded passage, though ocean surges can make this dangerous. Around the arch's base, the sea swirls stones, grinding circular holes in the bedrock. Such grinders are called millstones and their depressions, potholes.

Also on Burnaby Island, Swan Bay is of minor interest. This idyllic setting was once the homestead of some families seeking an alternative lifestyle. They struggled for six or seven years before deciding to move elsewhere. One of their homes resembled a large mushroom, but little evidence remains of their venture. Today, this is the site of a Youth Cultural Camp sponsored by the Skidegate Band Council. Young people in attendance learn about traditional Haida culture. Visitors are requested to give the bay a wide berth.

We had an enjoyable time motoring around Skincuttle Inlet, exploring the bays and walking the beaches. Even hiking to the ridge above Jedway was interesting. Everyone in our party had a measurable appreciation of geology and, consequently, enjoyed examining what remains of the mines. You may not share this same interest, particularly if natural history is the focus of your visit. Nevertheless, Skincuttle Inlet will certainly add another dimension to your Gwaii Haanas visit.

HOUSTON STEWART CHANNEL

Many people begin or complete their Gwaii Haanas explorations in Houston Stewart Channel since this area is as far south as most groups go. The channel has suitable pickup and drop-off places, offers refuge from poor weather and is close to a major place of interest—SGang Gwaay, an ancient village with a UNESCO World Heritage designation.

Early sailing ships also sought shelter in Houston Stewart Channel, anchoring here on trading visits. At first, trade dealings with the Haida were friendly, but unfortunately hostilities did occur. At least four ships were attacked, and two were burned. There was considerable loss of life on both sides. These tragic events are retold from a Native perspective in Christie Harris's novel *Raven's Cry*.

In 1853, sailors aboard the *Virago* discovered fresh stream water on the north side of the channel. They also found lush red salmonberries, which they called raspberries. Now known as Raspberry Cove, this is a good campsite. Unfortunately, tiny, biting flies called no-see-ums can be

GETTING THERE

Houston Stewart Channel separates Moresby Island from smaller Kunghit Island to the south. The channel is accessible to aircraft and boats. There are mooring buoys in Rose Harbour, as well as two within Louscoone Inlet. Rose Harbour has bed-and-breakfast facilities and offers a boat-tour service out to SGang Gwaay (Anthony Island). Parks Canada has a field warden station on the eastern side of Ellen Island. For emergencies, they monitor VHF channel 16 during the day or can be reached with a satellite phone at 1-877-852-3100.

No-access sites include Bowles Point on the eastern side of Kunghit Island, all of the rocks and islets surrounding SGang Gwaay, and Kerouard islands at the southern extremities of Kunghit Island. Camping is not permitted on SGang Gwaay. Water from a pipe can be found about halfway along the west side of Louscoone Inlet.

a problem, and the cove's popularity with kayakers means you may find this site rather crowded.

Directly across from the cove lies Rose Harbour, a former whaling station that employed as many as 100 men seasonally between 1910 and 1942. It was not unusual for management to bring their families in for the summer. Records indicate that in those 32 years more than 2,000 whales were processed and shipped as barrels of oil, mink food and fertilizer. The foul smell generated a lot of wisecracks about the station's floral name—named for the same George Rose who is commemorated at Nai-Kun (Rose Spit). The whaling company eventually went bankrupt and most of its machinery was dismantled. (W.A. Hagelund wrote an anecdotal history of whaling here and on Graham Island in his book, *Whalers No More*.)

Two digesters, used to render whale blubber and bones, still sit rusting on the beach at Rose Harbour. A plain monument nearby is dedicated to Asian workers who died while employed here. Steam boilers remain hidden behind the trees and modern buildings, and several homes are now built on this site. Families have resided here since 1978, living off the land and sea. If you go ashore to see the remains of the whaling station, please respect the residents' property and privacy.

A pleasant trip ashore awaits nearby in five-kilometre-long Rose Inlet. Inflatables and kayaks require careful navigation through rocks and kelp to reach the broad salt marsh at the inlet's terminus. Such a large foraging area is rare in Gwaii Haanas, making this important habitat. Deer and bear graze in the meadow, and it's also popular with migrating waterfowl.

Beyond the western end of Rose Inlet, all that separate you from the Pacific horizon are small island clusters. Despite its name, this ocean is rarely pacific; boaters should be properly equipped and cognizant of its dangers before travelling far from shore. For this reason, both sides of Kunghit Island are usually avoided by smaller craft.

At the very mouth of the channel is Flatrock Island, a mesa-topped monolith alive with nesting glaucous-winged gulls and pelagic cormorants. We also spotted a rare horned puffin flying in wide circles around this rocky roost. Going ashore here is extremely difficult, so the birds are best studied from the water. The nearby Gordon Islands have some pretty nooks, but

Courtesy of BC Archives E-01609

In its day, whaling was an acceptable commercial enterprise. This marine behemoth was only one of over 2,000 whales processed at Rose Harbour. The whales were rendered into oil, cosmetics and fertilizer.

only kayakers can easily navigate through them. Sometimes glass fishing floats from Japan can be found in this remote coastal location.

The best-known island cluster west of Rose Inlet contains SGang Gwaay (formerly Anthony Island), which is the location of SGang Gwaay llnagaay, often referred to as Ninstints (described in the next section, SGang Gwaay World Heritage Site). Around SGang Gwaay, the smaller islets are excellent for birdwatching. Nine of the 13 species of seabirds that breed in B.C. nest in this one area: an estimated 35,000 pairs. They use every type of available habitat—burrows, rock crevices, open rock or thin vegetation. A nesting horned puffin was first recorded in B.C. at this location. Our favourite, however, is the tufted puffin. Their colourful faces and fat bodies, with wings that seem to revolve around their midsections, give them the look of stunt planes at an air show. The islets all around SGang Gwaay are protected areas for these birds, so please remain in your boat while exploring and birdwatching.

This is also a great place to see mammals. Northern sea lions rest on the outermost rocks, exposed to surf and spray, and you can watch for harbor seals among the islets or river otters within Houston Stewart Channel.

There is an exceptional diversity of submarine mammals as well. If you're hoping to see whales on your trip, either end of Houston Stewart Channel is a likely locale. Watch for spouting gray and minke whales near shore, or humpbacks breaching farther out. Killer whales will sometimes cruise right through the channel.

Houston Stewart Channel is one of the most remote locations in B.C. Birds and mammals are abundant. Most people return with an exciting story about breaching whales, whirling puffins or sharing a campfire with a kayaker from almost anywhere in the world.

Nowhere else on Haida Gwaii is quite like it.

SGANG GWAAY WORLD HERITAGE SITE

This tiny island seems an unlikely place to find the masterpieces of the Haida's creative genius, but SGang Gwaay has been recognized as having international significance for its artistic heritage. Some of the world's greatest totem poles still stand here in the ground where they were raised.

The Haida name of SGang Gwaay—the Wailing Island—is most appropriate. The name originates from the sound of surging waves forcing air through a hole in a rock—a sound like a woman keening or wailing. European traders called the village Ninstints—a mispronunciation of Nan Sdins, the name of the village chief. It is correctly referred to as SGang Gwaay llnagaay, the Wailing Island town.

The historic village, once the home of at least 300 Haida and one of the largest villages in the Gwaii Haanas region, is now abandoned and decaying. Archaeologists have compared it favourably to the lost jungle cities of Mexico and Cambodia. The United Nations finally recognized this legacy in wood in 1981 by declaring SGang Gwaay a World Heritage Site, ranking it alongside Egypt's pyramids and France's palace at Versailles. SGang Gwaay presents an exceptional testimony to a civilization that very nearly disappeared.

This village was the last homeland of the Gangxid, a subdivision of the Haida Nation whose territory was the southern Gwaii Haanas region. They occupied this site for at least 2,000 years, using it as a year-round residence. During the summer, people scattered throughout the territory to hunt, fish and gather edible plants. They occupied their time in winter with carving, construction and social ceremonies, usually in conjunction with other villages.

SGang Gwaay was a difficult place for guests and enemies to approach. The winds of winter, and sometimes those of summer, are among the strongest in Canada. Yet the village itself is sheltered on the lee side of the island. A smaller island lies in front, restricting passage to a concealed cove behind. Here canoes once lay beached before numerous houses. When low tide dries the bay, you can still see the canoe runs cleared through the beach cobbles.

Visitors are often humbled into silence upon arriving here. Decaying wooden faces on the poles stare out to sea as if to ignore the intrusion, and a straggling row of bestial eyes can be intimidating. You feel like asking permission from the spirits to tread among these towering relics. The

GETTING THERE

SGang Gwaay (Anthony Island) is home to the famous Haida village of SGang Gwaay llnagaay (Ninstints). The island sits 3 km off the western end of Houston Stewart Channel, on the edge of the Pacific Ocean. It is accessible only by boat. Please note that the shore in front of the village is off limits to all boats; the landing site is a small cove on the north end of the island. A trail leads through to the totem poles and house sites.

Camping is not allowed on the island. Also, all of the rocks and islets surrounding SGang Gwaay are closed to visitors. Good campsites exist at nearby Louscoone Point and within Louscoone Inlet, where there is also fresh water. A pipe is hooked up to a buoy about halfway along the west side. Kayakers may want to consider staying at these sites. If you camp in Houston Stewart Channel, it is a challenge to tour SGang Gwaay and paddle both ways in a day.

Seasonal Haida watchmen live on SGang Gwaay. You are requested to radio ahead on VHF channel 6 to advise them of your arrival.

Toad or frog? The Haida never separated the two. This one peeks from a pole at SGang Gwaay llnagaay.

presence of the dead is pervasive, so perhaps it's fitting that the majority of the standing poles are mortuaries, honouring the people who led this village. The bodies of the dead were entombed in enclosures at the top of the poles. Other poles include tall memorials commemorating an ancestor lost at sea or elsewhere.

These poles do not depict pagans or demons, nor were they worshipped. The animal and human figures on them represent family crests and mythology, and are similar to European coats of arms or Scottish tartans. These symbols make a statement about genealogy and possibly the individual commemorated. Tragically, many of these meanings were forgotten or lost when, during the 1800s, raging smallpox epidemics nearly wiped out the entire population. We were able to identify some of the figures such as bears, whales and birds.

Oddly, some of the animals symbolized on the poles weren't residents of Haida Gwaii in those days or, in some cases, even to this day. These include the beaver (with cross-hatched tail), the frog (with toothless grin) and the grizzly bear (with protruding tongue). These animals strongly suggest the Haida were familiar with mainland creatures. Other figures are recognizable as eagles and killer whales. Some poles are virtually unidentifiable, having been damaged by fire in 1892.

Of the 26 poles remaining at SGang Gwaay llnagaay (many were removed to museums), several have begun to lean and a few have toppled. This decay is part of a cultural progression. Traditionally when poles aged, they were removed and replaced. The old ones would be cut up and given out at a potlatch. Recently, Parks Canada has worked together with the Haida elders to straighten some of the leaning poles.

Decay has seriously affected the remains of the dwellings. Collapsed beams and posts lie behind the poles, the remnants of 20 houses. The largest of these was 14.3 metres by 14.9 metres and had an excavated floor.

Dr. Marius Barbeau, speaking on Haida culture in 1954: "Their genius has produced monumental works of art on a par with the most original the world has ever known." Most of these leaning poles have now been straightened to their original posture.

Only two houses here had such terraced interiors. George MacDonald's booklet, *Ninstints: Haida World Heritage Site,* provides excellent drawings of their design, while artist Gordon Miller renders the village in exquisite detail as it may have appeared during its peak. This is an excellent onsite guide to identifying the houses and poles.

The G̲angxid suffered more than other Haida in their early contacts with Europeans and Americans. Led by a prideful and embittered chief, they attacked four trading vessels in as many years, twice destroying entire ships and crews. In the last conflict, which occurred in 1795, the chief, Koyah, and 50 warriors were killed with no loss to the traders.

Following Koyah's death, the G̲angxid kept much to themselves for many decades. Their isolation, however, was no protection from the new diseases White men brought. Smallpox first struck late in the 18th century, probably transmitted by Russian fur traders. A subsequent epidemic was thought to have been deliberately introduced in 1862 when a "sick" man was sent ashore in Skincuttle Inlet. The Haida social fabric was torn further apart when they obtained liquor and when many of their young people moved to a temporary camp on the outskirts of Victoria on Vancouver Island. By 1884, SGang Gwaay llnagaay had only 30 surviving residents. They were eventually invited to move to Skidegate. Today only a few descendants can trace their family back to the once-great Gangxid tribe in B.C. and Alaska.

The rainforest soon took over. For many years the village site was largely forgotten, visited only by the occasional hunter or fisher. In 1938, a few poles were removed and taken to Prince Rupert. During the 1950s, after negotiations with descendants from SGang Gwaay llnagaay, even more were removed under an initiative by the Royal BC Museum. Eventually, some of these poles were returned to the islands and can now be seen at the Haida Gwaii Museum at Skidegate. Seven remain at the Museum of Anthropology at the University of British Columbia. Thankfully, enough poles were left onsite to give visitors a glimpse into one of the Haida traditions from years past. The plan now is to keep the poles in place and slow their deterioration as much as possible. Native watchmen come each summer to monitor the thousands of visitors passing through here.

This is both a blessing and a curse. While no one will argue with the necessity of tourism to justify the poles' preservation, large numbers of people can have a detrimental impact. Visitors are reminded to tread carefully and keep to the established paths. In addition, the limit of only 12 people ashore at any one time will help keep the whole site as natural and intact as possible.

This legacy, richly deserving of our respect, was admirably summarized by Wilson Duff and Michael Kew in their 1957 *Report of the Provincial Museum*:

> A few fragments of memory, a few bright glimpses in the writings of the past, some old and weathered totem-poles in a storage shed, and the mouldering remnants of once-magnificent carved post and houses on the site of the old village—these are all that

survive of the tribe and village chiefs Koyah and Ninstints. What was destroyed here was not just a few hundred individual human lives. Human beings must die anyway. It was something even more complex and even more human—a vigorous and functioning society, the product of just as long an evolution as our own, well suited to its environment and vital enough to participate in human cultural achievements not duplicated anywhere else. What was destroyed was one more bright tile in the complicated and wonderful mosaic of man's achievement on earth. Mankind is the loser. We are the losers.

PART FOUR

THEIR PLACE TO BE

P eople come to the Charlottes from all over the world, never imagining that the islands' spell may descend upon them and they may never be able to leave. We heard first-hand how strong a pull this place can exert, even on the casual visitor, and we present 10 profiles of folks who stayed and who help contribute to the special character of Haida Gwaii.

Betty Dalzell,
Author and historian
Peter Hamel,
Anglican minister and ornithologist
Margo Hearne,
Naturalist
Carolyn Hesseltine,
Tourism consultant
Joy LaFortune,
Entrepreneur
Garner Moody,
Haida carver
Amanda Reid-Stevens,
Community activist
Faith Thorgierson,
Retired teacher
Kimiko von Boetticher and Andrew Merilees,
Islands enthusiasts

Betty Dalzell

To fully understand the present, we must first explore our past. Likewise, to really understand the Charlottes today, you must look into the islands' history. This is relatively easy to do, since every bookstore on these islands offers at least one of Betty Dalzell's three volumes. During the last 20 years she has methodically and effectively chronicled the islands' history.

Growing up in Port Clements, Betty often heard her parents talk about family ties to Wales and her distant aunts and uncles. She also listened to the stories of her neighbours, many of whom had European roots. One day, her father opened his detailed diary. "It was so interesting," she recalls, "and too good to go back in a drawer." This was all the incentive she needed.

Soon Betty enrolled in a writers' workshop led by established author Christie Harris, a decision that was to mark the beginning of her writing career. For now, her father's diary would have to wait. She started out writing short stories and articles for newspapers and magazines. Eventually she was persuaded to record the stories of people she knew from her childhood in Port Clements.

"Why don't you write something about the pioneers of the Charlottes?" persisted one of Betty's friends. "You know we're all dying and first thing you know all our stories are going to be gone and that will be the end of it. Why don't you do a book?"

The challenge of such a task was doubly daunting, says Betty, because at the time, few women were writing history books. Thankfully, Victoria archivist Willard Ireland was more interested in history than gender roles. He and his staff offered Betty willing assistance as she began to sort fact from fiction, put names to photographs and arrange stories in a meaningful order. After

Photo courtesy of Queen Charlotte Observer

Betty Dalzell

five years of dedicated effort, *The Queen Charlotte Islands 1774-1966* appeared on the bookstands. A sequel, *The Queen Charlotte Islands—Places and Names*, followed. Both provide excellent reading and detailed accounts of history and adventure throughout the islands.

The Beloved Island completes the trilogy. Based on her father's diary, the book begins with her father's family life in Wales, then follows his travels to South Africa, South America and across Canada, ultimately detailing his life as a homesteader on the Queen Charlottes. It relates much more than just a personal quest. Describing life at the turn of the century and introducing characters that helped shape countries and continents, *The Beloved Island* brought her father's diary out of the drawer for good.

Betty has done more than document the island's history. In 1985 she and her husband, Albert, helped spearhead a plan to build a historical museum in Port Clements. Two years later, a modest building was erected and volunteers began to collect, sort and display historical artifacts and photos. The museum has now tripled in size and is the main tourist stop in Port Clements.

In 1998 several residents of Port Clements wanted to recognize Betty and Albert's contribution to their community, to the Queen Charlottes and to the province. A few folks secretly filed nomination papers for the distinguished Order of British Columbia. This is given only to persons who have served with the greatest possible distinction and excelled in their field of endeavour. On July 23, 1998, Betty and daughter Joan (representing her father) arrived at Government House in Victoria, B.C., to accept this well-deserved award.

Recognition has not tempted Betty to leave. Even though she quietly admits she could live anywhere, the Charlottes have some big advantages. "I like being near the saltchuck," she says. "I love the beaches. Albert likes to go crab and trout fishing whenever he wants. I like the beauty of the islands and that they're small in population. You can make a difference in a small town."

Peter Hamel

In 1982 Peter Hamel was living in Toronto, working hard at the Anglican Church's head office. His job kept him extremely busy, applying church policies to corporate finances, as well as to environmental and Native land issues. This spectrum of responsibilities eventually brought him to Terrace, B.C., for a regional conference. Before the meetings ended he had been invited (divine intervention, perhaps?) to spend a few days on the Charlottes. This spontaneous side trip marked a new beginning in his church life. Soon he was ministering to the islands' parish and indulging his love of natural history—particularly birds.

"The first day I was here I went across the road, over the bank and looked across the inlet at all the seabirds," he recalls. "A yellow-billed loon, in breeding plumage, flew by along with Cassin's auklets and marbled murrelets. It was really quite exciting."

For a keen eastern bird-watcher, this was too much to ignore. He made some phone calls, met with his supervisors, then contacted the bishop. Three months later he began a one-year sabbatical as priest at the Masset church.

"I got involved in a number of things right away. A few of us started the first Christmas bird count. Nobody could believe what we saw here. There was a cattle egret in the sanctuary, a Townsend's solitaire on the beach, and I found a thick-billed murre! I fell in love with the place."

One year was not nearly long enough. He returned again in 1994, this time for a longer term. "One of the main things I wanted to do was to really explore, in depth, the spirituality of the islands and nature. I wrote a column for the national church for five years

Peter Hamel

on environmental spirituality. It would be great to rewrite these and connect them with some other theological writings."

The pastorate, however, involves more than just personal endeavours. Many members of his congregation are involved in the community, in political life, in education, or they work as fishers, caregivers or at the hospital. "I see the church as giving support and meaning to what these folks are doing. That is, supporting them in a spiritual way."

He also foresees the church playing a role in the new society that is developing here. The downsizing of the armed forces base meant a loss of civilian jobs, but invigorated community spirit. The artistic community seems to have revived, and residents have more control over decisions in their community. On the flip side, economic change in the fisheries and forest industries has hit people hard, like a mean-spirited punch. Many people are hurting, out of work and with limited prospects.

The church makes its building available for community arts events and has established a successful thrift shop along with a quaint drop-in cafe. The shop is staffed by volunteers, people who want to contribute positively to their community's need. In no small way, the church also promotes the spiritual connections of humanity's place in creation.

Peter eloquently ties all these observations together when asked what the Charlottes mean to him. "The islands are the vortex of creation. To me, they are the centre of the unfolding universe. It is a place where heaven and earth meet, and where they dialogue. To me, in a real way, you can sense the heartbeat of creation here, and the pivotal point is Rose Spit, where the land and the sea and the sky meet."

Margo Hearne

Visitors to Haida Gwaii soon hear about the Delkatla Wildlife Sanctuary. This relatively compact tidal marsh nestles next to the community of Masset and offers leisurely walking trails, viewing towers and well over 100 species of birds. Margo Hearne has been a major influence in this sanctuary's preservation and development.

Twenty-five years ago, Margo left her native Ireland and immigrated to Canada. Short stops in Toronto and Banff National Park were just stepping stones en route to her ultimate goal: Canada's west coast wilderness. Arriving in the Charlottes, she knew she had found the right place to be.

"I came out here for the winter with the intention of staying—for the winter," she says. "I liked it a lot. Something about it touched me. It reminded me of

Margo Hearne

Ireland. I remember one time I was sitting where I had a view out over the sanctuary. It was a still evening with a sunset, a rose glow over the water and a little mist rising. I thought, 'This is *really* beautiful.' So I stayed."

She worked in the local hotel through the winter, and the following spring opened the first bookstore in Masset. Two years later she joined her husband on his fishboat. Her fishing career lasted more than 15 years, until new regulations drove her from the water. "The fish are still out there. There are so many new rules, however, that you can't even get out to the fishing grounds anymore."

Although fishing was her livelihood, her passion became the Delkatla marshes. In 1978, town council appealed for help to manage the marsh, which was a gift to the community from the Masset Rod and Gun Club.

The wetlands were in a far from pristine state, the result of indiscriminate dumping and digging, combined with wandering livestock. The most challenging problem was the causeway. Built in 1963, the earth dam provided a wonderful access to the military base, but it altered the tidal flows. The salt marsh was slowly dying.

Over the next decade, Margo was twice elected to Masset council and was chair of the Wildlife Sanctuary Committee. The area was cleaned up, viewing towers were built, trails constructed and trees trimmed to make it a bit more accessible. In order to fully restore the salt marsh, however, the causeway had to change. So a Canada-wide fundraising campaign was undertaken—they needed $1 million!

Margo persevered, undaunted by the immense tasks of raising the money and manoeuvring through multiple levels of government and private bureaucracies. Finally, in 1995, part of the causeway was removed and replaced with a 30-metre bridge. The rising tide flooded the marshes for the first time in three decades. The restoration of Delkatla took a huge leap forward.

If Margo has her way, there will be more changes to come. "There's nowhere in Masset at the moment for people to find out about what's in the natural world around us. They come here to find out about the outdoors, but there's not a lot of information available."

She hopes the new interpretive centre will highlight Delkatla and give visitors an overview of the island's natural history.

Even though she has made Masset her home and become so involved in community affairs, Margo admits it's not always easy living here. Nevertheless, "one of the things we love about Masset is its relative quietude," she says. "I don't think the word is isolation. There is a certain peace and a certain security in knowing that you're quite a bit off the beaten track.

"One of the major attractions for me, as a birdwatcher, is that you get some really wonderful and unusual birds coming through here," she remarks. "And there's that wildness that you're close to all the time. The ocean and the trees and the wind blowing through here. It's really very special."

Carolyn Hesseltine

In the early 1900s, an aspiring 40-year-old artist made a sea voyage along the coastline of B.C. and Alaska. At every village stop, her fascination with the design, beauty and mystique of Native culture grew; she became determined to capture it with paint and brush. Over the next two decades her art began to attract a great deal of attention and her name, Emily Carr, rose through the ranks of the very best Canadian artists.

When she was attending grade school in Toronto, Carolyn Hesseltine and her class visited the Art Gallery of Ontario, where Emily Carr's art, now world-famous, was being displayed. She was awestruck by the intensity of Emily's coastal landscapes and Native villages. She knew right then that the Charlottes were a place she had to visit.

Carolyn Hesseltine

The route there, however, was not exactly direct. Carolyn recalls this period of her life: "I spent most of my life wandering. After I finished high school, I came west to work. Edmonton, Calgary, Banff and Whitehorse were some of the stops along the way. Ultimately, I ended up on the Charlottes."

When Carolyn first arrived on Haida Gwaii, her stay was short. Although she had realized her long-held goal of visiting this place, she wasn't quite sure whether she had the right to be here. "So I left and returned to Ontario."

Carolyn became aware that for her, "The islands were not so much a place that needed changing so much as they were a place that changed you." After a year of contemplation, she returned to stay.

After coming to Haida Gwaii for the second time, she soon reconnected with the tourism industry, her main area of work experience. While travelling across Canada and living in places like

Banff and Skagway, she had seen some of the negative effects of the burgeoning tourism industry. She felt that if she came to Haida Gwaii, things could be handled differently there.

"I wanted to work in the tourism industry, but if I was to promote the islands, it should be balanced with an educational component." Some of her other island work will certainly go a long way to accomplishing that goal. In addition to working in tourism, Carolyn also worked as a research assistant, examining the effects of introduced animals to the islands; deer were the target species. They are almost as numerous as thistle seeds, and live on virtually every island. Studying them also provided the opportunity to see the islands from many different directions.

She recalls, "From that job, I had the opportunity to visit a huge part of the islands—places where most long-term islanders have never been. I also worked as a crew member aboard a 52-foot schooner that navigated the many islands and channels comprising Haida Gwaii."

In a very short period of time, she had gained an intimate knowledge of the islands and knew, as much as anyone, that this was a very special place. But, as special as it is, Haida Gwaii must be self-sustainable, and tourism alone will not accomplish this.

"There's really no excuse for us not to have other kinds of businesses on these islands. It's up to us to take the initiative." Carolyn is emphatic as she states further: "We've sort of waited around for the government or others to do it. It should be islanders who make the decisions."

When Carolyn reflects on the time she has lived on the islands, she realizes that the islands have changed her.

"Here, there is a sense of family, of friendship, and a lifestyle that is pretty hard to beat. It has also taught me to appreciate a different set of values. Eventually I may feel the pressure to be back in the city and closer to my family. But I will be hard-pressed to actually move. This is my home. There is a sense of belonging and this is where I want to be."

Carolyn works at the Queen Charlotte Visitor Centre. If you have inquiries, you can email her at info@qcinfo.ca.

Joy LaFortune

In 1980 the first scheduled ferry arrived on the Queen Charlotte Islands. With it came tourists and car traffic never before experienced on these most isolated islands in Canada. Recognizing a great opportunity, Joy LaFortune turned part of her beachside home into an information centre and gift shop. Over the last quarter-century, Joy has been the first person many visitors meet en route to their favoured island destination. Living most of her life on the islands has given her a unique perspective and love for the Charlottes.

Both her parents' families arrived in the very early 1900s. Although born in the Village of Queen Charlotte, at age five she and her immediate family moved to Port Clements. They firmly grasped the pioneering spirit, carved out a life for themselves, and began to make things happen. Her father was both a fisherman and trapper, while her mother became the agent for the government telephone and telegraph. She also started the first credit union for the islands. "Our living room was a telephone office and a credit union all through my childhood," Joy recalls.

Children faced the additional problem of obtaining schooling, as there were seldom enough kids to fill a classroom. She took more than five years of school by correspondence, then boarded in Masset to complete Grades 10 and 11. "There was no road between Port Clements and Masset, so you had to go by gas boat. It took me as long to get to school in Masset as it takes the kids now to fly to Vancouver."

The phrase "pioneering spirit" may have a romantic ring, but it usually means hard work. In addition to finishing Grade 12 by correspondence, Joy worked as a school janitor for an income of

Joy LaFortune

$40 a month. Then, like both her grandfathers before her, she took on the job of postmaster for Port Clements.

With school, the teenage years and early work experience behind her, Joy followed the lure of greener pastures in Vancouver and the Caribbean. Her life abroad, however, did not last long. After living in such exotic locales and travelling the length and breadth of North America, why return to the Charlottes? "The weather," she quickly replies. "I live on the beach and it's always beautiful. The beaches: I really, really envy Masset's beaches. And the people: they are a different kind of people. I don't know whether special people come to islands or islands turn them into special people—we have an awful lot of very talented people here."

Joy would like to see more growth and more people. A bigger population base would improve the education system, reduce stress on the hospital and build on the tax base. "People do not know how wonderful it is here. This is the real problem. If anybody had a clue how gorgeous it is from the first of April till the end of October, we would have a lot more people here."

After 23 years in business, Joy has seen just about everything. Her first customers were the local fishers and loggers. The ferry service brought a whole new clientele, and the creation of Gwaii Haanas National Park Reserve and Haida Heritage Site promised to give tourism a huge boost. Unfortunately, leaner years and economic slowdowns have not helped the islands.

A lot of people who jumped on the tourism bandwagon did not last. Joy, however, has adapted with the times, moving her store into "downtown" Charlotte while keeping an ocean view from her shop window. Her neat, compact shop, Joy's Island Jewellers, features Charlottes apparel, books, Haida jewellery and plenty of island advice and stories.

You can also visit her website at <www. qcisland.net/joys/>.

Garner Moody

*T*he Raven and the First Men, *Loo Taas* and *Spirit of Haida Gwaii* are only three among the many striking creations by the late Bill Reid, a gifted and internationally renowned Haida artist. These later achievements, although awesome in size, complexity and detail, may ultimately be eclipsed by another outstanding accomplishment—inspiring a new generation of Haida artists. Garner Moody is one such artist.

Garner was fortunate. His Uncle Rufus, renowned for argillite carving, helped him get started. "The old school wasn't being used any more, so Rufus set up a night class. This was just in argillite," Garner explains. "Everybody that kept on [after the night class finished] moved to his house. He let 8 to 10 kids go into his bathroom and wash up after playing with slate [argillite]. We were just black. The washroom was a mess, as was

Garner Moody

the kitchen after serving candies, cookies and hot chocolate."

For the 1986 Expo in Vancouver, B.C., Bill Reid was commissioned to carve a large cedar canoe, one measuring more than 16 metres. A canoe of this size had not been carved for more than 70 years, and most of the skills and knowledge had been lost. So Bill hired four promising carvers, including Garner, to help take on this immense project.

"I guess we worked pretty good because Bill picked four guys from Skidegate to go down to Vancouver and work for him down there. He had his workshop on Granville Island and was just starting the Spirit Canoe. We learned how to melt down silver, make silver wire and solder. It was really good. He taught us as he worked on his projects."

Garner spent three months working on the canoe, starting with the raw log. By the time he left to go herring fishing, the canoe's sides were being honed down to less than two inches thick and it had been hollowed out and steamed. The sanding and painting were yet to come.

Bill had a unique style for teaching his students, Garner recalls. "I was working on the human—a bear with a man between his legs with a hat on. So Bill said do the nose. I looked at all the books and everything. All the old-style noses are big, fat, flared noses. So that's what I put on. When Bill saw it, he got his axe and went all over it, chopping it away. I cleaned it up, but when he returned he again said, 'No,' then chopped some more away. Four times he did this. The next thing I know I'm gluing the nose on. It was real discouraging. In the end he was happy with it, but he wondered why we were so darn slow. He was ready to fire us."

After apprenticing in Bill's studio for a year, Garner had had enough of Vancouver, even though the city served him well. "We got to know most of the Vancouver stores: we got to know the buyers, and they got to know us. I don't care for Vancouver now. I'm happy here—it's home. It's good for the kids to grow up here. They have a lot more freedom here than in the city."

Garner has now made Skidegate Village his home. Elected to the village council, he admits it takes a lot of work. "You have to be in the chambers from 9:30 to 4:30, every day. It's a big commitment. I never realized what it took to run a village."

The future of Skidegate Village looks immensely promising, particularly with the planned building of the Qay'llnagaay Heritage Centre. This will house a Bill Reid teaching centre, tool-making room, performance space and archives—all linked to the nearby Haida Gwaii Museum. It will be like a university. Ultimately, it is expected to display 16 poles outside, 6 of which are scheduled to be underway in September 2000. The best carvers in the world will soon be on Skidegate's doorstep.

Garner's sense of belonging means all he needs and wants is right here. "You grew up with everybody around here. You know everybody. So why leave?"

Amanda Reid-Stevens

Anyone who visited Haida Gwaii 10 years ago would be pleasantly surprised by the islands today. The downsizing of the armed forces base has actually revitalized the entire Masset community. The museum at Port Clements has tripled in size, Tlell has some new gift shops, Naikoon Provincial Park has improved facilities and the inside of Sandspit Airport has been given an impressive historical facelift. The most dramatic changes, however, have occurred at Skidegate Village. Amanda Reid-Stevens is a village resident who has made a significant contribution to the transformation.

Amanda was born in Toronto, but spent most of her teenage years in Skidegate Village. She remembers having a great time on the islands. "We swam, played baseball, walked

Amanda with her daughter Nika and granddaughter Kuuyas.

the beaches and partied when my parents weren't watching me too closely. It was a good teenagerhood for me." Unfortunately, the school system of the day did not extend past Grade 10. Correspondence courses or moving away were the only options to complete grade school.

For her senior grades, Amanda spent a year attending a school in Maple Ridge, B.C., and her last year in Vancouver. Since returning to Haida Gwaii, she has been an enthusiastic village resident, and for seven years was the general manager of a proactive corporation.

"One of the most significant factors for Native people recently has been Bill C31. This federal law allowed many First Nations people to regain their status. Skidegate was one community that welcomed back, and is still welcoming back, as many people as it can. Over the last decade, the population has nearly tripled. In response to this influx, the band council established the development corporation Gwaalagaa Naay, meaning 'Ambitious House.' Its mandate is to generate economic development and employment opportunities. The corporation, along with the council, is responsible for a lot of the development in Skidegate today."

Skidegate Village has some excellent facilities. You can purchase gifts, supplies and staples at the new mini-mall, and perhaps take part in a recreational activity at one of the gymnasiums. The village has the islands' only cosmic bowling alley. Younger children enjoy a state-of-the-art school, one that would make most school districts envious.

For Amanda, the future for the village, and for the islands as a whole, looks exciting. "I see the leaders of Skidegate willing to work with other leaders on the island, through the Gwaii Trust Board, through island communities and through other island boards where representatives (both Native and non-Native) work together to make progress."

The showpiece for the new millennium will be the Qay'llnagaay Heritage Centre, the most ambitious project yet. "It's going to encompass an expanded museum, a Bill Reid teaching centre, a theatre, as well as resource, language, interpretive and administrative facilities. It will be great for the village, for the kids and for future generations that come along. It's going to hold a lot of our history and keep it safe."

Amanda has a special interest in the project, particularly since one component, the Bill Reid teaching centre, honours her late father. She is involved in planning for the centre along with a cross section of people from all over Haida Gwaii. The entire complex will be linked with larger educational institutions, including the University of Northern B.C., Emily Carr College of Art and Design, Northwest Community College and the local school district. People from all over the world will soon be arriving to study or be a part of this unique centre.

Regardless of the national or international attention that Haida Gwaii or Skidegate Village receive, Amanda is more than content with her life on the islands. "They are my home and always will be my home. I feel at peace here, I feel safe and I feel part of a very vibrant Haida and island culture. It's an exciting place to live right now and I wouldn't want to live anywhere else."

Faith Thorgierson

For most of her life, Faith Thorgierson has lived on the Queen Charlotte Islands. This was not always her plan; nor was the idea of pursuing a career as a schoolteacher in Old and New Masset. She was a reluctant recruit at first, filling in temporarily. After just a few months, however, she began to enjoy being in the classroom. Over the next 34 years, she experienced what it is like to teach on isolated islands and discovered why, for her, the Charlottes are the best place to be.

Faith arrived here when she was six weeks old. Her family took up residence in Naden Harbour, then moved to the more central location of Masset because her father ran canneries in various parts of the islands. Throughout her childhood, her father spoke of his dream—that one day one of his children would attend university. After her sister chose a career in nursing and her brother

Faith Thorgierson

became a commercial fisherman, it fell to Faith, under her father's encouragement, to leave for the academic halls of the University of B.C. Two years of teacher education later, she felt she had fulfilled her father's dream. She now had other things in mind.

At first, she and her husband lived in Victoria, then moved to Inuvik, Northwest Territories, for two years. This was followed by two years in Ottawa, before they decided to return to their roots on the Charlottes. They arrived on the Northlands dock in Masset with no job prospects and only $2 to their name.

"Three days later, there was a knock on the front door," says Faith. "There stood the superintendent of schools wanting to know if I would come and work for them. I hesitated. All I wanted to do was raise my two boys and have a wonderful time, so I compromised. I agreed to help, but only for one month. But after one month they still couldn't get anybody else. So I said I'd stay till Christmas, and then finally, yes, I was hooked. So I never had to apply for a job."

The starting salary was $300 a month. Teachers had to work in the classroom, of course, but in small isolated communities their role also extended beyond the school door. Faith was expected to have her class appear before the visiting dentist, doctor and public health nurse, and to participate in weekend community activities. She also had some rather unusual in-class expectations.

"When I started teaching, our school was one of the few buildings in the community with running water. We had a sink right in the room, and every morning when the students came in, they washed their face and hands and brushed their teeth. And while they were doing that, you opened up cans of soup. We had a space heater in the back of the room and you put the big pot of soup on the back of the stove. At lunchtime you fed your students their soup and—cod-liver-oil biscuits! We all did this. It was just part of the job.

"We also have a really good outdoor education program. In Grade 3 the students start with an overnighter at the provincial park. Each grade higher, the kids go farther afield for a longer stay. The Grade 7s finish their elementary years with a wilderness hike on the Cumshewa Head trail. The islands are a wonderful place to teach and raise your own children. They're so free. For a long time there was no television so they spent all their time outside—camping, fishing and exploring the beaches."

After a reluctant beginning, Faith continued teaching for nearly three and a half decades. "They threw a great big retirement party for us in Old Massett—potlatch-style with Haida dancing," she says. Few other school districts can match that.

"As a retirement gift to ourselves, my husband and I did a Panama trip: Vancouver to Fort Lauderdale and three weeks in Florida. But I don't think there is any place more beautiful than the Queen Charlotte Islands. Everybody's life is a little niche. This is my corner of the world."

Kimiko von Boetticher and Andrew Merilees

In the mid-1990s Kimiko von Boetticher left her hometown of Scarborough, Ontario, and her summer playground, the world-famous Algonquin Park. She headed to Vancouver, B.C., and enrolled in post-graduate studies at Simon Fraser University, where her interest focused on environmental education and First Nations philosophy. Before long, she had set her sights on a trip to the offshore islands of Haida Gwaii.

One of her professors happened to be teaching a master's degree course in the island community of Masset, and Kimiko went there, planning to audit it and to do a little exploring at the same time. She easily recalls what happened next.

"I met some friends through that program who lived in Old Massett. I was invited back to attend a potlatch and was encouraged to come and stay. I moved there a month later and have been here ever since."

During an off-island trip, Kimiko was introduced to Andrew

Andrew Merilees and Kimiko von Boetticher

Merilees, who was no stranger to the islands. He had first visited Haida Gwaii in 1982 with his father, who was leading a natural-history tour group around the islands. It was enough of an introduction to give him a feeling of what the islands were all about. As his partnership with Kimiko developed, he decided to make the move to Masset. "It didn't take a lot of convincing to get me to move here!" he adds quickly.

Folks moving to Haida Gwaii have several choices as to where they can live. Although Sandspit, the Village of Queen Charlotte, Tlell and Masset all offer services, each locale has some advantages over the others. Andrew and Kimiko chose Masset, a small community of just over a thousand and the largest municipality on the islands, as their home.

Everyone in the community is within walking distance of the inlet, since Masset is nestled near the entrance to Masset Sound on the north shore of Haida Gwaii.

It is exposed, however, to moody Dixon Entrance, where winter storms pass through, sometimes with hurricane-force winds. When asked, "Why Masset?" Andrew and Kimiko replied with almost identical answers.

"The community of Masset and particularly Old Massett really welcomed us into their fold. They made us feel we were part of the community. We've had a really good experience here and … we've wanted to give back to it."

As with all small communities, there is no shortage of volunteer work to be done or directorships on societies to be taken on. Kimiko works for the local community college and is involved with the Masset Eagles Swim Club and the Queen Charlotte Islands' Women's Society. Andrew has revitalized his roots with the tourism industry as president of the Haida Gwaii Tourism Association and as director of the Queen Charlotte Islands Chamber of Commerce—a busy job, because the islands are in a transition phase: their resource industries are in decline, so there is a hope that tourism and other businesses, will help offset the void.

Being involved in a community means much more than just doing a job or helping out with long-term plans. It also means that you develop a sense of place and a passion for your community, and the surrounding environment. None of this has been lost on either Andrew or Kimiko.

Asked what the islands mean to him, Andrew said, "Haida Gwaii has everything you need and nothing that you don't. To me, it's a community with a close relationship to the natural world and the resources that we have here."

Kimiko quickly agreed, adding, "This is a place where I can live in harmony and balance. I have some pretty strong connections with nature and the spirit world. I find living up here I'm not bombarded with consumerism. I'm not forced to work a 40-hour week to make bill payments. So I really find that living here allows me to balance work and play. Haida Gwaii is my paradise for sure! I wouldn't want to live anywhere else."

Andrew and Kimiko will gladly help if you or a group want to be guided through Haida Gwaii. Northwest Recreation Services, which offers "Discovery Tours" of the islands, can be contacted either at PO Box 798, Masset, BC, V0T 1M0, or visit their website: <www.northwestrecreation.com>.

PART FIVE

VISITING HAIDA GWAII

Preparing for your trip to Haida Gwaii should be an enjoyable and hopefully easy undertaking. In this section we have included as much information as possible to help first-time or returning visitors plan their excursion.

If your plans include a B&B, charter or tour, we highly recommend making advance reservations. Phoning, emailing or investigating the websites listed here will speed up this process. Haida Gwaii may seem to be off the beaten track, but tours, charters and accommodations can still fill quickly. Keep in mind also that names, park regulations or facilities can change faster than a swimming salmon. Phone ahead to avoid disappointment.

Some travellers prefer to go it alone. The tides and weather set their day's agenda. Even so, it still makes good sense to have a contingency plan. Whether you're travelling by car, boat, plane or bike, this section also has heaps of helpful suggestions to keep you warm, dry and on the right trail, hopefully with a salmon or crab cooking over the fire.

OVERNIGHTING ON HAIDA GWAII

Overnight accommodation on the islands ranges from modern hotels and motels to bed-and-breakfast facilities and simple campsites. These are located throughout the island communities.

The number of bed and breakfasts on Haida Gwaii has grown over the past decade, largely in response to tourist popularity. We have highlighted nine of them, and two fishing lodges, basing our selection on signage, the host's experience, quality of accommodation, special features and atmosphere—indicators that the operators are familiar with the islands and know how to cater to their guests.

The B&Bs listed here share several characteristics. All are close to a river or the ocean, offer comfortable rooms and, in most cases, look out on magnificent views. In addition, their hosts can link you up to aerial tours, fishing charters, kayak rentals or boat trips. Whatever you plan to do while you're on the islands, they'll help you make the right connections. Bear in mind that all these accommodations have a policy of no smoking indoors. They will not normally accept pets, either; if you travel with a pet, be sure to make special arrangements when you make your reservation.

The fishing lodges featured here cater mostly to off-island fishers. Both have excellent facilities and do their best to make sure your fishing trip is memorable. One doubles as both a B&B and fishing lodge.

For additional information, consult the annual *Accommodation Guide* or *Bed and Breakfast Directory* published by the BC Ministry of Tourism. Both guides (available free from any of the more than 140 Visitor Centres located throughout the province) list accommodation only if it meets preset standards.

The Village of Queen Charlotte Visitor Centre can be contacted at:

P.O. Box 819, 3220 Wharf St.,
Village of Queen Charlotte, BC V0T 1S0
Phone: 250-559-8316
Fax: 250-559-8952
Email: info@gcinfo.ca
Website: <www.qcinfo.ca>

BED & BREAKFASTS

Jean's Beach House
Hosts: Mike & Jean Juhas
Box 147
Masset, BC V0T IM0
Ph/Fax: 250-626-5662;
Toll free: 1-888-273-4444
Units: 3
Rates: $70-$80

Features: Lunches and dinners may be available upon request.

While driving out along Tow Hill Road, you'll be more than tempted to stop and stay at Jean's. The beach rolling up to her doorstep is one of the longest and wildest in Canada. Dig for clams, watch for whales, identify shells and marvel at the twisted, weathered driftwood. Stay the night in a guest cottage suite or in the main house. A complete gourmet breakfast is served with Queen Charlottes hospitality.

Guest Comments: We thank you for your warm and caring hospitality during our stay. It was like visiting good friends. We look forward to a return visit.

Moresby Island Guest House

Host: Della Beldessi
Box 485,
385 Beach Rd.
Sandspit, BC V0T IT0
Ph/Fax: 250-637-5300
Email: migh@telus.net
Website: <www.moresbyisland-bnb.com>
Units: 10
Rates: $35-$75

Features: Locked storage for backpacking gear, secure and free car parking while guests are away touring, mountain bike rentals and coin laundry facilities. Rooms are wheelchair accessible. Golf course nearby. Any traveller wanting a home-like atmosphere will enjoy this guest house. Savour your self-serve breakfast out on the roomy deck, watching eagles soar by. Sip hot tea and marvel at the sunset over Skidegate Inlet. You're close enough to the airport to be on time for flights, but far enough away to sleep soundly.

Guest Comments: Beautiful and peaceful. A home away from home.

Seaport Bed and Breakfast

Host: Bonnie Wasyleski
Box 206
Sandspit, BC V0T IT0
Phone: 250-637-5698
Fax: 250-637-5697
Units: 3
Rates: $35-$55

Features: Library of local books, horses kept on site that you can watch swim off the beach, secure parking.

The island's first B&B. Stay in cozy comfort year-round in a waterfront home with private accommodations and cable TV. Full kitchen facilities, self-serve wholesome breakfast, homemade baked goods and even farm-fresh eggs.

Guest Comments: Pretty spiffy ... slept with both eyes shut.

Spruce Point Lodge

Hosts:	Nancy Hett and Mary Kellie Box 735 Village of Queen Charlotte, BC V0T IS0
Ph/Fax:	250-559-8234
Email:	sprpoint@qcislands.net
Website:	<www.qcislands.net/ sprpoint>
Units:	7
Rates:	$70-$80

Features: Great view of Skidegate Inlet. Onsite pottery shop, boat tours, kayak rentals and fishing charters. All tours leave right from Spruce Point.

Spruce Point's location at the west end of the Village of Queen Charlotte offers a panoramic view of the inlet. Each room is self-contained, quiet and comfortable. A full breakfast, including home baking, is delivered to your room each morning. Sip your coffee on the balcony, or relish your morning feast in the quiet of your room.

Guest Comments: The room with the best view, and the best breakfast we've ever had. I will definitely be back.

Dorothy and Mike's

Hosts:	Dorothy and Mike Garrett Box 595, 3125 2nd Ave. Village of Queen Charlotte, BC V0T IS0
Ph/Fax:	250-559-8439
Email:	doromike@qcislands.ca
Website:	<www.qcislands.net/ doromike>
Units:	9
Rates:	$40-$90 (kids under 12 free)

Features: Relax on the deck overlooking the ocean, surrounded by flowers and forest.

It would be hard not to enjoy this oasis in the middle of the Village of Queen Charlotte. Choose from queen, twin or single rooms, all with private entrances and fully equipped kitchens. You can look forward to complimentary coffee and tea served with a full breakfast.

Guest Comments: This was a great respite from windy beaches—a wonderful place, and a great host. We will return.

Riverside Lodging

Host: Margaret Condrotte
Box 89, Richardson Rd.
Tlell, BC V0T 1Y0
Phone: 250-557-4418;
Toll free: 1-888-853-5522
Fax: 250-557-4412
Email: margaret@qcislands.net
Website: <www.qcislands.net/
margaret>
Units: 4
Rates: $75 and up

Features: You can't get much closer to the Tlell River without falling in. Perfect for anglers. Margaret welcomes visitors to her riverside accommodations, certain they will enjoy the peace and quiet of the Tlell area. The central location allows you to cast a line in the river, walk to nearby shops and galleries or drive to Naikoon Provincial Park in just a few minutes. Adult oriented.

Self-contained rooms are all non-smoking, but each has access to a private balcony. A common kitchen is available for all guests to prepare their meals.

Guest Comments: Fantastic! Just like home, but better fishing.

Cäcilia's Bed and Breakfast

Host: Cäcilia Honisch
Box 3, Highway 16
Tlell, BC V0T 1Y0
Ph/Fax: 250-557-4664
Email: ceebysea@qcislands.net
Units: 5
Rates: $30-$50 per person

Features: From this rustic log house or cabin nestled behind the dunes, 11 acres of beachfront property await you. Bring your camera, paintbrush or binoculars. There is also room inside for larger groups if you plan a seminar, workshop or meeting. Start your day with either muesli or waffles topped with your choice of huckleberry jam or real maple syrup. What a treat!

Guest Comments: Hospitality was superb. The best B&B we've been in since Britain. Wonderful atmosphere.

Alaska View Lodge

Hosts: Rick and Dana Bourne
          Box 227, Tow Hill Rd.
          Masset, BC V0T IM0
Phone: 250-626-3333;
Toll free: 1-800-661-0019
Fax: 250-626-3303
Email: info@alaskaviewlodge.com
Website: <www.alaskaviewlodge.
          com>
Units: 4
Rates: $85-$210
          (off-season rates)

Features: Hot tub, satellite TV, bed and breakfast or all meals.

The south beach has its own personality. Why not get to know it better by staying right on the beach itself? Explore the drift line, splash in the surf, watch eagles soaring by and scan the distant horizon for the Alaskan mountains. Two of the units have separate baths. When you awaken, a complete breakfast is served at your convenience.

Guest Comments: We enjoyed our stay here immensely—the rolling surf, the long walks on the beach, agate searches (addictive) and the peace and quiet so difficult to find in Vancouver.

Harbourview Lodging

Host: Lynne Holland
          Box 153,
          1608 Delkatla St.
          Masset, BC V0T IM0
Ph/Fax: 250-626-5109;
Toll free: 1-800-661-3314
Email: lholland@mhtv.ca
Units: 5
Rates: $50 and up

Features: Crab pot cooker on site. Sauna and fax services available to guests. Laundry room available for suite guests only.

Whether you fly, boat or drive to Masset, staying at Harbourview puts you at the centre of things, literally overlooking the small boat harbour and marina. Delkatla Wildlife Sanctuary and several restaurants are only a short walk away. You have a choice of one- or two-bedroom suites, or can opt for three rooms that share two bathrooms. Each suite has a private phone and cable TV. A fresh cup of tea or coffee will get you off to a great start in the morning.

Guest Comments: All fishermen should bring their wives here to shop, collect shells and search for agates. Had a ball!

FISHING LODGES

Naden Lodge
Hosts: Chris and Brian Hillier
            Box 648, 1496 Delkatla Road
            Masset, BC V0T IM0

Phone: 250-626-3322   Toll free: 1-800-771-8933
Fax: 250-626-5465
Email: info@nadenlodge.com   Website: <www.nadenlodge.com>
Units: 5   Rates: $2,495-$3,295
B&B rates: $80-$129 (in season)   (3- to 4-day packages)

Features: Experienced local guides, return airfare from Vancouver, all gear and tackle included. Taxidermy services also available. Doubles as a B&B from September through May. Anglers will appreciate either ocean or steelhead fishing options.

For fun, fishing and food, you'll have to travel a long way to beat Naden Lodge. Within minutes of the lodge, you'll be hooked by some of the best ocean fishing in North America. The rates at Naden include virtually everything you'll need. Following your day out on the chuck, you can look forward to hearty home-cooked meals, complete with fine wine and plenty of stories. When the sun sets, settle into the easy chairs, shoot some pool or relax in the hot tub. Your comfortable quarters will allow you to rise from a great rest primed for the new day's excitement. Your catch will be handled promptly and be ready upon departure.

Guest Comments: I've waited a lifetime to come to the Charlottes to fish, and the staff at Naden Lodge made the wait worthwhile. Had an awesome time.

Some of the best fishing in North America can be enjoyed within minutes of Naden Lodge.

Kumdis River Lodge

Host: James Bowie
            Box 419
            Port Clements, BC V0T IR0
Phone: 250-557-4217;
Toll free: 1-800-668-7544
Fax: 250-557-4216
Email: info@langara.com
Website: <www.langara.com>
Units: One cabin for up to 8 guests.
            Floating accommodation sleeps 10.
Rates: $2,395-$2,995 (3-, 4- and 5-day all-inclusive packages)

Special Features: Bike and kayak rentals, heli-tours to remote island locations. Optional packages upon request.

Kumdis River Lodge offers a true get-away-from-it-all experience. Located on the historic site of Graham Centre, the lodge is tucked away by itself, hidden along the shoreline of Masset Inlet. From this home base you can fish numerous lakes, rivers and estuaries for cutthroat, Dollies and some of the best steelhead anywhere. All fishing packages include airfare from Vancouver, full meals, great accommodation, guides, equipment and, of course, transportation to choice fishing spots.

Guest Comments: Wonderful environment. So peaceful. Well-stocked kitchen, a taste of huckleberries and then the hot tub!

CAMPING

Numerous private, provincial and forestry campgrounds are located throughout the two largest islands. Most are listed below. Forest recreation sites are free. Fees are collected seasonally at provincial sites, but year-round at private sites. Although there are no organized campsites within Gwaii Haanas National Park Reserve and Haida Heritage Site, fees are still collected for both day use or extended trips.

If you intend to travel within Gwaii Haanas National Park Reserve and Haida Heritage Site for longer than a day, you can choose your own site in most places. Any beach that looks suitable can be used as a campsite, except those in sensitive cultural or bird-nesting areas. Camping is not allowed on SGang Gwaay (Anthony Island), Gandll K'in Gwaayaay (Hotspring Island), House, Rankine, East Copper, Bolkus and Slug islands, or at Cumshewa, K'uuna llnagaay (Skedans) and T'aanuu llnagaay (Tanu) village sites. Burnaby Narrows is also closed due to the high possibility of interacting with the local black bear population. Each year the park reserve has seasonal or sporadic closures which visitors are informed of at their orientation. Be sure to ask at the Gwaii Haanas orientation for closures in other, less well-known areas (see "Planning Your Trip" for orientation information).

Where there are no services, backcountry campsite etiquette naturally applies: pack out your garbage, bury all sewage below high tide, light fires below the high-tide line and leave your site as clean or cleaner than you found it. Only your footprints should give away your overnight location!

Moresby Island

Moresby Camp Forest Rec Site	6 sites
Mosquito Lake Forest Rec Site	11 sites
Gray Bay Forest Rec Site	20 sites
Sheldens Bay Forest Rec Site	4 sites
501 RV/tent Park (private)	15 sites

Graham Island: Village of Queen Charlotte and area

Joy's Camping (private)	15 sites
Haydn Turner (Lions Club)	15 sites
Kagan Bay Forest Rec Site	6 sites
Rennell Sound/Cone Head Forest Rec Sites	10 sites

Graham Island: Tlell area north to Masset and Tow Hill

Misty Meadows Provincial Campground (Tlell)	40 sites
Sunset Park and Interpretive Trail (Port Clements)	10 sites
Hidden Island Resort RV Park and Campground (Masset)	22 sites
Agate Beach Provincial Campground	41 sites

13

PLANNING YOUR TRIP

TRANSPORTATION AND TRAVEL

ON THE WATER

BC Ferries' MV *Queen of Prince Rupert* crosses Hecate Strait four times a week (less frequently in winter) from Prince Rupert on B.C.'s northern mainland.

The crossing takes six to eight hours on daylight cruises, depending on marine conditions. Staterooms, dayrooms, cafeteria and a video lounge are provided. The ship docks at Skidegate Landing on Graham Island. A smaller, open-deck ferry, MV *Kwuna*, shuttles vehicles back and forth between Graham and Moresby Island. A schedule is posted at both landings.

A water taxi crosses Skidegate Inlet after ferry hours. Kayak rentals are available at Spruce Point Lodge (see "Bed and Breakfasts" section of Overnighting on Haida Gwaii).

BC Ferries
For information, call toll free from within B.C.: 1-888-223-3779
From outside B.C., call 1-250-386-3431
Website: <www.bcferries.bc.ca>

IN THE AIR

Three companies provide scheduled service from Vancouver to Haida Gwaii. There is a regular floatplane service from Prince Rupert that serves both island airports and the Village of Queen Charlotte. A private airline with fixed-wing airplanes is based at the Village of Queen Charlotte and there is also one helicopter company based at Sandspit Airport.

Vancouver to Haida Gwaii (serving Sandspit Airport):

Air Canada Jazz	**Hawkair**
1-888-247-2262	1-250-624-4295
	Toll Free: 1-800-487-1216
Website: <www.aircanada.com>	Website: <www.hawkair.ca>

Vancouver to Haida Gwaii (serving Masset Airport):

Pacific Coastal Air
1-800-663-2872
Website: <www.pacificcoastal.com>

Prince Rupert to Haida Gwaii (serving Sandspit and Masset airports, Village of Queen Charlotte):

North Pacific Seaplanes
PO Box 99, Prince Rupert, BC V8J 3P4
Phone: 1-800-689-4234
Seal Cove Seaplane base, Prince Rupert
Website: <www.northpacificseaplanes.com>

Serving inter-island locations:

South Moresby Air Charters
Box 969, Village of Queen Charlotte, BC V0T 1S0
Phone: 250-559-4222 Fax: 250-559-4223
Toll Free: 1-888-551-4222
Email: info@smair.com
Website: <www.smair.com>

Vancouver Island Helicopters
Box 333, Sandspit, BC V0T 1T0
Phone: 250-637-5344
Website: <www.vih.com>

ON LAND

A minivan meets all scheduled flights at Sandspit and transports passengers between the airport and the Village of Queen Charlotte. Cars and trucks can be rented in Sandspit, the Village of Queen Charlotte and Masset. Taxis are available in the Village of Queen Charlotte and Masset.

Hitchhikers usually succeed in getting a ride on most paved roads. On logging roads, you had better keep a book handy. Reaching some of the locations described in this book means travelling on private, gravel-surface back roads owned by logging companies. These all-weather roads are usually well maintained and open to the public. Information on logging activity and company maps can be obtained from their local offices.

On Graham Island contact Western Forest Products; on Moresby Island, contact the Teal-Jones Group. It is advisable to stop at these offices on weekdays to ask about current logging activity.

Western Forest Products
Queen Charlotte Division,
Box 10, Juskatla, BC V0T 1J0
Phone: 250-557-6825

Teal-Jones Group, Sandspit Ltd.
453 Aliford Bay Road, Sandspit, BC V0T 1T0
May-September, phone: 637-5362
October–April, phone: 250-637-5323, ext. 4

Follow the companies' instructions carefully. Off-highway trucks bearing loads larger than those hauled by most semi-trailers use these roads. Unexpectedly meeting a loaded logging truck on a tight curve can be a heart-thumping experience. Always drive with your headlights on. Never venture onto private logging roads during working hours without prior permission. After receiving the OK to proceed, follow all directional signs.

CHARTERING AND TOURS

Visitors who want to explore isolated areas may need to charter a plane, helicopter or boat to help take them to their destination. If you have your own small boat, a one-way charter is worth considering. Split among a group, a charter is relatively inexpensive and not that difficult to organize.

FLYING

Chartering an aircraft is a simple enough task, but you will need to be well organized before making a reservation. You must have the weight of each group member plus all your personal gear, folding kayak, paddles and miscellaneous items. You must also know your desired destination, alternate sites and whether you plan to make additional stops en route. Once you have all the necessary information, make your call to the airlines.

Charter rates are determined by the hour or by the distance flown, not by the number of occupied seats. Expect additional charges for any landings en route to your final destination. It will probably be cheaper if your pilot can pick up a second party for the return flight rather than flying back empty. Smaller airlines might be willing to arrange this, but you may have to be flexible on your departure times.

Two of the larger airplanes available in the Charlottes are the de Havilland Beaver and the de Havilland single-turbine Otter. Beavers can carry 453 kg, or 4 passengers and gear. The turbine Otters can carry 816 kg, or 10 passengers. One party had no trouble loading the turbine Otter with 6 passengers and 136 kg of gear, then flying directly to Rose Harbour.

Helicopters (also chartered on an hourly rate) can't carry such heavy loads, but can get you into places where fixed-wing craft can't land. The company at Sandspit usually has fixed tour itineraries and prices. Helicopters are great for a short flight but keep in mind you will be restricted to the amount of gear you can take with you. Nevertheless, what a great way to fly!

Keep in mind a few additional things when flying. There are restrictions as to where aircraft can land in Gwaii Haanas National Park Reserve and Haida Heritage Site. For instance, aircraft are not permitted to land at cultural sites such as SGang Gwaay but can touch down in nearby Rose Harbour or Louscoone Inlet.

Aircraft can also carry outboard motors and fuel. If you need to have such equipment transported, then gasoline must be in approved containers and motors drained of fuel to prevent vaporization into the cabin. Most airlines have special conditions related to hazardous cargo, so be sure to get clearance well ahead of your departure time.

Most importantly, safety is always stressed while in and around aircraft. Your pilot will help you enter the plane, show you your seat and make sure you are buckled in. The pilots fly throughout Haida Gwaii year-round and, more than anyone, they know that weather may delay arrivals or departures. Check in early, but be prepared to wait if conditions prevent you from taking off. It is also possible your flight will be delayed due to fog or heavy seas at your rendezvous point. Be certain to have a contingency plan in place and go over this with your pilot before departing. Delays of a day or so have occurred in the past. You would be wise to carry extra rations for such an event.

Airlines servicing Haida Gwaii are listed in this section.

BOATING

Chartering a boat to go fishing, scuba diving or touring for the day is a relatively simple and safe venture. Numerous islanders specialize in this service. Some have been guiding for years—others not so long. Increased tourism has resulted in improved service over the years, but you should still shop around and compare what you get with what you pay.

For both fishing charters and adventure tours, inspect your prospective vessel beforehand, noting safety equipment and level of maintenance. Ask how long the owners have been in business and how familiar they are with the waters surrounding Haida Gwaii. It's also worthwhile finding out whether the company is insured, and under what conditions a refund would be granted.

Those wishing to tackle a scrappy coho or monster halibut will need to have a fishing licence. Ask your guide if they issue them, or where you can get one easily. Guides provide you with a rod and reel, but we suggest you inquire about extras such as rain gear, food and refreshments. You should also ask about having your fish processed and sent on to a desired location. If you want to take a side trip—perhaps to an old village

If your trip to Haida Gwaii includes a boat trip, pack rain gear and sunscreen. May is the month with the highest average of sunny days.

site—you will need to make this arrangement ahead of time. Your guide may need to get permits in order to go ashore at ancient Haida sites.

Adventurers wanting to transport their kayaks, zodiacs and related gear to locations such as the west coast or Gwaii Haanas may require a longer charter. If you or your group need an extended trip, ask whether food costs are included, who prepares the meals and what kind of menu can be expected. In one of our charters, there was an "extra" passenger aboard, which was not made known to us. This made a difference when it came to sleeping arrangements. We also needed to make an extra stop to stash food and fuel before reaching Rose Harbour. Fortunately, we made this request to our skipper ahead of time. He helped us pick our hideaway and, upon arrival, we quickly paddled ashore with little wasted time.

Similar inquiries will help you select an organized tour operator. Several companies, both on and off Haida Gwaii, lead tours throughout the islands every summer. If possible, request the company's literature before booking. In addition to the questions noted above, ask whether expert guides will be along, what the guide-to-participant ratio is, and what your sleeping quarters will be. Unexpectedly having to share a cabin with a fellow shipmate may result in unwanted stress.

We recommend you first contact the Visitor Centre in the Village of Queen Charlotte. They will have a current list of who is leading both fishing charters and adventure tours. They can be reached by phone at 1-250-559-8316. You can also visit their website <www.qcinfo.ca> and follow the links to fishing and diving charters, or land tours and adventures. Travel agents, major newspapers and outdoor magazines often list Haida Gwaii fishing and adventure tours.

Adventure holidays aboard a chartered vessel can provide a memorable lifetime experience—but remember—you'll be further ahead if you check your options long before you check your bags!

NAVIGATION AND SAFETY

The sea poses a constant challenge to all boaters, regardless of the size of vessel you're travelling in. Wind is usually considered to be the greatest hazard: it can come up suddenly, blow powerfully and not die down for days. Waves, swells, tides and currents may also present challenges, particularly if you are forced to paddle or motor against them. The best rule of marine safety is to obtain the latest weather information, equip yourself with charts, VHF radio, GPS and onboard survival gear, then be prepared for anything.

A wise first step is to obtain a portable VHF radio, readily available in marine supply or electronics shops. For safety, emergencies and convenience, anyone travelling into Gwaii Haanas or other remote parts of the islands should be equipped with one. Before starting your trip, become familiar with how to use it to both receive and transmit. In addition to using it to obtain regular weather reports, you can use the radio in an emergency to contact the Coast Guard, or nearby mariners, on channel 16. You will also need one to contact Haida watchmen before landing at villages or other cultural locations where they are posted.

Some people like to carry an altimeter—a barometer that indicates changes in atmospheric pressure. For reference purposes, the pressure at the centre of a very deep low will be about 950 millibars (mb). The centre of a very strong high will read about 1035 mb.

Before launching our boat, we always check to make sure our marine charts were with us. Unlike topographic maps, marine charts mark navigational aids, current flows and marine hazards. They measure depths in fathoms, which will assist in finding suitable anchorages. Depths are recorded during tidal lows, enabling predictable passage through shallow areas. These charts are indispensable—don't leave your camp without them!

A compact method of keeping them dry in an open boat is to seal two maps back-to-back within plastic. Commercial laminators can do this, or do-it-yourselfers sometimes use clear Mactac or a paint-on coating. Handy clear plastic sleeves are also sold in many outdoor stores.

Tide tables are just as important as charts. Published annually by the Department of Fisheries and Oceans, they list the height and time of high and low tides each day. The closest measuring station to Haida Gwaii is Prince Rupert on the mainland. Since tides reach Prince Rupert ahead of the islands, add one hour for Skidegate Inlet and two hours for Masset Inlet. Add another hour during Pacific Daylight Saving Time, in effect from April through October. If you wish to buy tide tables or charts before arriving on the islands, a list for all the areas mentioned in this book is listed at the end of this section.

We further recommend you obtain a copy of *Exploring the North Coast of British Columbia* by Don Douglass. For boaters unfamiliar with the islands, this book provides detailed maritime information for the most visited areas of southern Haida Gwaii. *Boat Camping Haida Gwaii* by Neil Frazer goes one step further by covering many marine locations around Graham and Moresby Island. His main focus is pointing out camping spots for kayakers and small boaters, but he also includes helpful navigation and safety information.

Even if visitors in small boats plan to stay within the protected channels of Moresby Island, they should always bring along extra supplies in the event they find themselves wet, weather-bound or exhausted. Extra food and clothing alone can be a lifesaver; either for you or some unfortunate fellow explorers.

Before heading into remote areas, it is advisable to file a sail plan with a reliable family member or friend. If you miss your return date, it is nice to know that someone will be watching for you and can contact the Coast Guard on your behalf. The Coast Guard can be reached by calling 1-800-567-5111. Be certain to contact your family or friends immediately upon your return, or you may cause much grief, not to mention unnecessary search-and-rescue costs.

Tide tables and charts are available in most sporting goods and marine supply stores, on the Internet or can be mail-ordered from:

Canadian Hydrographic Service, Chart Distribution & Sales
Box 6000, Sidney, BC V8L 4B2
9860 W. Saanich Rd.
Phone: 250-356-6358   Fax: 250-363-6841
Email: chartsales@pac.dfo-mpo.gc.ca

Tide tables covering Haida Gwaii are found in the *Canadian Tide and Current Tables, Volume 6: Barkley Sound and Discovery Passage to Dixon Entrance.* Tide tables can also be found online by visiting a link to the Fisheries and Oceans website at: <www.waterlevels.gc.ca>.

The marine chart reference numbers for the marine areas mentioned in this book are as follows:

Masset Area
Dixon Entrance 3802
Masset Sound and Inlet 3805
Plans–Dixon Entrance 3895
Port Luis to Langara Island 3868
Masset Harbour and Naden Harbour 3892

Skidegate Area
Skidegate Inlet and Channel 3806
Skidegate Channel to Tain Rock (Rennell Sound) 3869

Gwaii Haanas National Park Reserve and Haida Heritage Site
Cape St. James/Cumshewa Inlet/Tasu Sound* 3853
Houston Stewart Channel 3855
Juan Perez Sound 3808
Carpenter Bay–Burnaby Island 3809
Houston Stewart Channel/Cape St. James 3825
Lawn Hill–Selwyn Inlet 3894
Atli Inlet–Selwyn Inlet 3807

* *This chart is helpful but inadequate for navigation purposes as the scale is too small.*

MUSEUMS

For one of the best introductions to life on the islands, visit the Haida Gwaii Museum at Skidegate. A showpiece for small museums, it is built on a rocky point overlooking Skidegate Inlet. (From the deck you can spot migrating gray whales in spring.) Inside the cedar building are displays of Native art, poles, natural history and European settlement.

The collection is attractively laid out and easy to view. You may also want to check out their selection of books pertaining to Haida or pioneering history. The museum is open every day during the summer but closed Sunday and Monday during the winter. Hours are posted outside and there is a small entrance fee.

Port Clements' museum focuses on logging, commercial fishing, homesteading and farming equipment. Though open year-round, check for times listed outside the front door. If you arrive outside of scheduled openings, feel free to look at the antiquated logging machinery on the outside grounds. Some of these pieces date back to the 1930s.

The Dixon Entrance Maritime Museum, located at the north end of Masset, boasts an impressive collection of maritime and pioneer artifacts. The cream-coloured building is a museum piece in itself: it was Masset's first hospital. Parents with children will enjoy coming here: eager young fingers are welcome to touch virtually anything they like! An added bonus is that persons under 16 are admitted free.

Although not a museum, the displays and photographs in Sandspit Airport are certainly worth a close look.

An exciting Haida cultural complex—the Qay'llnagaay Heritage Centre—is scheduled for opening in 2007. It will be located adjacent to the Haida Gwaii Museum. Although still in the construction phase as this guide goes to print, it promises to be a cultural and artistic complex unlike anything else in Canada.

PERMITS FOR HAIDA RESERVES

You must obtain permission from the appropriate band office before entering ancient Haida villages. The village council office in Old Massett governs sites on the northern sections; phone: 250-626-3337 or fax: 250-626-5440. The Gwaii Haanas National Park Reserve and Haida Heritage Site administers most villages in the southern parts of the islands. It can be reached at 250-559-8818. The Skidegate Band Council monitors southern villages outside of Gwaii Haanas and can be reached at 250-559-4496.

You must radio ahead before landing at any village sites in Gwaii Haanas. The number of visitors ashore at any time is limited.

You must make a reservation in advance before independently visiting any Haida cultural sites in Gwaii Haanas National Park Reserve and Haida Heritage Site. This includes K̲'uuna llnagaay (formerly Skedans) on Louise Island. Further details are described below.

ORIENTATION AND RESERVATIONS FOR GWAII HAANAS NATIONAL PARK RESERVE AND HAIDA HERITAGE SITE

Visitors not booked with tour companies to Gwaii Haanas must make advance reservations, or take a chance for a standby spot. Those who are booked with tour companies may not need reservations. Advance reservations can be made by calling Super Natural British Columbia's toll-free number, 1-800-HELLOBC (1-800-435-5622). In the Greater Vancouver area, call 604-435-5622. For anyone living outside of North America, call 1-250-387-1642. If you choose not to make an advance reservation, only six standby spots are awarded each day on a first-come, first-served basis at the Village of Queen Charlotte Visitor Centre.

All independent visitors entering Gwaii Haanas or K̲'uuna llnagaay (Skedans) for the first time must attend an orientation. These sessions take about 90 minutes. Presenters will show an enjoyable movie and discuss topics relevant to travelling in the park reserve. When the orientation is over, your name will be registered on the park's computer and kept on file for three years, during which you need only register and make reservations for subsequent visits. After three years, you must attend another orientation.

Boaters entering Gwaii Haanas from the south must also make advance reservations. An orientation can be done over the phone and a video will be mailed out to you. All other orientations are held at either the Visitor Centre in the Village of Queen Charlotte or in the Sandspit Visitor Centre (at Sandspit Airport). (Note: Orientations are expected to move from the Village of Queen Charlotte Visitor Centre to the new Qay'llnagaay Heritage Centre when it opens in 2007.)

Scheduled times for orientations are:
June:
Queen Charlotte Visitor Centre, Monday to Friday: 11:00 a.m.
Sandspit Airport (beginning June 19), Monday to Friday: 3:00 p.m.
July 1 to August 13:
Queen Charlotte Visitor Centre, daily: 11:00 a.m.
Sandspit Airport, daily: 3:00 p.m.
August 14 to September 1:
Queen Charlotte Visitor Centre, Monday to Friday: 11:00 a.m.

Orientation sessions may also be booked individually outside of scheduled times, but within normal working hours. The centre will try to accommodate you, provided they have at least 24 hours' notice and available staff. Sessions sceduled outside of normal hours cost $75.

When making plane or ferry reservations, plan to arrive 24 hours prior to your departure for Gwaii Haanas to be certain you have time to attend the orientation.

Commercial tour operators may offer the orientation as part of their customer service. Be sure to ask them for this in writing and, to be on the safe side, plan your arrival so there's enough time to participate in an orientation if necessary.

Reservations and orientation sessions are subject to changes at short notice. We suggest you call the following numbers to confirm dates and times.

For the latest information, contact:

The Superintendent
Gwaii Haanas National Park Reserve and Haida Heritage Site
Box 37, Village of Queen Charlotte, BC V0T 1S0
Phone: 250-559-8818/Fax: 250-559-8366
Email: gwaii.haanas@pc.gc.ca
Website: <www.pc.gc.ca/gwaiihaanas>

or:

Village of Queen Charlotte Visitor Centre
P.O. Box 819, 3220 Wharf St.,
Village of Queen Charlotte, BC V0T 1S0
Phone: 250-559-8316
Fax: 250-559-8952
Email: info@qcinfo.ca
Website: <www.qcinfo.ca>

There are no stores or public services in the Gwaii Haanas region. Plan your meals carefully and have extra supplies in case you are weather-bound.

COMMUNITIES AND FACILITIES

There are eight communities on the islands today: Old Massett, Masset, Port Clements, Tlell, Skidegate, Skidegate Landing, the Village of Queen Charlotte on Graham Island and Sandspit on Moresby Island.

If you're not travelling with an organized tour, most of the things you might need are available in one or more of these communities. Prices are naturally higher than they might be back home. In fairness, however, a day on the Charlottes will probably cost you a lot less than a day at West Edmonton Mall.

Local businesses welcome the influx of tourists, but their variety and quantity of supplies are limited by shipping costs and retail space. If you can't find what you're looking for, don't be afraid to ask. Some stores and attractions have no signs, because the people who live here know where things are.

The Village of Queen Charlotte, Sandspit and Masset all have modern docking facilities for small craft. As with most marinas, it's best to call ahead to reserve a berth.

FACILITIES TO BE FOUND IN EACH COMMUNITY

Old Massett
- ❖ Gift and artist shops
- ❖ Village office
- ❖ Automotive fuel
- ❖ Internet café
- ❖ Convenience store

Masset
- ❖ Scheduled seaplane service daily
- ❖ Vehicle rentals and taxi service
- ❖ Marine and automotive fuels, parts and services
- ❖ Government pier and floats
- ❖ Boat ramp at seaplane base
- ❖ Motel, cabin and B&B accommodation
- ❖ RV park with showers and hookups
- ❖ Sani-dump and car wash at Visitor Centre
- ❖ Restaurants, pub and grocery stores
- ❖ Laundromat, pharmacy, liquor store, credit union
- ❖ Hospital and public health nurse
- ❖ Royal Canadian Mounted Police
- ❖ Nine-hole golf course
- ❖ Fishing guides, licences and tackle
- ❖ Airport
- ❖ Library
- ❖ Maritime Museum
- ❖ Royal Canadian Legion
- ❖ Delkatla Interpretive Centre
- ❖ Sightseeing and cultural tours
- ❖ Indoor swimming pool

Port Clements
- ❖ Automotive fuels and parts
- ❖ Government pier and float, boat ramp
- ❖ Motel with laundromat
- ❖ Sani-station
- ❖ Grocery store with liquor sales
- ❖ Licensed restaurant and pub
- ❖ B&B
- ❖ Gift shops
- ❖ Post office
- ❖ Library
- ❖ Pioneer and logging museum
- ❖ Campground and interpretive trail, wildlife viewing

Tlell
- ❖ Provincial park campground and headquarters
- ❖ Lodge, B&B
- ❖ Gift and craft shops, farm and country store

- ❖ Take-out restaurant
- ❖ Laundromat
- ❖ Post office, fishing licences

Skidegate area
- ❖ Scheduled ferry service
- ❖ Water and road taxi service
- ❖ Boat ramp and boat charters
- ❖ Automotive fuels
- ❖ B&B
- ❖ Grocery store, marine and fishing supplies
- ❖ Haida Gwaii Museum
- ❖ Sightseeing and cultural tours
- ❖ Gift and artist shops

Village of Queen Charlotte
- ❖ Vehicle rentals
- ❖ Taxi service
- ❖ Automotive fuels, parts and service
- ❖ Government wharf and floats
- ❖ Hotel, motel and B&B
- ❖ Campgrounds
- ❖ Restaurants and grocery stores
- ❖ Laundromat, pharmacy, liquor store and credit union
- ❖ Hospital and public health nurse
- ❖ Royal Canadian Mounted Police
- ❖ Boat charters and rentals
- ❖ Gift shops
- ❖ Travel agent
- ❖ Library
- ❖ Provincial and federal government offices
- ❖ Seaplane charters

Sandspit
- ❖ Airport with scheduled daily flights and charters
- ❖ Helicopter and seaplane charters
- ❖ Vehicle rental, fuel and parts
- ❖ Small-craft harbour
- ❖ Government pier and boat ramp
- ❖ Hotel, motel, lodge and B&B accommodation
- ❖ RV park
- ❖ Restaurants and lounge
- ❖ Grocery stores, one with liquor sales
- ❖ Outdoor supplies and licences
- ❖ Hunting and fishing guides
- ❖ Nine-hole golf course
- ❖ Library
- ❖ Health clinic

EMERGENCY SERVICES

In case of emergency, here are the phone numbers for the police, the hospitals on the islands, and the Coast Guard station in Prince Rupert.

RCMP
Masset area and Port Clements: 250-626-3991
Village of Queen Charlotte and Sandspit: 250-559-4421

Hospitals
Masset: 250-626-4700; emergency: 250-626-4711
Village of Queen Charlotte: 250-559-4300; emergency:
  250-559-4506
Sandspit Clinic: 250-637-5403

Prince Rupert Coast Guard
Air and marine emergencies: 1-800-567-5111

Helicopters and fixed-wing aircraft service the islands and connect with Prince Rupert or Vancouver on the mainland.

CLIMATE AND CLOTHING

The climate of Haida Gwaii is extremely variable. The Queen Charlotte Mountains attain elevations of 1,050 metres—high enough to disrupt tumultuous storm clouds driven in by offshore winds. Coastal areas near the mountains can be particularly windy and wet, while just a few kilometres inland the wind tapers off, the air temperature rises and rainfall is significantly less. This rain-shadow effect is most noticeable on Graham Island, disappearing altogether where the land narrows toward southern Moresby Island. Less than 1 percent of Canada experiences this unusual blend of oceanic storms, cloudy skies, cool summers and relatively mild, wet winters.

Overall, weather on the islands has two patterns. From mid-May until September, prevailing winds blow from the northwest. In late September, a new system begins to form in the Gulf of Alaska, and the wind blows from the southeast for the rest of winter. Storms are worst from October to January. Cape St. James, the windiest place in Canada, bears the brunt of this force (average wind speed over the past 26 years has been 37.7 km/h).

Rainfall measurements here do not set national records but they are impressive. The average annual precipitation of 4,218 millimetres at Tasu on the west coast makes it the wettest spot on Haida Gwaii. The east-coast communities overall receive less than a quarter of the rain that the west coast experiences. May, June and July are the driest months. Tlell and Sandspit are recorded as the driest (and the warmest) places on the islands.

Although we encountered some weird weather on some of our summer trips to Haida Gwaii, it was nothing we couldn't handle. In anticipation of at least one rainy day, a rain jacket with a hood was always included. We also packed

If you plan on tenting, make sure you have a water-repellent fly. In the summer, rain squalls are often followed by sunny breaks. Wet clothing dries quickly when hung on a tree or clothesline.

toques, gloves and pullover fleeces, which occasionally came in handy. Rubber boots, intended for beach and bog walks, were appreciated if it rained when we were camping. Numerous residents told us, "If you don't like the weather, then wait five minutes and it will change." This proved correct on most of our trips.

CYCLING ON HAIDA GWAII

Cycling has to be one of the nicest ways to explore Haida Gwaii. Whether you are cycling the highway from Skidegate Landing to Tlell, riding the sandy expanse of North Beach or mountain biking the island railbeds, you will have unique experiences. The hardest decision may be what kind of bike to bring along; the trusty tourer or the rugged mountain bike.

TOURING

Probably the cheapest way to go! BC Ferries has very low rates for cyclists, and your bicycle travels free aboard MV *Kwuna*, the ferry that crosses Skidegate Inlet. The roads connecting Sandspit, the Village of Queen Charlotte, Skidegate, as well as north to Tlell, Port Clements, Masset and Old Massett, all have asphalt surfaces. Visiting any other island location, however, means travelling on gravel roads.

Cycling on Haida Gwaii is very enjoyable, especially along North Beach. Carry an extra backpack to hold beach treasures. You might have to use fresh water to rinse off sand and salt.

Newly arrived cyclists tend to spend their first evening near the Village of Queen Charlotte. B&Bs, motels and a few campgrounds are close by. The next day is usually spent around town or riding to Tlell, about 41 km north along Yellowhead Highway (#16). It is 21 km farther to Port Clements, and an additional 40 km to reach Masset. Some cyclists leave their bikes in Masset and catch a ride to North Beach; others choose to tackle an additional 25 km of mostly gravel road.

Cycling time between the communities varies according to the rider and the weather conditions. You can expect hard rain and strong winds, even during summer months. Make sure your bike is in excellent condition, and carry an emergency repair kit. Bicycle service is almost non-existent here, and stores carry very few parts.

MOUNTAIN BIKING

On almost all our trips to Haida Gwaii, we took our mountain bikes along. Our main purpose was to ride the North Beach (Hiellen River toward Rose Spit), almost 10 km of hard, smooth sand that is suitable for bikers of every age and ability. This is an excellent way to beachcomb and explore this section of Naikoon Provincial Park. Be extra careful to keep the sand out of your gears and chain. Afterwards, you can wash your bike with tap water in Agate Beach Campground.

Recently, several biking enthusiasts have promoted a route that leads to the abandoned Aero logging camp on Cumshewa Inlet. If you like a more challenging ride, this is an excellent way to view this area, which has the only railroad system built on the Charlottes.

The trail begins at Skidegate Lake trestle, 4 km east of the Moresby Camp turnoff. It heads south on the old railbed, then follows some logging roads. The initial portions of the trail are suitable for most riders. As you approach Aero, you may have to dismount for fallen trees, or possibly wait for the tide to drop. Explore the rusty remains of Aero on foot.

Most riders should return via the same route; only very experienced and hardy individuals should attempt the "loop" via Allison Lake. This stretch is bumpy, with numerous ravines, deadfall and half-buried rail ties. The entire loop is about 25 km; four hours should be ample time for most bikers to ride the rails.

FISHING

The waters surrounding these islands supply the traditional protein source for islanders, offering, as they do, the very best in fresh seafood. The rod-and-reel recreation is renowned: access is easy and the fish are abundant. In recent years, however, salmon fishing has come under such immense pressure that closures are now common in all B.C. coastal areas. Be sure to consult the latest fishing regulations before wetting your line.

Fishing can be divided into lake, stream and saltwater categories. Steelhead, salmon and halibut are of greatest interest to most anglers, but rockfish and cod also live in the waters around Haida Gwaii. On the freshwater side, there are rainbow and cutthroat trout as well as Dolly Varden char in most streams and lakes. Small boats can be launched at Mayer Lake in Naikoon Park, and at Mosquito and Skidegate lakes on Moresby Island. The latter two offer trout up to 1.4 kg and Dolly Varden weighing in at 0.5 kg. If you lack a boat, you can still dangle your line along the lakeshore or head to the nearest river and cast for steelhead or sea-run trout.

Former U.S. president Jimmy Carter includes a chapter on Moresby fishing in his book *An Outdoor Journal* describing his steelhead experiences and heralding this fishing as among the best in North America. The season for these fighting fish starts in November, climaxes during the Christmas holidays then declines toward spring. The timing of the runs varies somewhat from river to river, and techniques vary according to the angler and the nature of the water. The Yakoun and Tlell rivers on Graham Island, and Pallant Creek on Moresby Island, are among the best producers.

Mid-September is when coho salmon aficionados arrive for stream fishing, so accommodation and vehicle rentals can be scarce at that time of year. Coho return to fresh water when fall rains raise river levels to a point where the fish can swim up from the ocean to spawn. The Tlell, Yakoun, Copper and Deena rivers offer good water. Since their stream gradients are low, they have tidal action as far as one kilometre upstream. Check for triangular markers indicating the boundary of tidal fishing. Here, as throughout B.C., separate fishing licences are required for salt and fresh water.

Saltwater fishing is a year-round activity if you can tolerate the winter weather. We detailed some specific locales earlier in the sections on Tow Hill, Langara Island, Louise Island and Skidegate Inlet.

There is great fishing for salmon and bottom fish in many other locations as well. Bottom fish include halibut (easily as desirable as salmon from a culinary point of view), ling cod and red snapper. These species can be caught by jigging on simple handlines: reef raiders and buzz bombs are popular lures. Bottom fish aren't always that easily caught, and you really have to know what you're doing to land a large halibut. Counting on fresh fish for an expedition menu has meant going hungry for more than a few intrepid travellers.

In the last decade, numerous floating lodges, land lodges and roaming ships have attracted fly-in clients for extended saltwater fishing. Most of these fancy facilities are on the west and north coasts of Graham Island. Coho and spring salmon are the major attractions, but halibut is also high on the list. All bookings must be made in advance through companies in Victoria or Vancouver. Consult the *Saltwater Fishing Guide* (free from almost any fishing store) for their locations, or look in recent fishing magazines for their ads. Inquire locally for the names of people who have smaller boats available for casual charter fishing. The Village of Queen Charlotte website lists local charter operators. Log on at <www.qcinfo.ca> then click on "great adventures," then on "fishing and diving charters."

If you don't have a boat or the budget for a guide, you can still catch saltwater fish from shore. Surf-casters have brought in halibut from the rocks at the foot of Tow Hill in Naikoon Park, although there's an equal chance of landing dogfish—a small, undesirable shark. Other anglers report success catching young coho and pink salmon from the spit at Sandspit, from southside beaches in Skidegate Inlet and in Rennell Sound.

Once spawning starts, the local salmon derby gets underway as salmon begin to concentrate at the mouths of their home streams. On the four September weekends each year, the Sandspit Rod and Gun Club sponsors a coho derby. To be eligible, fish must be caught between Gray Bay and the Deena River on Moresby Island. The coho, though much smaller than spring (also called king or chinook) salmon, has a reputation as the wildest fighter of the salmonid family. A fish in the 3- to 5-kg range can

Small boats are easily launched on both sides of Skidegate Inlet. This area is within the fishing boundaries of the annual Sandspit coho derby. There are prizes for kids as well as for competitive anglers.

create tremendous excitement when caught on light tackle. Many anglers concentrate on the Copper River estuary, where a sizeable encampment of the devoted suddenly appears during the derby. The competition is open to visitors and residents alike, and prizes are awarded in various categories. The largest coho caught is usually in the 9-kg range.

Saltwater fishing also includes shellfish, but as with finfish, you need a licence before you can set a crab trap or dig for razor clams. Remember that the islands are under a permanent closure for all other bivalves due to the paralyzing toxins found in some molluscs. Thankfully, shrimp, prawns and crabs aren't affected. Dungeness crabs are the favourite (or should we say "flavourite"?). A collapsible crab trap baited with any smelly fish or tinned meat should produce a cracking good meal off North Beach, in Naden Harbour or in Masset Inlet. The key is to find sandy ocean bottoms, preferably with eelgrass as cover for the crabs.

Licences and regulations are available from most sporting goods stores or the government agent's office in the Village of Queen Charlotte. We further recommend having a copy of *Fishing the Queen Charlotte Islands*, by former resident Bob Long (see "Further Reading"). His book has numerous maps giving away the best fishin' holes on the islands.

FISHING IN GWAII HAANAS NATIONAL PARK RESERVE AND HAIDA HERITAGE SITE

Limited saltwater fishing is allowed within the park reserve. During orientations or when registering for a visit, inquire about any current fishing closures. There is a permanent closure in all freshwater rivers, lakes and creeks. In addition, Rockfish Conservation Areas exist in two locations. One of these is in the waters north, south and east of SGang Gwaay (Anthony Island). The second is generally north, east and south of Lyell and Tanu Island, and throughout Crescent Inlet. Parks Canada or the Village of Queen Charlotte Visitor Centre can provide you with a map showing the exact boundaries of these two areas.

The harvesting of any bivalve shellfish is not permitted due to the high risk of Paralytic Shellfish Poisoning (PSP).

ON-THE-SPOT PREPARATION AND RECIPES FOR CRAB AND CLAMS

Please note: Fisheries and Oceans lists possession limits for both crab and clams. We hope you will respect these and take only what you can eat while visiting Haida Gwaii. When we visit, it's nice to know there will be some for us!

RAZOR CLAM PREPARATION

If possible, transport live clams in a bucket of seawater, in which clams tend to purge themselves of some sand. Cover the bottom of a large pot with 1.5 cm of salted water and bring to a boil. Place clams in pot, leave lid ajar and steam for 1 to 3 minutes until clams open. Remove and allow to cool. With a sharp knife, open the clams and remove all meat. Separate the foot and siphon from other body parts. Wash thoroughly to remove sand. Cut into small, tasty pieces.

CREAMY CAMPFIRE CHOWDER

2 cups of diced clams

1 medium onion, chopped

2 slices of bacon (cooked)

¼ cup of diced green pepper

1 cup diced potatoes

½ tsp salt and a dash of pepper (preferably cayenne)

¼ tsp thyme

2 cups of milk or tomato juice

In a clean pot, add all the ingredients with presteamed clams, stir until creamy and the vegetables are tender, then serve.

DUNGENESS CRAB PREPARATION

Transport live crabs in a bucket of seawater and keep them intact and submerged until you are ready to eat. For those unfamiliar with handling crabs, first place the live crab on its back and hit the underside dead centre with a rock or knife handle; the crab will die instantly. Next, grasp the legs and pincers in each hand, twisting first inwards and then out. The limbs will separate quite easily from the shell. Remove any of the remaining gills and rinse in seawater. Submerge crab legs in boiling salted water for about 15 to 20 minutes, depending on the size.

CAMPFIRE CRAB

After the crab is cooked, remove from the water, allow time to cool, then separate legs from main body. Break each leg at the joints, then crack open the covering with nutcrackers or a rock. Strong fingers can sometimes break the shell. A small fork can help remove meat from narrow sections.

Remove the white meat and enjoy. For added delight, dip morsels in melted butter, garlic butter or a seafood sauce. Crab can also be added to salad or used as a side dish with your main meal.

HUNTING

Possibly the first recreational hunter in the Charlottes was Charles Sheldon, who searched for Dawson caribou here in November 1906. He endured three weeks of ghastly weather in the unsuccessful pursuit of that now-extinct animal. Despite his failed quest, he writes with a keen interest in natural history, and his observations in *The Wilderness of the North Pacific Coast Islands* provide an interesting perspective on those times. (see "Further Reading")

Modern hunters like the Charlottes for their nine-month season and high limits on deer. Mule (Sitka) deer were originally introduced to provide islanders with a fresh meat source. With no natural predators on the islands, however, they soon became overabundant. Though relatively small, these deer are tender and flavourful. Hunting has reduced deer numbers near populated areas, but they are still plentiful on back roads. Their tolerance of people makes them particularly popular with bow hunters, although larger bucks are more cautious about showing themselves. Locals claim that deer hunting is most productive during the rut in November. When it snows, the animals will forage for kelp washed up on the beaches. At any time of year they can be found grazing in grassy meadows, along roadsides and in estuaries.

There is also limited hunting for a small elk herd that was introduced on Graham Island. Unlike their deer cousins, these animals have not expanded their numbers and rarely stray from their territory on the upper Tlell River watershed.

Black bear (*Ursus americanus*) tracks beside a 15-centimetre ruler. The skull measurements of the Charlotte subspecies are the largest on this continent. Bears can be expected on any island, so campers should always keep a clean campsite and store food beyond a bear's reach.

Hunters interested in black bears are attracted to the Charlottes by the trophy-sized animals taken here. The particular subspecies resident on the islands is the largest in North America. Hunters concentrate their search on the beaches and tidal estuaries of Moresby Island, where bears feed on crabs and grasses. In the fall, the bears feed along salmon streams. They are occasionally found on small islands, too, but these are poor locations to hunt. The question of continued hunting within Gwaii Haanas National Park Reserve and Haida Heritage Site is presently under review. All out-of-province big-game hunters are required to hire a licensed guide. Such guides live on the Charlottes; the Visitor Centre in the Village of Queen Charlotte can supply their names and contact numbers.

Some waterfowl hunting is permitted on the Charlottes as well, though not on a scale to warrant planning a trip exclusively for this purpose. Protected bays with large estuary flats are favoured habitat for Canada geese and ducks. These birds stage here when storms keep them off migration flights.

No hunting or discharge of firearms is permitted in Naikoon Provincial Park between April 1 and September 1. For more information, contact:

Village of Queen Charlotte Visitor Centre
P.O. Box 819, 3220 Wharf St.
Village of Queen Charlotte, BC V0T 1S0
Phone: 250-559-8316
Fax: 250-559-8952
Email: info@qcinfo.ca
Website: <www.qcinfo.ca>

or

Ministry of Environment's Conservation Officer Service
126 2nd Ave, Village of Queen Charlotte, BC V0T 1S0
Phone: 250-559-8431

THE FIVE-DAY GUIDE

Faced with so many intriguing options, tourists with a limited amount of time can be a bit overwhelmed trying to figure out how to make the most of their visit. One of the most frequent questions we hear from people planning their first trip is: "We're going to the Charlottes for few days. Where should we go?" The following day planner is designed to provide an overall perspective of the variety of shops, sights, beaches, restaurants and available accommodation. On your second visit, you will no doubt head straight for a favoured location. This planner assumes you will have five full days, are travelling in a motorized vehicle and are either camping or staying in a B&B.

- ❖ Disembark from the ferry and drive to either Misty Meadows Campground or a B&B.
- ❖ First morning: hike to *Pesuta* shipwreck or take the beach walk from Misty Meadows Campground. Afternoon: visit nearby gift shops.
- ❖ Second morning: tour Old Massett and Masset. Be sure to visit Haida gift shops. Afternoon: drive to Agate Beach Campground and Tow Hill. Hike to the top of Tow Hill.
- ❖ Third morning: drive to Skidegate Landing, take the ferry to Alliford Bay and Sandspit. Walk the short trail to Onward Point. Later, allow some time to view the displays in the Sandspit Airport. If you have additional time and a suitable vehicle, drive on to Gray Bay and perhaps Moresby Camp.
- ❖ Fourth morning: drive to the Village of Queen Charlotte. Visit Haida Gwaii Museum, Visitor Centre and local shops. If there's time, hike the Spirit Lake Trail, beginning at Skidegate Village.
- ❖ Fifth morning: head north to Port Clements and view the old blank canoe. Also drop by the pioneer museum or visit Sunset Park and Interpretive Trail. In the afternoon, tour Delkatla Wildlife Sanctuary in Masset. Before settling on the beach for a picnic dinner, drop by the Maritime Museum at the north end of Masset.
- ❖ Sixth morning: if you have good tires, drive to Rennell Sound. This will be your only glimpse of the west coast. Allow ample time to return to the Village of Queen Charlotte. Prepare to board the ferry in the evening.

USEFUL WEBSITES

Air Canada Jazz: <www.aircanada.com>

BC Ferries: <www.bcferries.ca> or <www.bcferries.bc.ca>

BC Parks: <www.env.gov.bc.ca/bcparks>

Hawkair: <www.hawkair.ca>

North Pacific Seaplanes: <www.northpacificseaplanes.com>

South Moresby Air Charters: <www.smair.com>

Parks Canada—Gwaii Haanas National Park Reserve and Haida Heritage
   Site: <www.pc.gc.ca/gwaiihaanas>

Village of Queen Charlotte Visitor Centre: <www.qcinfo.ca>

Weather Office: <www.weatheroffice.ec.gc.ca>

APPENDICES

APPENDIX 1: THE METRIC SYSTEM

In 1975 Canada began its conversion to the international method of measurement, the metric system. By 1984 most of us were using this standard, much to the confusion of our U.S. visitors and those Canadians who felt they were too old to bother learning new tricks. For the uninitiated, here are the abbreviations and conversions for the metric weights and measures that appear in this book.

METRIC CONVERSIONS

Weights and Measures (multiply by)

Miles to kilometres (km) 1.6
Kilometres to miles 0.6

Nautical miles to kilometres (km) 1.9
Kilometres to nautical miles 0.5

Feet to metres (m) 0.3
Metres to feet 3.3

Acres to hectares (ha) 0.4
Hectares to acres 2.5

Inches to centimetres (cm) 2.5
Centimetres to inches 0.4

Fathoms to metres (m) 1.8
Metres to fathoms 0.6

Gallons to litres (l) 4.6
Litres to gallons 0.2

Pounds to kilograms (kg) 0.5
Kilograms to pounds 2.2

Temperatures (follow formula below)
Fahrenheit to Celsius (C)
    subtract 32, multiply by ⅝

Celsius to Fahrenheit (F)
    multiply by ⅝, add 32

APPENDIX 2: BIRDS OF HAIDA GWAII

BR - Breeding SP - Spring SU - Summer AU - Autumn WI - Winter • - denotes breeding or occurence in season					
	BR	SP	SU	AU	WI
Red-throated loon	•	•	•	•	•
Pacific loon		•	•	•	•
Common loon	•	•	•	•	•
Yellow-billed loon		•	•	•	•
Pied-billed grebe	•	•	•	•	•
Horned grebe		•		•	•
Red-necked grebe		•	•	•	•
Eared grebe		•			
Western grebe		•	•	•	•
Laysan albatross		•	•	•	•
Black-footed albatross		•	•	•	•
Short-tailed albatross		•			•
Northern fulmar		•	•	•	•
Murphy's petrel			•		
Pink-footed shearwater		•	•	•	
Flesh-footed shearwater		•	•	•	
Buller's shearwater			•	•	
Sooty shearwater		•	•	•	•
Short-tailed shearwater		•	•	•	•
Manx shearwater			•	•	
Black-vented shearwater			•	•	
Fork-tailed storm-petrel	•	•	•	•	•
Leach's storm-petrel	•	•	•	•	•
Brandt's cormorant		•	•	•	•
Double-crested cormorant		•	•	•	•
Red-faced cormorant		•			
Pelagic cormorant	•	•	•	•	•
Magnificent frigatebird			•		
American bittern				•	•
Great blue heron	•	•	•	•	•
Great egret		•	•	•	
Cattle egret		•		•	
Greater white-fronted goose		•	•	•	•

	BR	SP	SU	AU	WI
Emperor goose		•		•	•
Snow goose		•	•	•	•
Ross's goose		•			
Canada goose	•	•	•	•	•
Brant		•	•	•	•
Trumpeter swan		•		•	•
Tundra swan		•	•	•	•
Wood duck				•	•
Gadwall		•	•	•	•
Eurasian wigeon		•		•	•
American wigeon		•	•	•	•
Mallard	•	•	•	•	•
Blue-winged teal	•	•	•		
Cinnamon teal		•			
Northern shoveler		•	•	•	•
Northern pintail	•	•	•	•	•
Baikal teal		•			
Green-winged teal	•	•	•	•	•
Canvasback		•	•	•	•
Redhead		•	•	•	•
Ring-necked duck		•		•	•
Tufted duck				•	
Greater scaup		•	•	•	•
Lesser scaup		•		•	•
Steller's eider				•	
Spectacled eider		•			
King eider		•	•	•	•
Common eider		•	•		
Harlequin duck	•	•	•	•	•
Surf scoter		•	•	•	•
White-winged scoter		•	•	•	•
Black scoter		•	•	•	•
Long-tailed duck		•	•	•	•
Bufflehead		•	•	•	•
Common goldeneye		•	•	•	•
Barrow's goldeneye	•	•	•	•	•
Hooded merganser	•	•	•	•	•

	BR	SP	SU	AU	WI
Common merganser	•	•	•	•	•
Red-breasted merganser	•	•	•	•	•
Ruddy duck				•	•
Osprey		•	•	•	
Bald eagle	•	•	•	•	•
Northern harrier		•		•	•
Sharp-shinned hawk	•	•	•	•	•
Northern goshawk	•	•	•	•	•
Red-tailed hawk	•	•	•	•	•
Rough-legged hawk				•	
American kestrel	•	•	•		
Merlin		•	•	•	•
Gyrfalcon				•	
Peregrine falcon	•	•	•	•	•
Rock ptarmigan		•			
Blue grouse	•	•	•	•	•
Virginia rail		•	•	•	•
Sora		•	•	•	
American coot		•	•	•	•
Sandhill crane	•	•	•	•	
Black-bellied plover		•	•	•	•
American golden-plover		•	•	•	•
Pacific golden-plover		•	•	•	•
Mongolian plover		•			
Snowy plover			•		
Semipalmated plover	•	•	•	•	•
Killdeer	•	•	•	•	•
Black oystercatcher	•	•	•	•	•
Greater yellowlegs		•	•	•	•
Lesser yellowlegs		•	•	•	•
Wood sandpiper				•	
Solitary sandpiper		•	•		
Wandering tattler		•	•	•	
Spotted sandpiper	•	•	•	•	
Upland sandpiper		•	•		
Whimbrel		•	•		
Hudsonian godwit		•	•		

	BR	SP	SU	AU	WI
Bar-tailed godwit		•	•		
Marbled godwit		•	•	•	•
Ruddy turnstone		•	•	•	•
Black turnstone		•	•	•	•
Surfbird		•	•	•	•
Red knot		•	•	•	
Sanderling		•	•	•	•
Semipalmated sandpiper		•	•		
Western sandpiper		•	•	•	
Red-necked stint			•		
Least sandpiper	•	•	•	•	•
White-rumped sandpiper		•			
Baird's sandpiper		•	•		
Pectoral sandpiper		•	•	•	
Sharp-tailed sandpiper			•	•	
Rock sandpiper		•	•	•	•
Dunlin		•	•	•	•
Curlew sandpiper			•		
Stilt sandpiper		•	•	•	
Buff-breasted sandpiper		•	•		
Ruff			•	•	
Short-billed dowitcher	•	•	•		
Long-billed dowitcher		•	•	•	•
Common snipe	•	•	•	•	•
Wilson's phalarope		•	•		
Red-necked phalarope		•	•	•	
Red phalarope		•	•	•	
South polar skua		•	•	•	
Pomarine jaeger		•	•	•	
Parasitic jaeger		•	•	•	
Long-tailed jaeger		•	•		
Franklin's gull		•	•		
Bonaparte's gull		•	•	•	
Heermann's gull		•			
Black-tailed gull				•	
Mew gull	•	•	•	•	•
Ring-billed gull		•	•	•	

	BR	SP	SU	AU	WI
California gull		•	•	•	•
Herring gull		•	•	•	•
Thayer's gull		•	•	•	•
Slaty-backed gull			•		
Western gull		•	•	•	•
Glaucous-winged gull	•	•	•	•	•
Glaucous gull		•	•	•	•
Sabine's gull		•	•	•	•
Black-legged kittiwake		•	•	•	•
Red-legged kittiwake					•
Caspian tern		•	•		
Arctic tern		•			
Aleutian tern		•	•		
Common murre	•	•	•	•	•
Thick-billed murre		•		•	•
Pigeon guillemot	•	•	•	•	•
Marbled murrelet	•	•	•	•	•
Kittlitz's murrelet			•		
Xantus's murrelet			•		
Ancient murrelet	•	•	•	•	•
Cassin's auklet	•	•	•	•	•
Parakeet auklet		•	•	•	
Rhinoceros auklet	•	•	•	•	•
Horned puffin	•	•	•	•	•
Tufted puffin	•	•	•	•	
Band-tailed pigeon	•	•	•	•	
Mourning dove			•	•	
Great horned owl		•		•	
Snowy owl				•	•
Long-eared owl				•	
Short-eared owl		•		•	•
Northern saw-whet owl	•	•	•	•	•
Common nighthawk		•	•		
Black swift				•	
Vaux's swift		•			
Anna's hummingbird	•	•	•	•	•
Rufous hummingbird	•	•	•	•	•

	BR	SP	SU	AU	WI
Belted kingfisher	•	•	•	•	•
Lewis' woodpecker				•	
Red-naped sapsucker			•		
Red-breasted sapsucker	•	•	•	•	•
Downy woodpecker		•	•	•	•
Hairy woodpecker	•	•	•	•	•
Northern flicker	•	•	•	•	•
Hammond's flycatcher		•			
Pacific-slope flycatcher	•	•	•	•	
Say's phoebe		•	•	•	
Eastern kingbird		•	•		
Northern shrike		•		•	•
Hutton's vireo		•			
Steller's jay	•	•	•	•	•
Clark's nutcracker				•	•
Black-billed magpie		•			
American crow			•		
Northwestern crow	•	•	•	•	•
Common raven	•	•	•	•	•
Skylark				•	
Horned lark		•	•	•	•
Tree swallow	•	•	•	•	•
Violet-green swallow		•	•		
Northern rough-winged swallow		•	•		
Bank swallow				•	
Cliff swallow		•	•		
Barn swallow	•	•	•	•	
Chestnut-backed chickadee	•	•	•	•	•
Red-breasted nuthatch	•	•	•	•	•
Brown creeper	•	•	•	•	•
Winter wren	•	•	•	•	•
American dipper	•	•	•	•	•
Golden-crowned kinglet	•	•	•	•	•
Ruby-crowned kinglet		•	•	•	•
Northern wheatear				•	
Mountain bluebird		•		•	•
Townsend's solitaire		•	•	•	•

	BR	SP	SU	AU	WI
Swainson's thrush	•	•	•		
Hermit thrush	•	•	•	•	
American robin	•	•	•	•	•
Varied thrush	•	•	•	•	•
Gray catbird		•			
Northern mockingbird		•	•	•	
Brown thrasher		•			
European starling	•	•	•	•	•
Yellow wagtail			•		
Red-throated pipit			•	•	
American pipit	•	•	•	•	•
Bohemian waxwing		•	•	•	•
Cedar waxwing	•	•	•	•	•
Orange-crowned warbler	•	•	•	•	
Yellow warbler		•	•	•	
Yellow-rumped warbler		•	•	•	•
Townsend's warbler	•	•	•	•	
Prairie warbler		•			•
Palm warbler		•	•		•
Blackpoll warbler		•	•		
Black and white warbler				•	
Northern waterthrush			•		
Common yellowthroat				•	
Wilson's warbler	•	•	•		
Western tanager		•			
Spotted towhee		•			•
American tree sparrow				•	•
Chipping sparrow			•		
Savannah sparrow		•	•	•	•
Fox sparrow	•	•	•	•	•
Song sparrow	•	•	•	•	•
Lincoln's sparrow	•	•	•	•	•
Swamp sparrow				•	•
White-throated sparrow		•		•	•
Harris's sparrow				•	
White-crowned sparrow		•		•	•
Golden-crowned sparrow		•	•	•	•

	BR	SP	SU	AU	WI
Dark-eyed junco	•	•	•	•	•
Lapland longspur		•	•	•	•
Smith's longspur		•		•	
Rustic bunting			•	•	
Snow bunting		•		•	•
Black-headed grosbeak			•	•	
Red-winged blackbird		•	•	•	•
Western meadowlark				•	
Yellow-headed blackbird		•	•		
Rusty blackbird				•	•
Brewer's blackbird		•	•	•	•
Great-tailed grackle		•			
Brown-headed cowbird		•	•	•	
Brambling		•	•	•	•
Gray-crowned rosy-finch		•		•	
Pine grosbeak	•	•	•	•	•
Purple finch				•	•
Cassin's finch				•	
House finch			•		
Red crossbill	•	•	•	•	•
White-winged crossbill		•		•	•
Common redpoll				•	•
Hoary redpoll				•	
Pine siskin	•	•	•	•	•
American goldfinch		•	•		•
Evening grosbeak		•		•	•
House sparrow	•	•	•	•	

Based on records from Peter Hamel and Margo Hearne
and *Birds of BC*, volumes 1-4

APPENDIX 3: LAND MAMMALS AND AMPHIBIANS OF HAIDA GWAII

MAMMALS	NATIVE	INTRODUCED	EXTIRPATED
Dusky shrew	•		
Silver-haired bat	•		
California myotis	•		
Keen's long-eared myotis	•		
Little brown myotis	•		
Muskrat		1925	
Beaver		1936, 1949	
Keen's mouse	•		
Norway rat		early 1980s	
Black rat		date unknown	
Red squirrel		1950	
River otter	•		
Marten	•		
Ermine (weasel)	•		
Raccoon		1940s	
Black bear	•		
Red deer (from New Zealand)		1918	•
Elk (Rocky Mountain)		1929–30	
Mule deer (Sitka deer)		1901, 1925	
Dawson's caribou	•		•

Based on Royal British Columbia Museum handbooks
by David W. Nagorsen and David Shackleton

AMPHIBIANS	NATIVE	INTRODUCED	EXTIRPATED
Western toad	•		
Pacific treefrog		1960s	

Based on Royal British Columbia Museum handbooks
by David W. Green and R. Wayne Campbell

APPENDIX 4: MARINE MAMMALS AND REPTILES OF HAIDA GWAII

MAMMALS	NEARSHORE	OFFSHORE
Sea otter	•	
Northern fur seal	•	
Northern sea lion	•	
California sea lion	•	
Northern elephant seal	•	
Harbor seal	•	
Right whale		•
Minke whale	•	
Sei whale		•
Blue whale		•
Fin whale		•
Humpback whale	•	
Short-finned pilot whale	•	
Risso's dolphin		•
Pacific white-sided dolphin	•	
Killer whale	•	
Gray whale	•	
Harbor porpoise	•	
Dall's porpoise	•	
Sperm whale		•
North Pacific bottle-nosed whale		•
Bering Sea beaked whale		•
Goose-beaked whale		•

REPTILES	NEARSHORE	OFFSHORE
Leatherback (marine turtle)		•

Based on records from the Royal British Columbia Museum and the Department of Fisheries and Oceans

FURTHER READING

Brown, A. Sutherland. *Geology of the Queen Charlotte Islands*, BC. Victoria: Department of Mines and Petroleum Resources, bulletin #54, 1968.

Campbell, R. Wayne, et al. *The Birds of British Columbia—Loons through Woodpeckers*, Volumes 1 & 2. Victoria: Royal BC Museum, 1989.

———. *The Birds of British Columbia—Flycatchers through Vireos*, Volume 3. Victoria: Royal BC Museum, 1997.

———. *The Birds of British Columbia—Wood Warblers through Old World Sparrows*, Volume 4. Victoria: Royal BC Museum, 2001.

Carey, Neil G. *Puffin Cove*. Vancouver: Hancock House, 1982.

Carr, Emily. *Klee Wyck*. Toronto: Clarke, Irwin & Co., 1971.

Carter, Jimmy. *An Outdoor Journal*. Toronto: Bantam Books, 1988.

Collison, William H. *In the Wake of the War Canoe*. Victoria: Sono Nis Press, 1981.

Collison, F., M. McNamara and J. Nelson, eds. *Yakoun, River of Life*. Council of the Haida Nation, 1990.

Dalzell, Kathleen E. *The Queen Charlotte Islands*, Volume 1 (1774–1966). Queen Charlotte City: Bill Ellis, Publisher, 1968.

———. *The Queen Charlotte Islands*, Volume 2 (Of Places and Names). Queen Charlotte City: Bill Ellis, Publisher, 1973.

———. *The Beloved Island*. Madeira Park: Harbour Publishing, 1998.

Dawson, George M. *Report on the Queen Charlotte Islands, including Appendix A: On the Haida Indians*. Montreal: Geological Survey of Canada, 1880.

Douglas, Sheila. *Trees and Shrubs of the Queen Charlotte Islands: An illustrated guide*. Queen Charlotte City: Islands Ecological Research, 1991.

Douglass, Don and Reanne Hemmingway-Douglass. *Exploring the North Coast of British Columbia: Blunden Harbour to Dixon Entrance including the Queen Charlotte Islands*. Fine Edge Productions, 1997.

Duff, Wilson and Michael Kew. *Anthony Island: A Home of the Haidas*. Report of the Provincial Museum. Victoria: Provincial Museum, 1957.

Ford, John, G. Ellis and K. Balcomb. *Killer Whales*. Vancouver: UBC Press, 1994.

Ford, John and G. Ellis. *Transients: Mammal-Hunting Killer Whales*. Vancouver: UBC Press, 1999.

Frazer, Neil. *Boat Camping Haida Gwaii*. Madeira Park: Harbour Publishing, 2001.

Green, David and Wayne Campbell. *The Amphibians of BC*. Victoria: BC Provincial Museum Handbook #45, 1984.

Gregory, Patrick and Wayne Campbell. *The Reptiles of BC*. Victoria: BC Provincial Museum Handbook #44, 1984.

Hagelund, William A. *Whalers No More*. Madeira Park: Harbour Publishing, 1987.

Haley, Delphine, ed. *Marine Mammals*. Seattle: Pacific Search Press, 1986.

Harris, Christie. *Raven's Cry*. Toronto: McClelland and Stewart, 1966.

Islands Protection Society. *Islands at the Edge: Preserving the Queen Charlotte Islands Wilderness*. Vancouver: Douglas and McIntyre, 1984.

Long, Bob. *Fishing the Queen Charlotte Islands*. Sandspit: Raser Enterprises Ltd., 1988.

MacDonald, George F. *Ninstints: Haida World Heritage Site*. Vancouver: UBC Press, 1983.

———. *Haida Art*. Vancouver: Douglas and McIntyre, 1996

Nagorsen, David W. and R. Mark Brigham. *Bats of British Columbia*. Royal British Columbia Museum Handbook. Vancouver: UBC Press, 1993.

Nagorsen, David W. *Opossums, Shrews and Moles of British Columbia*. Royal British Columbia Museum Handbook. Vancouver: UBC Press, 1996.

———. *Rodents and Lagomorphs of British Columbia*. Royal British Columbia Museum Handbook. Vancouver: UBC Press, 2005.

Osgood, Wilfred H. *Natural History of the Queen Charlotte Islands, BC*. Washington: Government Printing Office, 1901.

Poole, Francis. *Queen Charlotte Islands: A Narrative of Discovery and Adventure in the North Pacific*. London: Hurst and Blackett, 1872; reprinted Vancouver: J.J. Douglas, 1972.

Scudder, Geoffrey and Nicholas Gessler, eds. *The Outer Shores*. Queen Charlotte Islands Museum, 1989.

Sheldon, Charles. *The Wilderness of the North Pacific Coast Islands*. New York: Charles Scribner's Sons, 1912.

Shackleton, David. *Hoofed Mammals of British Columbia*. Royal British Columbia Museum Handbook. Vancouver: UBC Press, 1999.

Smyly, John and Carolyn Smyly. *Those Born at Koona*. Vancouver: Hancock House, 1973.

South Moresby Resource Planning Team. *South Moresby Land Use Alternatives*. Victoria: Queen's Printer, 1983.

Stewart, Hilary. *Cedar*. Vancouver: Douglas and McIntyre, 1984.

———. *Looking at Totem Poles*. Vancouver: Douglas and McIntyre, 1993.

INDEX

501 RV/tent park 192
abalone 33, 61, 152
Aero logging 122-23, 212
Agate Beach 86-87, 92
Agate Beach Provincial Campground 87, 93, 193, 212, 220
Agglomerate Island 145
Air Canada Jazz 195, 221
air travel 133, 194-95, 209, 221
airport. *See* Sandspit Airport, Masset Airport
Alaska View Lodge 189
albatross 25, 27, 51, 223
Alliford Bay 54, 57-59, 117, 121, 220
American Museum of Natural History 50
ammonites 54-55
An Outdoor Journal 213
Anderson, Ole 70
anemones 56
Anna Inlet 137
Anthony Island. *See* SGang Gwaay
Anthony Islets 33
argillite 22, 175
auklets 29, 31-32, 79, 167, 227

Bag Harbour 146, 149
bald eagles 25, 32-33, 65, 81, 143, 225
Bank of British Columbia 69
Barbeau, Marius 161
barnacles 61, 147
bats 43, 140, 231
BC Forest recreation sites 115, 119, 192
BC Forest Service 60
BC Packers 127
Beach Road 59
beach(es) 12, 14, 25, 28, 34, 38, 46, 54, 57, 59-61, 64-65, 68-70, 77-78, 84, 86-87, 89-93, 95, 97-101, 103, 105-15, 117-19, 121, 123, 126-27, 138, 146, 149, 153-54, 156, 166, 174, 177, 180, 185-87, 189, 192, 211-12, 214-15, 219-20
beachcombing 60, 64, 78, 84, 97, 99, 212
Beal Cove 76
bear(s) 129, 156, 176; black bear(s) 42, 149, 192, 218-19, 231
Bearskin Bay 57
beaver 44-45, 76, 160, 231
bed and breakfasts (B&Bs) 15, 133, 155, 183-90, 194, 208, 212, 220
Beitush Road 105, 112-13
Beresford Inlet 138
Bering Industries 72
Bigg, Michael 37
biking (cycling), bikes 49, 98-99, 101, 118, 186, 191, 211-12
Bill C31 177
Bischof Islands 135, 137-38
Bischoff, K.G. 137
boating 46, 54, 57, 60, 133, 138, 198-202
bog(s) 43, 72-73, 84, 91-93, 95-96, 107, 138, 211
Bonanza Beach 60-61

British Columbia Ferry Services (BC Ferries) 49, 60, 194, 205, 208, 211, 220-21
Brown, A. Sutherland 14, 125
Bruin Bay 76
Burnaby Island 13, 135, 146, 150, 154, 202
Burnaby Narrows 129, 146-49, 192
Burnaby Strait. *See* Burnaby Narrows

Cäcilia's B&B 188
camping, campsites, campgrounds 52, 60, 64-65, 76, 79, 86-87, 92-93, 105, 107-8, 110, 112-15, 117, 119, 127, 129, 137-38, 140-41, 146, 149-50, 155, 159, 180, 184, 192-93, 201, 208, 212, 218, 220
Canadian Hydrographic Service 202
Canadian Tide and Current Tables 109, 202
cannery(ies) 90, 100, 149-50, 152-53, 179
Cape Ball 95, 107
Cape Ball River 106
Cape Fife 91, 109
Cape Fife Trail 91-92
Cape Knox 76-77
Cape St. James 29, 38, 77, 132, 202, 210
caribou 23, 43, 218, 231
Carmichael Passage 121
Carr, Emily 126, 171, 178
Carter, Jimmy 213
cave exploration 77-78, 118, 154
Cedar 67
Chatham Sound 47
Chief Klue 139
Chittenden, Newton 114
Christmas bird count 28, 83, 167
Church Creek. *See* Mathers Creek
Clague, John 107
clams 54, 97-100, 147, 149, 185, 215-17
Cloak Bay 74, 76-77
Coast Guard 200, 202, 209
cod 65, 76, 87, 134, 213-14
Collison, William 19, 48, 67
commercial fishing 15, 39, 49, 73, 76, 88, 98-99, 124, 169, 179, 203
Cone Head forest recreation site 60, 193
Cook, James 18
Copper Bay 117
Copper Bay Road 59, 115, 117
Copper Island 33, 150, 154, 192
Copper River 213, 215
cormorants 29-31, 33-34, 90, 156, 223
Council of the Haida Nation 130
crab(s) 49, 87-89, 97-99, 148-49, 166, 183, 189, 215-17, 219; Dungeness 88, 98-99, 148, 215, 217
Crosby, Thomas 123
Cumshewa Head 117-18, 180
Cumshewa Inlet 36, 40, 59, 119, 121, 124-25, 202, 212
Cumshewa Village 22, 192
cutthroat trout 78, 86, 88, 90, 113, 191, 213
Cygnet Lake 92

Dalzell, Albert 166
Dalzell, Kathleen E. "Betty" 19, 70, 90, 164-65
Darwin Sound 135, 137
Darwin, Charles 24
Davidson, Alfred and Robert 66
Dawson, George 126, 137
De La Beche Inlet 138
Deena River 213-14
deer 43-44, 57, 91, 93, 118-19, 129, 156, 172, 218, 231
Delkatla Wildlife Sanctuary 28-29, 79, 81-83, 169-70, 189, 208, 220
Dentalium 61
Dixon Entrance 13, 21, 47, 74, 77, 87, 90, 97, 101, 104, 109, 182, 202-3
Dixon Entrance Maritime Museum 203
Dixon, George 18, 74
Dodge Point 141, 144
dogfish 123, 214
Dogfish Bay 119
Dolly Varden (Dollies) 88, 90, 113, 191, 213
Dolomite Narrows. *See* Burnaby Narrows
dolphins 35, 37, 232
Dorothy and Mike's 187
Douglass, Don 201
drinking water 17, 52, 63, 87, 108, 110, 117-18, 121, 127, 135, 138, 141, 146-47, 152, 155, 159, 208
Duff, Wilson 162

Eagle Creek 107
Eagle Hill 107, 109
East Beach 91-92, 95, 97, 99, 101, 105, 108-9, 114
Edenshaw pole 77
Edye Pass 47
elk 44, 218, 231
Ellen Island 133, 155
ermine 42, 231
Evans, Edward 70
Exploring the North Coast of British Columbia 201

Fairburn Shoals 125
farming 54, 70, 72, 203
fishing 12, 15, 17, 39, 49, 57, 60-61, 64, 66, 73, 76, 78, 84, 86-90, 99, 113, 119, 124, 134, 166, 169, 175, 180, 184, 187-88, 190-91, 198, 200, 203, 208, 213-16; licences 86, 88, 99, 113, 198, 208, 213, 215
Fishing the Queen Charlotte Islands 215
fish-packing plants 127-28
Five Mile Beach 60
Flatrock Island 156
forest industry 11, 15, 44, 127-28, 168, 196
fossils 14, 52, 54-56
Four Corners Trail 91
Frazer, Neill 201
frog(s) 44, 96, 160, 231
Fuller Point 141
fulmars 29, 33, 51, 223
fur trade 11, 18, 40, 74, 76, 162

Galapagos Islands 24, 29
Gandll K'in Gwaayaay 43, 132-33, 135, 138, 140, 192
Gangxid people 158, 161-62
George Brown Recreation Centre 58
Gillatt Arm 121, 124
glaucous-winged gulls 20, 30, 56, 151, 227
Gogit Point 141
Gooden Island 54
Goose Island 40
Gordon Islands 156
Gospel Island 65
government agent 109, 215
Graham Centre 191
Graham Island 13-15, 43-44, 46-114, 156, 193-94, 196, 201, 207, 210, 213-14, 218
Gray Bay 59, 115, 117, 119, 192, 214, 220
Gray Bay Creek 117-18
Gray Bay Forestry Site 115, 117, 192
Gray Point 117-18
gray whales 35-36, 58, 203, 232
Gray, Robert 18
great blue herons 119, 223
Gregory Beach 60-61
Gwaalagaa Naay Corporation 67, 178
Gwaii Haanas National Park Reserve and Haida Heritage Site 12, 15-16, 29, 46, 130-163

Haans Islet 125
Hagelund, W.A. 156
Haida Gwaii Museum 67, 69, 74, 162, 176, 203, 208, 220
Haida Gwaii watchmen 133, 135, 140-41, 159, 162, 200
Haida Heritage Site. *See* Gwaii Haanas
Haida Nation 130, 158; and cedar 20-22, 58, 66-68, 125, 143-44; art 22, 78, 84, 126, 161, 175, 203; Bill C31 177; canoes 18, 21-22, 42, 48-50, 66-69, 74, 142-44, 159, 175, 220; legends 17, 90; old villages 12, 20-21, 52, 56, 68, 74, 77, 123-27, 132, 134, 141, 149, 155, 158-63, 171, 192, 198, 200, 203-4; potlatch(es) 20-22, 69, 160, 180-81; totem poles 6, 56, 77, 124-27, 144, 158-59, 162
Haina Village 56
hairy woodpecker 28, 81, 228
halibut 49, 65, 76, 87, 198, 213-14
Hamel, Peter 164, 167, 230
harbor seal 38, 40, 232
Harbourview Lodging 189
Harriet Harbour 150, 152, 154
Harriet Island 152
Harris, Christie 165
Haswell Bay 138
Hawkair 195, 221
Haydn Turner Campsite 52, 193
Hearne, Margo 83, 164, 169, 230
Hecate Strait 13, 21, 27-29, 42, 44, 46-52, 55, 67, 97, 104, 106, 117, 119, 124-25, 130, 150, 194; birds 27-29, 51, 104, 107; fish 49
Henslung Cove 76
herring 59, 124, 146, 175
Hesseltine, Carolyn 164, 171
Hidden Island Resort RV Park 87
Hiellen River 88, 90-91, 97, 99-100, 212
hiking 58, 78, 87, 92, 101, 106-9, 115, 117-18, 143, 154, 180, 220

Hippa Island 18, 30
Hlk'yah GaawGa 132-33, 141-45
hospitals 168, 174, 203, 208-9
hot springs 135, 138-40
Hotspring Island. *See* Gandll K'in Gwaayaay
House Island 135
Houston Stewart Channel 133, 155, 157-59, 202
Hoya Passage 135
Hudson's Bay Company (HBC) 19
humpback whales 158
hunting 20, 44, 66, 86, 105, 208, 218-19
Huxley Island 133, 135, 137

Ikeda Cove 152
Ikeda, Arichika 152
In the Wake of the War Canoe 19, 48
Ireland, Willard 165
Island Bay 146-47
Islands at the Edge 24
Isozaki, Taniyo 153

Jean's Beach House 185
Jedway 150, 152, 154
Jedway Bay 150, 152
Jeffrey Island 33
Jewell Island 51, 57
Johnson, Alec 70
Juan Perez Sound 133, 135, 137-39, 146, 202
Juskatla 67-68

K'aaw (caviar) 147
K'uuna Ilnagaay 20-21, 46, 119, 121, 126-27, 132-33, 192, 204
Kagan Bay 29, 55
Kagan Bay Forestry Site 52, 193
Kerouard Island 30, 33, 155
Kew, Michael 162
killer whales (orca) 37-38, 104, 145, 158, 160, 232
Kiusta 74, 76-78
Koyah 161, 163
Kumara Lake 92, 108-9
Kumdis River Lodge 191
Kunghit Island 13, 155-56
Kwuna Point 56-57
Kwuna, MV 28, 54, 58, 194, 211

LaFortune, Joy 164, 173
Lagoon Inlet 127-29
Langara Island 13, 29-30, 74, 76-79, 202, 214
Langara lighthouse 77
Langara Lodge 76
Lawn Hill 17, 51, 202
Lepas Bay 33, 76-78
Limestone Islands 127
Lina Island 54, 55
Lina Village 54
ling cod 76, 214
Lockeport 137
logging roads 59, 117, 196, 212
Long, Bob 216
Loo Taas 67, 69
Looking Around and Blinking House 141
loons 25-26, 167, 223

Louise Island 13, 46, 119, 126-27, 129, 204, 214
Louise Narrows 119, 121, 129
Louscoone Inlet 137, 155, 159, 197
Louscoone Point 159
Lyell Island 13, 30, 40, 130, 133, 135, 137, 141, 145-46, 216

MacDonald, George 161
Maple Island 54
Marco Island 40, 138
marine charts 118, 125, 141, 201-2
marine touring 104, 200-2
marten 42, 231
Masset 15, 41, 28-29, 32, 43-46, 49, 72, 74, 76, 79, 81, 83, 86-87, 93, 97, 99-101, 167, 169-70, 173-74, 177, 179, 181-82, 185, 189-90, 193, 196, 202-3, 207, 209, 211-12, 220; facilities 208
Masset Airport 195, 208
Masset Eagles Swim Club 182
Masset Inlet 14, 40-41, 68, 70, 191, 201-2, 215
Masset Rod and Gun Club 169
Masset Sound 29, 32, 69, 72, 202
Mathers Creek 123-24
Mathewes, Rolf 107
Maude Channel 55
Maude Island 55-57
Mayer Lake 86, 213
McIntyre Bay 29
Merilees, Andrew 164, 181
metric system 17, 222
Mica Lake 92
Miller, Gordon 50, 161
mining 11, 15, 137, 150, 152-54
minke whales 158, 232
Misty Meadows Campgound 86, 105, 110, 113-14, 193, 220
Moody, Garner 164, 175
moon snail 147-48
Moresby Camp 46, 119, 121-22, 129, 133, 212, 220
Moresby Camp Forestry Site 192
Moresby Island 13-14, 16, 40-41, 52, 54, 58, 115-29, 135, 137-38, 150, 155, 192, 194-96, 201, 207, 210, 213-14, 219, 221
Moresby Island Guest House 186
mortuary pole(s) 21, 77, 126
Mosquito Lake 119, 213
Mosquito Lake Forestry Site 192
mosses 23, 32, 72, 77, 91, 93, 96, 112, 114, 126, 143
Murchison Island 135, 137
murrelets 31-33, 78, 135, 144, 167, 227
Museum of Anthropology (UBC) 84, 162
mussels 61, 65, 147

Naden Harbour 179, 202, 215
Naden Lodge 190
Nadu 69-70, 72-73
Nadu River 73
Nadu Road 69, 72
Naikoon Provincial Park 12, 14, 46, 8487, 89, 93, 96-97, 100, 103, 108, 113, 177, 188, 212-14, 219

Nai-Kun. *See* Rose Spit
Nan Sdins. *See* SGang llnagaay
National Museum of Canada 66
needlefish 65
New Kloo 123
Ninstints. *See* SGang llnagaay
Ninstints: Haida World Heritage Site 161
North Beach 87, 89-90, 92, 97-101, 103, 108-9, 211-12, 215
North Island. *See* Langara Island
North Pacific Seaplanes 195, 221
northern saw-whet owl 28-29
Northwest Recreation Services 182

Oeanda River 107
Old Massett 15, 27-29, 68, 91, 97, 179-80, 182, 207, 211; facilities 208
Onward Point Trail 59, 220
Osgood, William 143
oystercatchers 26, 56-57, 225

Pacific Coast Fisheries 127
Pacific Coastal Air 195
Pacific treefrogs 44, 96, 231
Pacofi Bay 127-28
Pallant Creek 59, 124, 213
Parks Canada 60, 133, 135, 140, 147, 152, 155, 160, 216, 221
Parry Passage 77
Parry, David 48
peat moss plant 72
Pelican Cove 154
peregrine falcons 25, 30, 32-33, 78, 81, 83, 104, 225
Perez, Juan 18
Pesuta 106, 114, 220
petroglyphs 77-78
picnic sites 57-58, 86-87, 90, 105-6, 110, 119, 146, 220
pigeon guillemots 27, 51, 56, 227
Pillar Bay 76-77
Plum Pudding Rock 77
Poole Point 153-54
Poole, Francis 66, 139, 153-54
porpoises 35-38, 58-59, 124, 232
Port Clements 15, 29, 46, 63, 67-68, 72, 86, 113, 165-66, 173-74, 177, 191, 193, 207, 209, 211-12, 220; facilities 208
Port Clements' museum 67, 166, 177, 203
Porthole Rock 77
prawns 215
Prince Rupert 47, 49, 65, 70, 162, 194-95, 201, 209
puffins 31, 156-58, 227
Pure Lake 86
Pure Lake Provincial Park 86

Qay'llnagaay Heritage Centre 176, 178, 203, 205
Queen Charlotte City. *See* Village of Queen Charlotte
Queen Charlotte Islands 11, 13, 166, 179-80, 185
Queen Charlotte Mountains 14, 65, 90, 97, 210
Queen Charlotte Sound 47

Queen of Prince Rupert 49-50, 52, 194

raccoons 33, 44, 149
railroad(s) 122, 212
rainbow trout 213
rainforest(s) 11, 15, 67, 77-78, 92, 127, 141, 143, 162
Ramsay Island 45, 135, 137
Rankine Island 30, 33, 150, 192
Raspberry Cove 155
rats 33, 42, 44, 78, 144, 231
Raven and the First Men 84, 175
raven(s) 101, 143, 149, 228
Raven's Cry 155
RCMP 208-9
red rock crabs 148
red snapper 214
Rediscovery program 76-77
Reef Island 38, 127
refugia 42, 44, 95, 107
Reid, Bill 69, 84, 175-76, 178
Reid-Stevens, Amanda 164, 177
Rennell Sound 60, 63-65, 202, 214, 220
Rennell Sound recreation site 60, 65, 193
Riley Creek bridge 61
river otter(s) 42, 118, 129, 157, 231
Riverside B&B 188
rock scallops 65
rockfish 213, 216
Rockfish Harbour 127
Roderick Island 54
Rose Harbour 133, 155-57, 197, 199
Rose Inlet 156-57
Rose Spit 24, 27, 29, 36, 38, 40, 49, 84, 97, 99, 101, 103-5, 108-9, 113, 156, 168, 212
Rose, George 156
Royal British Columbia Museum 231-32

Sac Bay 138
salmon 39, 49, 52, 65, 76, 86, 113-14, 117, 124, 134, 144,149, 152, 183, 213-14, 219; chum 76, 144; coho 57, 60, 76, 90, 113, 124, 144, 198, 213-15; pink 57, 144, 214; spring (king, chinook) 76, 214
Saltwater Fishing Guide 214
San Christoval Range 138, 147
sand dunes 84, 92, 97, 103-4, 106, 108, 110-13, 188
sanderling(s) 28, 226
sandhill cranes 25, 29-30, 81, 83, 91, 104, 119, 225
Sandilands Island 56
sandpipers 28-29, 83, 225-26
Sandspit 16, 29, 49, 52, 54, 57, 59, 117-18, 121, 133, 181, 186, 195-97, 205, 207, 209-11, 214-15, 220; facilities 208
Sandspit Airport 16, 52, 59-60, 117, 186, 195-96, 203, 205, 208, 220
Sandspit Inn 117
Sandspit Rod and Gun Club 214
Sangan River 86
Santiago 18
schools, schooling 52, 173, 177-80
sea lions 35-36, 38-39, 65, 104, 127, 157, 232
sea otter(s) 11, 18, 35, 40-41, 76, 232

sea stars 61, 65, 147
seals 35-36, 39-40, 65, 104, 118, 138, 145, 157, 232
Seaport B&B 186
Secret Cove 117
Section Cove 135, 146
semipalmated plovers 28, 106, 225
Sewell Inlet 127
SGang Gwaay 21-22, 30, 46, 132-33, 155, 157-59, 192, 197, 216
shark(s) 99, 147, 214
shearwaters 25, 27, 29-30, 33, 49, 51, 104, 223
Sheldens Bay 118-19
Sheldens Bay Forestry Site 192
Sheldon, Charles 44, 218
shrew 42, 231
shrimp 215
Shuttle Island 135, 137
Skedans Bay 126
Skedans Island 127
Skedans Point 119, 126
Skedans Rocks 38
Skedans. See K'uuna llnagaay
Skidegate Band Council 154, 204
Skidegate Channel 52, 55, 202
Skidegate Inlet 27-29, 36, 40-41, 51-52, 54, 57-58, 121, 186-87, 194, 201-3, 214-15
Skidegate Lake 59, 122, 212-13
Skidegate Landing 15, 49, 51-52, 54, 58, 113, 121, 194, 207, 211, 220
Skidegate Mission 56
Skidegate Village 6, 14-15, 20, 22, 36, 51, 57-58, 67-69, 123, 162, 175-78, 202, 207, 211, 220; facilities 208
Skidegate Village Museum 67, 162, 203
Skincuttle Inlet 146, 150, 152-54, 162
Skittagetan Lagoon 138
Slatechuck Mountain 22
Slug Islet 150; Slug islands 192
Smyly, Carolyn and John 126
South Moresby 40-41, 135
South Moresby Air Charters 195, 221
Spirit Lake Trail 58, 220
Spruce Point Lodge 187, 194
St. Mary's Spring 17
starfish. See sea stars
steelhead 86, 113, 190-91, 213
Steller's jay 28-29, 81, 228
Stewart, Hilary 67
stickleback 44-45, 84
storm-petrels 30, 32, 58, 223
Sunset Park and Interpretive Trail 193, 220
Sunshine-Town 56
Swan Bay 154
Swan Creek 92

T'anu llnagaay 123-24, 132-33, 192
Tar Islands 145
Tasu Sound 132, 150, 202, 210
Teal-Jones Group 117, 121, 196
Testatlints (Plum Pudding Rock) 77
The Beloved Island, 166
The Queen Charlotte Islands, 1774–1966 70
The Queen Charlotte Islands: Of Places and Names 90

The Wilderness of the North Pacific Coast Islands, 44, 218
Thorgierson, Faith 164, 179
Those Born at Koona 126
tide tables
Tlell 15, 36, 43, 46, 177, 181, 188, 193, 207, 210-12; facilities 208
Tlell Anvil Trail 114
Tlell River 84, 86, 103, 105-6, 108-10, 112-14, 213, 218
toads 44, 160, 231
topographic maps 91, 106, 108-9, 118, 141, 201
Torrens Island 51, 57
tourism 12, 15, 73, 133-34, 140, 162, 171-74, 182, 184, 198, 207, 220
Tow Hill 14, 86-93, 97, 100-1, 108-9, 193, 214, 220
Tow Hill Bog 92-93, 95-96
Tow Hill ecological reserve 92
Tow Hill Road 79, 185
trumpeter swans 29, 92, 119, 224
Tuft Islets 144
turban snails 61
turtles 41, 232

UNESCO 21, 155

Vancouver 66, 69, 84, 173-77, 180-81, 189-91, 194-95, 204, 209, 214
Vancouver Island 13, 38, 40, 47, 99, 140, 152, 162
Vancouver Island Helicopters 195
vehicle rentals 208, 213
Vertical Point 127
Victoria 21, 66, 72, 91, 109, 162, 165-66, 179, 214
Village of Queen Charlotte 15, 49, 52, 54, 60, 63, 109, 133-34, 173, 181, 185, 187, 193, 195-96, 200, 204-7, 209, 211-12, 214-16, 219-21; facilities 208
Virago 155
Visitor Centre (Village of Queen Charlotte) 133-34, 172, 185, 200, 204-6, 208, 216, 219-21
Von Boetticher, Kimiko 164, 181

Waterfowl. See Kagan Bay
weather reports 141, 200, 221
Western Forest Products Ltd. 63, 67, 127, 196
western red cedar 20, 67, 130, 142-43
Whalers No More 156
whaling 156-57
Windy Bay Creek 144
Windy Bay. See Hlk'yah Gaawga
Withered Point 55

Yakoun River 29, 213
Yatza Mountain 147

DENNIS HORWOOD

Dennis Horwood has always had a passion for birds and mammals and all things wild. He spent several years with Parks Canada and BC Parks, then moved to Kitimat in 1978. He works for the public school system and specializes in science and outdoor education.

On his days off, he canoes, hikes and explores Douglas Channel, always on the lookout for new or unusual birds. Over the years, he has collected thousands of bird records that formed the basis of *Birds of the Kitimat Valley*, released in 1992. Dennis continues to write a regular natural history column for his local newspaper.

As a member of the Kitimat Valley Naturalist Club, he has recently reactivated his marine-biology training and become involved with a coast-wide survey of marine eelgrass.

Dennis and Tom first met in Banff National Park while working as park naturalists. A chance encounter seven years later rekindled their friendship, which ultimately led to their collaboration on this guide.

TOM PARKIN

Once described as a Renaissance man because of his diverse and deep interests, Tom Parkin has followed his path of passions through careers as a naturalist for Parks Canada and BC Parks and as a professional writer and photographer. He has also worked in public relations for the government of British Columbia. During those creative careers, his work was published in books, magazines and newspapers across North America, and won three national awards.

Today Tom is self-employed as a stonemason on central Vancouver Island. His education and knowledge of the natural sciences and his creativity continue to serve his striving for excellence in his craft (see <www.ssmasonry.ca> for more details.)

When not occupied with upending stones or messing about in his garden, Tom keeps busy researching and writing his family history. He is also an unrepentant railroad historian and steam buff.